Research Methods in Librarianship:
MEASUREMENT AND EVALUATION

MONOGRAPH NUMBER 8

University of Illinois
Graduate School of Library Science
Monograph Series

Goldstein, Harold. Implications of the New Media for the Teaching of Library Science (No. 1). 1963. $2.00 paperback, $3.00 hardcover.

Stone, Elizabeth. Training for the Improvement of Library Administration (No. 2). 1967. $2.00 paperback, $3.00 hardcover.

1962 Statistics of Public Libraries Serving Populations of Less Than 35,000 (No. 3). 1966. $2.00 paperback, $3.00 hardcover.

Public Libraries in the United States of America. Part 1. 1876 Report. (Reprint.) (No. 4). 1966. $4.00 paperback, $5.00 hardcover.

Rules for Descriptive Cataloging in the Library of Congress. (Reprint of 1949 edition.) (No. 5). 1966. $2.00 paperback.

Grundt, Leonard. Efficient Patterns for Adequate Library Service in a Large City: A Survey of Boston (No. 6). 1968. $3.00 paperback, $4.00 hardcover.

Rhees, William J. Manual of Public Libraries, Institutions and Societies in the United States and British Provinces of North America (Reprint.) (No. 7). 1967. $4 paperback, $5.00 hardcover.

Goldhor, Herbert, ed. Research Methods in Librarianship: Measurement and Evaluation (No. 8). 1968. $5.00 hardcover.

Distributed by the Illini Union Bookstore
715 South Wright Street
Champaign, Illinois 61820

RESEARCH METHODS IN LIBRARIANSHIP:

MEASUREMENT

AND

EVALUATION

PAPERS PRESENTED AT A CONFERENCE
CONDUCTED BY THE UNIVERSITY OF ILLINOIS
GRADUATE SCHOOL OF LIBRARY SCIENCE
September 10–13, 1967

Edited by
HERBERT GOLDHOR

UNIVERSITY OF ILLINOIS GRADUATE SCHOOL OF LIBRARY SCIENCE

Copyright © 1968 by
The Board of Trustees of the University of Illinois

TABLE OF CONTENTS

Page

INTRODUCTION 1
       Herbert Goldhor

CHAPTER I: A THEORETICAL FRAMEWORK FOR PUBLIC LIBRARY MEASUREMENT 2
       Kenneth E. Beasley

CHAPTER II: MEASUREMENT AND EVALUATION OF THE PUBLIC LIBRARY 15
       Charles M. Armstrong

CHAPTER III: MEASUREMENT AND EVALUATION IN COLLEGE AND UNIVERSITY LIBRARY STUDIES: LIBRARY RESEARCH AT PURDUE UNIVERSITY 25
       John H. Moriarty

CHAPTER IV: RECENT TRENDS IN MARKETING RESEARCH 33
       Robert Ferber

CHAPTER V: TRENDS IN THE ACCREDITATION OF HIGHER INSTITUTIONS 40
       Charles M. Allen

CHAPTER VI: A REVIEW OF RESEARCH IN SCHOOL LIBRARIANSHIP 51
       Jean E. Lowrie

CHAPTER VII: MEASUREMENT AND EVALUATION IN SPECIAL LIBRARIES 70
       Eugene B. Jackson

CHAPTER VIII: MEASUREMENT AND EVALUATION IN ADULT EDUCATION 88
       Wilson B. Thiede

CHAPTER IX: STATISTICAL INFERENCE 95
       Robert E. Pingry

CHAPTER X: MEASUREMENT AND EVALUATION OF RESEARCH IN LIBRARY TECHNICAL SERVICES 105
       Maurice Tauber

CHAPTER XI: ATTITUDE MEASUREMENT 119
       Harry C. Triandis

INTRODUCTION

In September 1963 the Graduate School of Library Science sponsored a conference at Allerton House, the University of Illinois conference center, on research methods in librarianship. The proceedings of that conference were edited by Dr. Guy G. Garrison, Director of the Library Research Center of the University of Illinois, and were published as the July 1964 issue of *Library Trends*. That conference was general in nature and covered several different aspects of the subject. It was planned as the first of a series of conferences on research methods in librarianship, with the later ones to be focused on one aspect or another of the general topic.

The second conference on library research sponsored by the University of Illinois was held from September 10-13, 1967, at the Illini Union building on the Urbana campus. This volume includes the papers which were given at that conference. The subject of the meeting was "measurement and evaluation," not because there is so much to be said on these topics by library researchers (actually seven of the eleven papers were given by non-librarians, and five of these seven dealt with fields other than library science), but because they are so important and so difficult in all areas of research. No final answers were given to the complex problems involved, but hopefully insights were provided by speakers who were both experienced and knowledgeable.

Measurement and evaluation are technical matters, and the papers by Moriarty, Jackson, and Pingry deal in their own ways with some of the newer techniques — mostly mathematical — with which inevitably librarians will have to become familiar. In addition the problems of measurement and evaluation are much the same in all fields of study, and the lessons to be learned from the experiences of other and related fields justified the papers by Ferber, Allen, Thiede, and Triandis. Finally, measurement and evaluation depend essentially on the definition of a criterion — explicitly expressed as by Beasley and Armstrong, or implicit in the cumulative record of research to date as shown in the papers by Lowrie and Tauber.

These papers deal with issues which will greatly affect the success with which we in librarianship uncover the nature of the relationships between people and books. In publishing these papers, in holding these conferences, and in other ways, we at the University of Illinois hope to be increasingly identified with the efforts to discover and verify those relationships. Though the process is long and often apparently unsuccessful, there is no other known way than the scientific method by which to convert an art into a discipline.

The committee which planned this conference consisted of Dr. Frances B. Jenkins of the Library School faculty, Dr. Garrison, and the undersigned. We wish to thank Mr. T. W. Sineath of the Division of University Extension for his conscientious attention to the administrative arrangements for the conference. The speakers — and authors — made the major contribution, of course, and we are grateful to them for their willingness to give of themselves in this way. We hope that those who attended the conference profited by it; and if so the discussions with the speakers and the corridor talk undoubtedly contributed. And I wish to thank Mrs. Barbara Donagan for her help in seeing these manuscripts through the publishing process.

Herbert Goldhor

Urbana, Illinois
November, 1967

CHAPTER I: A THEORETICAL FRAMEWORK FOR PUBLIC LIBRARY MEASUREMENT*

KENNETH E. BEASLEY
Head of the Department of Political Science
The University of Texas at El Paso

An article in the July 1966 issue of the *Library Journal* begins with the statement: "The National Conference on Library Statistics, held in Chicago, June 6-8, raised more questions than it settled, as a healthy conference should."[1] Assuming in a broader context for the moment that raising more questions than are answered is indeed a condition of healthiness, one must conclude that library administration and service have much vitality and little chance of developing pathological conditions, because for at least thirty years there has been discussion about statistical reporting without observable evidence of progress. For every proposed reform suggested in the current literature, there are so many objections that one wonders if any of us really want what we say is essential for the future, namely more sophisticated tools (a) to measure the quantity and quality of service, and (b) to use in constructing standards.

One can appreciate the sense of frustration that pervades the profession about statistics. Research projects are proposed in large numbers, only a few of them are started, and a still smaller number are completed. Those that culminate in publication are too often disappointing because they are essentially a restatement of previous assertions. *Library Statistics: A Handbook of Concepts, Definitions, and Terminology*[2] is the most recent addition to this lengthening list. Born under auspicious circumstances, with a more than adequate financial inheritance, it created interest, caused discussion, produced raised eyebrows and wonderment, and then slowly and quietly adjusted to the world it found. One might say it continued the family line, but accomplished little more. Such an observation is not a criticism of the original intent of the project or its sponsors or the people who labored long in an effort to develop something new. Instead, it is merely a statement of a condition in which too many librarians, board members, political decision makers, and even members of the public apparently find comfort; or they do not understand the real issues. Successful research in social services which leads to change must nearly always be conducted in an environment where the desire to change already exists. Research itself rarely produces motivation.

It is not surprising, therefore, that the profession has tended increasingly to discuss and worry about standards, apparently in the hope that thereby some order could be generated and gradually a body of data could be developed for both self and public analysis. The hope has remained unfulfilled because almost by definition standards imply the ability to describe precisely both the present position and the changes necessary to attain a future position. They imply, furthermore, that there is general agreement on where one should go and why. None of these conditions exists in library service except in a most general sense.

This lack of agreement was clearly evident when the latest standards for public libraries were adopted at the ALA Conference in 1966. Many librarians expressed serious reservations about them, and consensus was reached largely by changing their title to imply they were applicable to systems first and individual public libraries second. In reading the standards, even the uninitiated can note the numerous compromises in the highly generalized language. A legislator, recognizing this situation, asked me recently what the standard for per capita expenditures really meant, as he could not see the relevance of the recommended level of expenditures for any city or system arrangement in his district. I had to reply honestly that the standard was designed to prod or scare most communities into raising budgets in the belief that improvement would be generated. Sometimes genuine improvement resulted, but in too many cases *pseudo*-advancement would be a more accurate description.

Although the efforts to set standards have been largely unsuccessful, the energy expended has not been wasted. Discussion of them at conferences and in the general literature has been a potent force in retraining the older generation and instructing the younger generation about the general trend they should support. This force must be preserved in essentially its present form, but perhaps with fewer bold statements, while a statistical reporting and measuring scheme is devised.

*This paper is a preliminary statement of a longer article now in preparation which will provide more details on several of the generalized points and propose additional measurements.

GENERAL FEATURES OF A STATISTICAL SYSTEM FOR LIBRARIES

The argument in this paper is that much of library service can be described accurately in statistical terms and that such a description would provide new insights about the variables of library service and would facilitate communication among members of the profession. The only limitation is the state of the statistical art, and there are many areas equally as complicated as library service or more so, where statistical analysis has been proved not only useful but almost essential (e.g., personality testing, psychiatric and medical diagnosis, intellectual achievement, cost-benefit ratios, etc.). Academic libraries have already made significant advances in the use of statistical tools.

A prerequisite for this development in library circles though, is a reorientation of thinking with special emphasis on identifying (a) the function of the public library, (b) the nature of stored knowledge, (c) the ways in which libraries are actually used, and (d) the inter-relationships of the various elements of a library program. These factors and their sub-parts must be examined objectively (and almost callously) in the abstract in order to identify the gross pattern, but at the same time one must recognize that reality produces the data and abstractions must eventually be translated into reality. It is this moving back and forth between two almost discrete types of thought processes that causes anxiety, frustrations, and fear for individual librarians as well as the entire profession. Yet, from such a movement come the insights that produce the new order.

In 1964 in *A Statistical Reporting System for Public Libraries*,[3] I implied rather strongly that a statistical system is not created but is developed like a library. This paper continues that theme by advancing some ideas at one higher level of abstraction in the shape of formulae that purport to describe library service. The formulae reflect at this point only the first of several steps, namely an identification of major variables and their relationship to each other. They are a product of some checking of current statistical reports, conversations with librarians, review of library literature, listening at conferences, and intuition. Unfortunately, because of the scarcity of data covering all of the elements, they have not been subjected to the rigors of field testing. That is the next step.

Interrelationship of Standards and a Statistical Reporting System

In some cases the elements reflect my judgments about standards. While these hopefully have been kept to a minimum and are clearly identified, they cannot be completely avoided because a reporting system and standards are themselves a function of each other. The intent of this approach is, therefore, to raise questions about standards in specific contexts in order to determine if their premises are sound.

Such a scrutiny has not always been made in the past in articulating guidelines. For example, standards in general suggest a lower per capita book ratio for large cities than small ones. This assertion, however, can be questioned if the known sociological and economic data about metropolitan areas are accurate. These data suggest that urban groupings are highly dynamic and complex with considerable personal interaction. Both of these conditions suggest in turn that the need for information is greater in both quantity and quality because there are proportionally more economic, social, and political decisions. Testing the accuracy of this latter interpretation is difficult if not impossible with current data because the profession has "decreed" the former analysis with the consequent effect that metropolitan cities have tended to formulate their development to agree with the analysis.*

Two other areas which have confounded the professionals for many years can be cited as examples of the need to question current standards. One is what happens when a standard is greatly surpassed, as in per capita support. In many sections of the profession, such surpassing is not considered *ipso facto* "good" or "superior"; instead, how the money is used is questioned — and here deficiencies are usually found. There is also a tendency to raise the standards at the next revision, and some librarians frankly admit that standards should always be set slightly above the ability of anyone to reach them. One might argue, accordingly, that the first two laws of public library development are: (1) all libraries must meet standards to be considered good or acceptable and (2) if a library meets the standards, it is still poor because the standards must be wrong.

*A current research project at the Graduate School of Library Services, Rutgers University, may shed some light on this point. It will attempt to determine information needs and the communication network in a metropolitan area.

The other area that has confounded librarians is that of small libraries. In these libraries, there is so much variation in administration and organization that one is tempted to hypothesize that they do not pay attention to and accept the advice of their "elders" as leaders of the profession in the centers of urban culture. Or it is possible that current standards are not relevant for their activities, and they know it and act accordingly.

Finally, general note must be made of four features of any statistical reporting systems for libraries, or other social services:

1. The expressions should be stated in such a way that they themselves do not set values. Values are imputed by the manipulators. Neither are the products of statistical computations norms or an ideal.

2. If developed or used properly, there should be a statistical or mathematical formula for each discrete element of a library program. This process admittedly creates seemingly artificial units which are then analyzed internally. They must be assembled for general program decision-making, and obviously can be assembled in different forms. These units, also, should be discrete enough to be subjected to testing.

3. A general statistical system does not need to reflect all sub-units or all of the possible variables in a total service. For one thing, there is generally no purpose in refining relationships beyond the accuracy of the raw data; and secondly, the end goal is *general* program decisions, which must be adjusted as they are exposed to the real social and political forces of a community. In short, enough variables must be used to delineate clearly the total pattern, but no more.

4. The statistics should state clearly the characteristics of the present — where we are now — and in such a manner as to facilitate forecasts of the future. The word "forecast" rather than "prediction" is used for a special reason. "Prediction" implies a degree of accuracy that cannot be achieved at this time with the known tools of social science research. "Forecast" carries the connotation of reducing the degree of uncertainty. While this approach may appear to be begging the issue, reducing the error of one factor in a complex social system by a small amount may increase the effective use of total public resources significantly. For example, preventing the establishment of a small library where it is not needed, at an annual operating cost of $20,000, means a saving of $200,000 to $300,000 in ten years plus the freeing of at least one employee for more productive ventures.

A Formula For Potential Public Library Service

The major elements of public library service are stated below in a form partially recognizable by most librarians. Each element has a rather specific meaning, is related to the others in a precise way, and is in turn composed of other factors. In understanding the formula,

$$\frac{B}{P} \cdot \sqrt{\frac{C}{P} \cdot S} = \text{Potential Service}$$

one must first accept the concept that the end product is potential service, meaning that the components for a definable type (level) of service are present. This type of service might not be attained in practice because of numerous factors, but they would be primarily personal ones such as attitudes of the library personnel or rejection of service by some groups in the community. If one wanted to be more general, potential service is also similar to the concept of the impact of the library on the community. It is not a standard *per se* even though it has overtones of good and bad, since a greater potential is usually desired for social services be they medicine, mental health, education, or libraries.

Material-Population. "$\frac{B}{P}$" is similar to the familiar expression of books per capita but sufficiently different that the appellation may create the wrong impressions. "B," for example, includes all resource materials which convey information or feelings to the recipient. A resource item, therefore, may mean a book, pamphlet, periodical, record, tape recording, framed picture, etc.* No distinction is made at this point in the relative numbers of each type for the simple reason that we do not know what the proper weighting or descriptive

---

*Guides must be established so that such things as cut-out pictures for elementary school teaching are not counted. Printed material should be counted as much as possible in terms of the standard concept of volumes. Ephemeral pamphlets, retained only for short periods and not fully cataloged, can be counted as (1) equivalents of 50 or 100 pages, or (2) feet of file or shelf space.

terms should be. The communication arts are changing so rapidly, as both a cause and effect of technology, that the library is taking on a different hue, much as one moves gradually from violet to indigo to blue in the color spectrum. Where we will be in five years is almost pure conjecture. We can be certain, though, that the traditional books will continue to be important but less significant in many settings such as language instruction, technical research in dynamic subjects, and art and music appreciation. Moreover, public libraries are becoming more and more only one of several institutions sharing the same responsibilities (e.g., with school, academic, and other special libraries), but with a specialized role as an important supplementary depository and a stimulus for the development of a broad-based and coordinated system.

In such a setting, one can argue at the moment that any one discrete item in any of the media of communications is equal to its counterpart in another, and if no counterpart exists it still has real meaning for a community. There is no one mold applicable to all communities; and indeed the systems concept, although bringing libraries together, is actually making greater diversity and decentralization possible. Unfortunately many librarians do not yet understand that systems have this merit. As long as libraries are staffed by presently trained professionals, there will be few instances where an array of collected material violates "good library conduct." By conduct is meant those universals in library teaching and literature which are not only recognized by the profession but actually practiced by all but an extremely small number of librarians. Included among these universals would be a recognition of the uniqueness of the *public* characteristic, maintenance of material in an orderly manner to permit easy identification and use, acceptance (at least at the conscious level) of the need for a variety of material, and identification with the profession. Differentiating conduct and standard allows a more precise definition of the latter.

No attempt is made to measure quality in most of this survey, on the assumption that it is primarily a function of the type of personnel. Besides, it seems, as discussed below, that there is a high positive correlation between quality and quantity, in which case quality becomes of serious concern only in the small library.[4] If one desired to identify types of material in this segment of the formula, he could do so easily by assigning weight factors, say .9 for a book and 1.1 for a periodical, etc.

Population. The population used in the denominator means only the area for which there is truly service, as distinguished from "access." This means that only that population should be counted which does not exceed the number of resource items, and provided that these people live within an average traveling time of thirty minutes of the library.[5] The effect of this definition would be to reveal areas that are actually unserved, but reported now in most statistics as merely a low level of service. Stated differently, there is a level of service that is so low that it should be recognized as clearly as the fiction on the bookshelves and so reported. One metropolitan library in the central United States, to use a specific example, claims service for the county in which it is located; but its book-population ratio is only .75 for the county and just barely over 1 for the city. The people in this area are being deceived in being told they have service. In one major state, 1.2 million people (slightly over 10 percent of the total state population) would be reported as unserved whereas now service is claimed for them.

This limitation in counting population serves several useful purposes that I have noted elsewhere:[3] (1) it protects the librarian from the pressure to overstate service in order to show that the library is moving onward and upward; (2) it states clearly that a ratio of less than 1 means service is really being provided to a select group of fortunates since many people could not utilize the facilities even if they so desired; and (3) it recognizes that political boundaries are an anachronism in modern library service, and that just because a library is located in a political jurisdiction that community does not necessarily have full service. Equally important, the simple act of forming districts or regions does not increase service — at most it only creates greater access, except in cases where there is one large library in a district with small libraries nearby.

Branches. For purposes of this method of analysis, branches in cities of approximately 50,000 population and over are considered separate libraries with their own service areas distinct from the central unit. As metropolitan areas become larger, the central library begins to change its character and cater to a more specialized clientele. It can so change that in some respects it ceases to be a public library because its very size makes it a forbidding institution to be revered and held in awe like the cathedral, but not to be used except on specific and urgent occasions. Any system of measuring library service, therefore, should contain a factor which distinguishes between *public* and *quasi-public* libraries, branches being the former.* If central libraries were truly used as the branch concept intends, most of them would sink in their own administrative mire in their efforts to send books to requesters. This conclusion in no way challenges the validity of branches but only raises the question whether we have the proper theoretical underpinning for them.

Circulation. Circulation is defined simply as a measure of the people who enter the institution for some purpose; and in most cases the total number would be a product of sampling procedures. Many of the discussions in the current literature and much of the expressed dissatisfaction about circulation have added to our confusions because they did not assert clearly what should be measured. Are we interested in (a) a facility's pattern of use (direct demand for service) for purposes of program decision-making, or (b) the number of people in the community who have gone to the library at least once in a given period? Although the two interests are not mutually exclusive, for purposes of this paper the former is of more concern. The latter is less accurate as a measure of direct library service because the public library is in part a symbol and safety valve, i.e., it is available if needed. Therefore, the percentage of the population using a library understates actual community demand and expectation. This measure also understates demand by the frequency of use per person, a factor which will be even more important in the future in shaping the character of library service.

Actual personal use, as distinguished from check-outs or cardholders, show rather accurately the total demand on a particular facility and the library personnel. Under this definition, any use of material, no matter how simple, is considered a circulation; and it is assumed that in only rare cases would a person going to a library not produce some direct "use" even if it were nothing more than browsing or reading a magazine. Counting persons also lends itself to analysing both the nature of the use and the type of the user. No distinction is here made between residents and non-residents, the basic reasoning being that this factor should be considered completely separate from a general evaluation of the potential of a library. A library used predominantly by non-residents is no better or worse than one used by residents. The non-resident problem, if such really exists, is one more of economic justice than anything else.

Square Root Function. The square root factor contains one of the value judgments noted earlier that must be included in almost any library statistical system. In effect, it states that circulation has a decreasing importance as it increases. The reasoning is simply that part of a library's value is a function of the probability that any one item will be available immediately on demand. As usage increases, the social value may go up, but the collective decrease in individual values as a result of not being able to get what is needed may equal the former and perhaps even produce a total negative effect. At the moment, I believe that a cube root would show a more accurate relationship, and at some point a negative value should be assigned to C; but application of these would be a drastic departure from some current thinking, and I have no substantiating test results.

Study-Research. The most important element in the formula, discussed in detail in the next section, is S, which stands for study or research capability. It means much more than reference and is based on an assumption that the usage pattern in the future will (a) reflect more on-site activity, (b) tend to be non-recreational,** and (c) require the participant to be more self-sufficient in his search but at the same time will also add to the discretionary responsibilities of the librarian in acquiring and retrieving material.

In one sense, the S factor is measured by $\frac{B}{P}$ and $\frac{C}{P}$, and inclusion of it in the formula leads in part to circular reasoning, i.e., the actual use may also reflect the capability of the institution to provide study or research opportunities. Poor study facilities, for example, should show up in a reduced $\frac{C}{P}$ and perhaps even

---

*I cannot myself decide whether "a circulating collection" among branches is proper. Basically, I do not like the approach because it implies a timetable for reading, or a definite reading pattern for each community. Someone should test the hypothesis that a permanent collection in each branch is preferred even at the price of slower growth. The volumes counted for a branch in this formula should be the volumes located permanently therein plus a percentage of the central collection. With the increase in branches, this percentage would drop rapidly since a book can be sent to only a given number of branches in a year regardless of the demand in all branches. As an example, a library with two branches might assign 30 percent of the collection to each branch, but if there were eight branches only 5 percent might be assigned to each.

**Recreational reading is primarily fiction and hobby materials. The need for these materials may be relatively high in communities where the educational level is low and economic opportunities are minimal. Higher educational attainment and income results in self-sufficiency in these items and diverse leisure time activities reduce the demand for hobby literature.

in B. The S factor is retained, nevertheless, because it reflects a special use with certain independent characteristics that describe and determine a library program and, equally important, it resolves the thorny issue of how to counterbalance the high values in most statistical reporting systems caused by collections with a high percentage of fiction or children's volumes and their consequent high circulation.

General Application. In a general application:

1. The factor $\frac{B}{P}$ would have a range of zero to about eight with perhaps few very small community libraries having a higher figure due to large area and sparse population.

2. Circulation would have an upper limit of four in nearly all instances, a limit which reduces markedly the great variation in circulation that one notices in current state reports.

3. Children's libraries and small community libraries with primarily a fiction collection would have a low product because of a low $\frac{B}{P}$, or because of the new way of measuring circulation, or because of a low S value.

4. Some metropolitan libraries now thought to be excellent would also tend to have a smaller product relative to other libraries because each branch would be considered a separate library. Instead of counting "identical" collections of 100,000 volumes each in four branches plus 500,000 in the central unit as a 900,000 volume library, as under the present method, they would become four modest efforts at library service, and one marginal collection. One can contend that the branches do not have identical collections. However, they cannot differ too much under present concepts of proper book selection which emphasize *good* items, good being defined in the same value structure by most librarians. The increasing nationalization of the population adds to the demand for the uniformity, as does the educational system.

5. The use of the multiplication function to show the relationships between the three factors is only suggestive although I believe it is realistic.* All three tend to be given equal weight except that the normally higher absolute value for a computed S makes it a major determinant of the final product. More refined processes, including calculus, would certainly be desirable at a later stage of development.

6. $\frac{C}{P}$ and S both reduce the need for a library to retain old or other non-usable items in order to keep its reported books-per-capita ratio high enough to give it stature among other institutions.

Further Notes on B. At this point two parenthetical comments on B are appropriate. First, some librarians would probably be more comfortable intellectually if B were divided into sub-units with perhaps a different weight being given to each. A fiction volume, for example, could be counted as one-half the value of a non-fiction one. Or, one could say that only the first 10,000 or 20,000 fiction volumes would be counted as a part of B. In this way small libraries would receive credit for their primary function of circulating recreational reading, but beyond this point they would not be considered any better as a result of further acquisitions (particularly duplicate copies). Such a limit would probably compel a more critical evaluation of new additions for their literary quality and probably would encourage weeding. If this approach were used, the 10,000 or 20,000 limit should be higher for larger urban areas, although they would catalog many fiction items as 800's, in order to accommodate the greater variation in reading habits.

Secondly, with the current size of the publishing industry, and with every indication of continued growth, quality almost of necessity must be considered a direct correlate of quantity. Academics find it difficult to maintain a current knowledge of their disciplines and often make decisions about acquisitions on a random and personal basis. A similar process goes on in public library circles although it is not obvious because of the use of recommended lists and printed reviews. The interesting question in this connection is how a book gets on a list, and who decides when a book is reviewed and by whom. These are not new questions to librarians and will probably not be new ones to the next generation.

Further compounding any effort to define quality is that a poor collection for Community A may have important items that supplement an integrated district collection. Should this collection be rated poor in terms only of the community in which it is located? Should the supplementary books be removed from Community A to the district center, thus raising the over-all community rating, but making access to them more

---

*Other illustrative possibilities with readily apparent different results would be: $\frac{B+C}{P} \cdot S$; $\frac{B+C}{P} + S$; $B \cdot \frac{(C \cdot S)}{P}$, etc.

difficult to A? I do not claim to know the answers but would hypothesize for the sake of identifying a desired test that marginal resource items (e.g., outdated books) detract from library service only if they occupy needed space or require more than routine maintenance by semi-professional personnel.

In the absence of these two demands, there is nothing wrong with retaining books and other material as long as possible and letting time be more active in the decision-making process. In short, quality is a nebulous concept which is so disturbing to many people that it cannot be accepted in daily administration. To these individuals, some libraries *must* be better than others; and there are surely some identifiable reasons which distinguish them. The argument in this paper is that the reasons are a combination of quantity and trained personnel, "a trained librarian" being defined by the author as a person who is knowledgeable about and identifies fully with both the social system in general and the communication arts in particular.

A Formula For The Study Factor

The capability of a library as a study or research center can be described first as the interrelationship of three items: (a) physical facilities measured in terms of desk (table) space (D); (b) periodicals (F); and (c) size of the non-fiction collection (B_1). All three of these are then related as one unit to personnel (Q), and hours of service (N):

$$S = (D \cdot B_1 \cdot F) \ (Q \cdot N)$$

Study Space. Wheeler and Githens advanced nearly two decades ago a formula for determining space needs as follows:*[6]

$$\frac{\text{Area in feet for}}{\text{entire building}} = \left(\frac{\text{Volumes}}{10}\right) = \left(\frac{\text{Seats} \cdot 40}{}\right) + \left(\frac{\text{Circulation}}{40}\right)$$

In their approach, space was made a function of volumes and circulation; but more important, a standard was built into the formula that presumed a certain need characteristic of all communities. The approach in this paper is very different in that it does not purport to set a standard but instead emphasizes the description of what exists by relating study space to resources according to the following simple expression: $\frac{X}{B_1}$, where X is the area for a study space in square feet (table or desk, chair, and aisle) and B_1 is the non-fiction collection (with collections under 10,000 volumes having a negative value). The larger the quotient the more effective the service that can be provided. This simple division itself will produce a very small fraction in nearly all libraries, but this should not detract from the basic principle because it can be adjusted by other computations to produce any magnitude desired.

Study space is used instead of total floor area — although the two are interdependent — because while a library grows in volumes its need for total area and study facilities does not increase in the same proportion. The direct economy of size in library service is limited because of the short distance people will travel to a library and impediments in retrieving from a large collection. However, unlike one publication, which suggests that the need for study space declines per 1,000 population in an almost straight line, I believe a more meaningful expression is the percentage of study space to total area. The curve depicting this relationship is probably as shown below** (Figure 1). The two places where the slope is less steep essentially mean that added volumes will not generate a major immediate demand for research, and at some point new stack facilities and processing and administrative offices must receive a higher priority. The flattening at the upper level, in particular, partly reflects the fact that added materials at this point are the more rare items used by special clienteles; and a public library of this size is in a metropolitan area where there are alternative

---

*The 10 represents 1 square foot for each volume. One seat is presumed to require 40 square feet. One square foot is also the space necessary to circulate 40 volumes per year.
**Wheeler and Goldhor advocate the following needs:[7]

Population	No. of Seats per 1,000 Population
Under 10,000	10
10,000 – 35,000	5
35,000 – 100,000	3
100,000 – 200,000	2
200,000 – 500,000	1¼
500,000 and over	1

facilities.* In addition some flattening must be expected if the previous hypothesis is true, that there is a definable maximum use of a given quantity of materials.

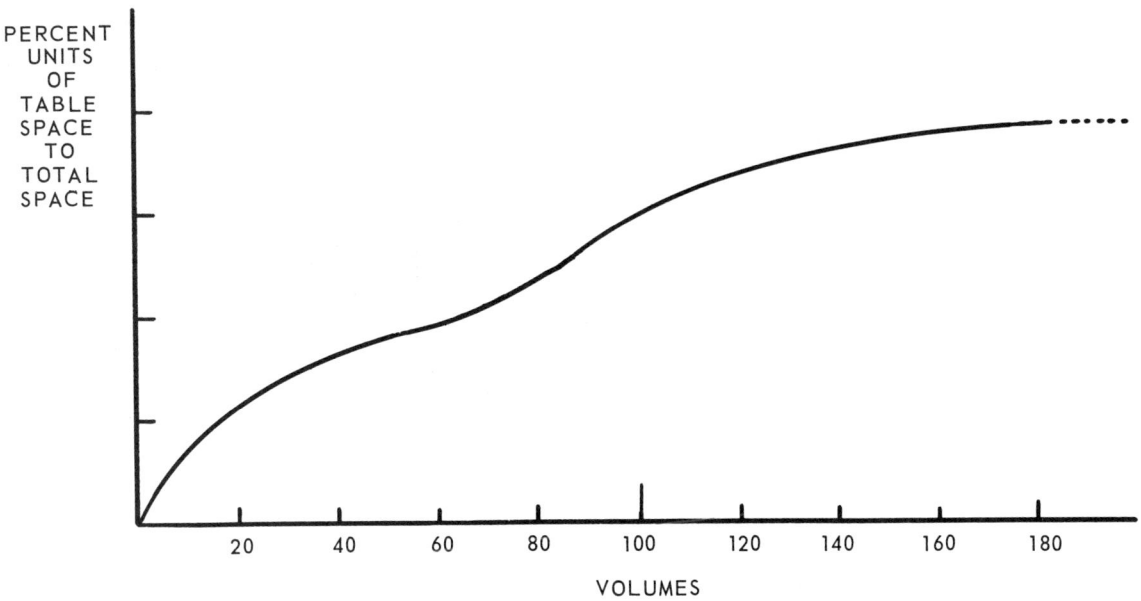

Figure 1.
Relationship between study space and volume growth.**

**In this chart the slope of the curve is set to agree with the volumes. The vertical scale is labelled "Percent Units" because there is no data to indicate the exact percentages — e.g. whether the first unit should be one, five, ten, etc. percent. As stated in the text, this curve is an "hypothesis."

The sharp rise in the curve for libraries with about 20,000 volumes (non-fiction) represents in part a backlog of demand to be expected in any new small library; particularly in small communities with few other alternative resources, each added non-fiction item would have a high marginal value which would be reflected almost inevitably in increased total library use. At about the 80,000 volume point, the library begins to change its character by offering materials to a wide variety of specialized and technical clienteles, with each added volume sometimes appealing to more than one clientele. In the 80,000 to 300,000 class, therefore, use will rise faster than the increase in resource items, thereby increasing the marginal utility of each added increment. The incremental units in a large library also have a high marginal value, but of a different type which should not be confused with that of the smaller library. The former is highly personal while the latter is more social, and total personal value is not the same as total social value.

The correctness of this curve could be tested rather easily in select communities by developing unit measurements of staff space per volume and measuring patterns of use in facilities of different and the same size. Measurements also could be made of the frequency of occupation of table space at the 80 percent level, noise factor, and time and motion necessary to acquire, use, and return a resource item.

B_1, the reader should be reminded, includes only those non-fiction volumes over the first 10,000.*** The assumption is that no collection of less than 10,000 volumes has enough reference or research potential to warrant assigning a positive value. For purposes of the formula, collections under this figure would be assigned a minus value equivalent to the deficit, i.e., the divisor for a 15,000 volume collection with 8,000 non-fiction items would be a $-2,000$.

*Librarians in large libraries will argue that they are grossly over-crowded, and that a flattening of the slope is therefore not correct. Where school libraries are underdeveloped or improperly administered, a larger than normal influx into the public library system is likely. Here, the problem of proper evaluation lies in the fact that many librarians view almost any concerted use as an intrusion. I would argue, to the contrary, that a *public* library by definition should expect major use by students.
***Resources are measured in this instance in standard volumes since at this time records and pictures are not for the most part research materials. They become so at a later date.

Limit on Study Space. At the other extreme, a limit could be set by saying that the study space would be reduced to the level where total circulation through this space did not exceed three times the number of non-fiction volumes, with circulation in this case being defined as each study space multiplied by the factor of 1 volume times 60 (the number of hours open each week) times 52 (weeks in a year). This would mean that a library open 60 hours a week during the entire year would generate a maximum countable circulation of 3,100 and with a collection of 20,000 non-fiction volumes would be permitted to count 19 to 20 study spaces regardless of the actual number. The purpose of this modification is to emphasize, again, that there is a limit to which a library can be used; adding study space in excess of this limit is not only uneconomical if it is not used, but also causes a decrease in the total value of the library if occupied maximally. The 60-hour factor is a way of saying to libraries open for fewer hours that increased hours of service are one way of making better use of the capital investment. The circulation factor as stated here is arbitrary and could be tested by observation to obtain a true value.

I might add parenthetically that some librarians will claim vociferously that uneconomical use of a library is impossible because all library service is controlled by a third natural law that says: No library shall knowingly be financed adequately.

Non-Fiction Collection. Although the non-fiction collection is a factor in the study space, it should also be considered an independent variable contributing some value to the community even if there are no opportunities for on-site use. The measurement proposed is a simple per capita ratio with one exception. Any collection under 10,000 volumes, as noted before, is presumed to have little intrinsic worth. The recorded amount in these instances, therefore, is proposed as a negative number indicating a fundamental deficiency.

Periodical Index. The periodical index will be treated briefly here. In essence, this index is an attempt to measure the general quantity and research potential of a periodical collection by dividing all periodicals into six classes: (1) sponsored, (2) current popular feature, (3) news magazines, (4) technical-special audience, (5) current serious features, and (6) professional journals.

$$\left[0.1 \frac{(M_6 - N_6)}{T_6} + 0.0005\, M_6 \right] + \left[0.09 \frac{(M_5 - N_5)}{T_5} + 0.0004\, M_5 \right] + \left[0.08 \frac{(M_4 - N_4)}{T_4} + 0.0003\, M_4 \right] +$$

$$\left[0.07 \frac{(M_3 - N_3)}{T_3} + 0.0002\, M_3 \right] + \left[0.06 \frac{(M_2 - N_2)}{T_2} + 0.0001\, M_2 \right] *$$

Two computations are made for each class. The first one is $\frac{M-N}{T}$, which is a short way of referring to average volumes per title that are at least five years old. The higher the average volumes per title the higher the computed value. Since, however, all libraries with the same average would have identical values, a factor for total volumes must be inserted. This is done by weighting and counting them separately. The application of the entire formula can be illustrated as follows:

1. If a library had 100,000 volumes in class 6, with an average of 100 volumes per title, its index would be about 59.5.** If it only averaged 50 volumes per title, the value would be about 54.7.

2. If a library had 100,000 volumes in class 2 with an average of 100 volumes per title, the computed value would be about 5.7. If it had 10,000 volumes, with an average of 20 volumes per title, its index would drop to about 1.9.

In its present form, the formula essentially says that only a very few large libraries should keep back issues of class 2 titles, and of course no credit is given to sponsored publications.

Limitation. This approach to measurement has a limitation in that a library with a small collection of a higher class could have the same index as another institution with many volumes of a lower class. In particular this could occur if the collections are primarily in the two middle classes. But from another point of view, this coincidence is exactly what should happen — a point is reached where it is not possible to say

---

*"M" represents the total volumes of periodicals; "N" is those volumes less than five years old; and the subscripts refer to the class of periodicals. "T" is the number of titles. The expression $\frac{M_6 - N_6}{T_6}$ is therefore the total volumes of all periodicals in class six (professional journals), minus those volumes less than five years old, and divided by the total number of titles of class six periodicals.

**The computation is based on the following: 100,000 total volumes, 1,000 titles, and 5,000 volumes less than 5 years old (five volumes per title).

that one combination of volumes is more valuable than another except as those volumes are related to other factors which cannot be expressed easily in this formula. To offset this limitation, tables could be computed showing the possible variations that would produce similar indices so that an observer would have some clues for interpretation. I suspect also that from such a table ranges could be set within which there would be a high probability that certain collections were similar. For nearly all titles, for example, there is a maximum of eighty to a hundred volumes (one volume per year). Regardless of the many titles now available, I would hypothesize that small libraries would tend to have a similar index number because librarians have fairly set standards of the proper titles that ought to be held.

Personnel. How to evaluate personnel, with particular reference to certification, has been a thorny problem for many years for nearly all professions. This paper does not address itself directly to the desirability of certification for librarians since the question has many ramifications, but instead proposes a way to express the general quality of a library's staff. It is frankly assumed that quality is directly related to educational training and experience in the vast majority of cases. These are also about the only factors which can be quantified easily in every state.

The statistical expression for the measurement is:*

$$Q = \frac{\frac{H \text{ (not to exceed 210)}}{30} + .2E \text{ (not to exceed 15)}}{A}$$

where H is the number of semester hours of college credits not to exceed 210 (which is approximately the Ph.D. level) divided by 30 in order to equate to academic years. To this value is added a factor of .2 of the total years of experience up to 15 years. This limit means that experience has value separate from education but that most persons have a definite peak of intellectual development in a job based on this one element alone. There is nothing magical about 15 except that it roughly correlates with the age of 40 for a person starting his working career at around 25 years of age — it could be 21 or 25 with no harm to the over-all proposal. A is the total number of employees who have a direct service contact with the public; and by using it as a divisor, an *average* value can be computed for each employee.

In the application of this formula, the maximum value for a library would be 10, with education counting for as many as 7 of the total points if the average educational attainment was at the Ph.D. level. A library would receive a maximum credit of 3 if none of its employees had been to college and if all had been librarians for at least 15 years. As a third example, an average of 4 years of college and average experience of 10 years would produce a result of 6. On a general basis, libraries with well-trained persons and low turnover would rate higher than institutions with primarily young graduates. Also, a library with employees with long experience only would approximate the same value as those with only 4 years of college work. The small library which will never be able to afford to employ at the M.A. level, or possibly even the B.A. level, is in effect told that it should get a person with as much education as possible and then retain and develop him by in-service training.

Two special features of this formula need individual attention. One is that A represents personnel who make direct decisions on library service. In some libraries this would include check-out employees and some secretaries, while in others the inclusion would be greater or smaller. This definition has been criticized for its vagueness since I first proposed it in 1964.[8] To a certain extent, the charges are true, but in defense I would argue that it is also closer to reality than other definitions. A member of the public is concerned primarily with the actual quality of service that he receives and pays for, and the librarians have an obligation to tell him as accurately as possible who determines service. Non-degree people *per se* are not always unqualified, as the above experience factor implies, even though some librarians feel insecure personally and professionally if *any* admission of this type is circulated. I am convinced personally that head librarians can apply this definition easily with a few guidelines — if they cannot, one might hypothesize they do not know what their subordinates are doing.

Secondly, this formula makes no distinctions between types of curricula or degrees. Considering the breadth of public library service today, a very persuasive argument can be made that a wide variety of cur-

---

*This formula is basically one devised for the School Foundation Program adopted in 1965 by the Kansas State Legislature. State aid is distributed in part on the basis of the quality of school personnel in each district.

riculum patterns would train potential librarians. One could be, for example, a good reference librarian without knowing how to catalog or acquire books. At the same time, other things being equal, knowing a little about all aspects of library service is valuable. In specifics, a person with three years of social service work and one year of concentrated library subjects might be equal to another person with a regular degree in library service.

If this proposal is too innovative, though, the formula can be changed very easily by counting only certain courses in the 210 semester hour limit.

Hours of Service. The last major proposal in this paper is to add a factor for hours of service. Its primary value in the over-all scheme is to produce a higher value for a library that is identical to another one in all respects except the number of hours during which the public has access to the resources. This factor is also a way to show the total number of personnel. In present statistical reports, total employees are reported as a raw number, with the reader being left with the chore of evaluating its meaning. It seems much more desirable to say at the outset that the number has meaning only as it is related to hours open and the nonfiction collection; the latter is that segment of the resources with which the user is likely to need help. It is suggested therefore that the relationship be expressed as:

$$\frac{\text{Employees . Hours Open Over 1500}}{\text{Non-Fiction Volumes}}$$

Employees is the same number used in the previous expression, and the 1500 hours represent approximately 30 hours per week in a year. Below this number, a library would receive no credit, which also means a zero for the entire study factor, on the basis that the public does not have adequate opportunity to use the facilities and thus really to make the library program a viable one. Stated differently, an excellent collection with highly-qualified employees means little in the modern setting if the hours of service are so restricted that an excessively large number of patrons would have to use the facilities at the same time. Crowding not only reduces professional service per patron but also creates adverse conditions for use of materials on the site. The relationship to volumes should be obvious: resources have meaning to the extent there is personnel to acquire, select, and locate individual items. Theoretically, one could overstaff a facility, but this is very unlikely and need not be of concern to us at the moment; such an occurrence would be obvious anyway if the data were reported as suggested above, since in a simplified way the formula is a statement of man hours per volume of resources.

CONCLUSION

Although there are many other relationships, such as branch service, which can be described in statistical terms, the ones presented above are sufficient to illustrate the concept proposed in this paper. This writer is convinced that this approach, despite its limitations, must be employed if there is to be any real breakthrough in developing meaningful standards. Before standards can be formulated, we must think much more clearly and precisely about the elements of library service. This thinking must then be articulated in some type of "neutral language" and in such a way that ideas or conclusions can be tested empirically. Developing library service in terms of intuition as we have been doing is an anchronism that must be recognized at once. Political decision-makers, among others, are not accepting this approach in other areas of social service, and there is no reason to believe they will make an exception for library programs.

The statistical expressions in this paper are not final but only an introduction, with the hope that several people will join the movement and start testing them. If any one is proved erroneous or needs modification to express reality more accurately, I will be among the first to discard it. I am convinced, though, that such a demonstration will have a by-product which will lead to other more accurate expressions.

No mention is made about expenditures or income. Both of these are merely tools to accomplish the desired purpose. Income and expenditures state what can be bought but they do not tell us what *should* be bought. Further, they can be used to acquire such a variety of things that they do not describe accurately what is actually occurring. In short, the dollar amounts are of concern after the program has been evaluated.

The formulae can be expressed as one unit or the components can be treated as independent units. At places in these expressions, my own concept of a standard is obvious. The reader may disagree, but again the burden is to test concepts, not merely to assert disagreement as an article of faith. Each person may insert his own standard as long as he too agrees to submit it to testing.

Finally, there is no pretense that the ideas in this paper are new. They may suggest, however, that there is a different way to examine library service and that a different approach may result in new insights long hidden by traditional thought processes.

REFERENCES

1. Chicorel, Marietta. "Statistical Ammunition. A Report on a National Conference on Library Statistics," *Library Journal*, 91:3363, July 1966.
2. Statistics Coordinating Project, American Library Association. *Library Statistics: A Handbook of Concepts, Definitions, and Terminology*. Chicago, ALA, 1966.
3. Beasley, Kenneth E. *A Statistical Reporting System for Public Libraries*. (Pennsylvania State Library Monograph No. 3.) University Park, Pa., Institute of Public Administration, Pennsylvania State University, 1964.
4. *Ibid.* See p. 8 for a further discussion on quality-quantity. Quality factors could be added to the formula if one disagreed with this line of reasoning. To do so, though, would probably add a complexity that would not be offset by improved practical measurements.
5. *See* Lowell Martin's forthcoming *Progress and Problems of Pennsylvania Libraries* (p. 78 of mimeographed advance copy). The thirty minute maximum has never been tested under controlled circumstances. There is general professional agreement, though, about a limit of approximately this magnitude.
6. Wheeler, Joseph L., and Githens, Alfred M. *The American Public Library Building*. New York, Charles Scribners, 1941, p. 41. For an application of the formula, *see* Wheeler, Joseph L., and Goldhor, Herbert. *Practical Administration of Public Libraries*. New York, Harper & Row, 1962, pp. 554-555.
7. Wheeler and Goldhor, *ibid.*, p. 554.
8. Beasley, *op. cit.*, p. 23.

CHAPTER II: MEASUREMENT AND EVALUATION OF THE PUBLIC LIBRARY

CHARLES M. ARMSTRONG
Associate Statistician, Division of Evaluation
New York State Education Department, Albany

The measurement and evaluation of the public library is an elusive problem. The nature of the library operation makes this inevitable. A brief discussion of the theory of evaluation will make the characteristics of the problem clear and will simplify and integrate the subsequent discussion. The ultimate point of measurement and evaluation in an institution is its product. Does it produce what it is designed to produce, and does the product meet the requirements of the customers? The ultimate product of the library is intangible. The stimulation of the human mind cannot be measured by any objective method. It has the elusiveness of all education, but this elusiveness is re-enforced by the spontaneity of the relationship between the library and its user. The librarian seldom knows exactly why a given individual comes to the library or exactly what he secured. A sample of users can be questioned and an idea of the product can be secured by ingenious questions, but many people are inarticulate and the usual questionnaire is a cold device that can only partially penetrate to the essence of the relationship.

Of the measures that we have used in New York State, one of the most successful in really measuring what the heavy users of the small library secured was a record of each book drawn by each borrower so that at the end of a year the evaluator could summarize the use made by individuals, at least to the extent of seeing the titles of the books drawn. A special study was made to identify outstanding types of borrowers. A few case studies from the report of the Watertown experiment will make the elusiveness of the ultimate product clear:

Case 1. Dr. _____ is a practicing physician in his forties. He seldom comes to the library but sends his wife or daughter. He borrowed 56 nonfiction books and 11 fiction books.

Case 4. Miss _____, a nurse, borrowed 147 books. They were for patients in her nursing home but taken out in her name.

Case 6. Mrs. _____ is a mother and teacher in a rural school. She borrows for her family, her school and herself. She borrowed 279 adult and 276 juvenile books.

Case 8. Mr. _____ lives alone some distance from the library. In the winter months he gets books and lends them to his neighbors. He borrowed 9 nonfiction, 89 fiction and one juvenile book.

Case 9. Rev. _____ and his wife are avid readers of books on many topics. They borrowed 119 books of which 98 were nonfiction.

Case 10. Mr. _____ is a farmer of Indian descent and has been educating himself. He has borrowed books such as Bolton's *Poor Boys That Became Famous* and *How to Build a House*. He has actually built a house and made furniture using public library books as guides. His borrowing includes 35 nonfiction, 14 fiction, and 9 juvenile books.

The key point in the case studies is that the borrowing of the book is not the real ultimate product of the library. The real product is the house built by the Indian, the improved sermons of the minister, or the stimulated children taught by the rural school teacher. The ultimate measure of a library is the kind of community it serves. In other words, the public library is an important element in the complex of forces that keeps a community interested in education and the advancement of knowledge. Perhaps any community that lacks strong cultural activities should look to its library to see if it is actually performing its job.

There are many essential steps or processes in a public library operation. Staff has to be hired, books have to be purchased, and buildings acquired before a library can serve its public. Before the community is stimulated, users must actually come to the library and use the facilities. All of these are facilities or processes that are essential to the library operation. The existence of these facilities and processes indicate that library service is possible, but they do not prove that library service exists. The lack of one of these essentials will largely preclude the possibility of service, or a poor facility or process may narrow service sharply.

Therefore, in all that follows, the discussion will deal with measuring facilities and processes, and the data obtained must be reviewed to see if they presumably resulted in the desired ultimate product.

The Intensity of Library Use-User Surveys

Of all the generally feasible process measures, the one that comes closest to establishing a product is the user survey. As used in the recent New York State two-year evaluation of regional public library systems, the user survey consisted of a questionnaire secured from everyone coming into the library for a week. This universal questionnaire was short and was supplemented by a longer questionnaire given to every tenth person. The short questionnaire included questions establishing the residence of the user in accord with the political subdivisions used by the U.S. Census, the education of the user by the definitions in the census, and the purpose of the person in coming to the library. The longer questionnaire secured more details on use and satisfaction. With the short questionnaire a number of crucial measures of library effectiveness could be obtained. The key measure is what proportion of the people living in a community and having a specific educational background come into the library. The results obtained in the New York State study surprised the evaluation staff and gave it some new perspectives. The surveys were run in thirty-nine libraries of various types; as expected among the adults over twenty-five, the more education, the more intense the use of the library.

The surprise came in the wide variation in use from library to library and in the kind of library that encouraged intensive use. The highest intensity of use among women college graduates was 31 percent visiting the library in a week. The low intensity libraries showed 3 and 4 percent or even a little less. These low figures are subject to some correction because of bookmobiles and branches in some cases, but there is little question that some use levels are as low as 4 percent. Many libraries are at the 10 percent level. The highest intensity of use seems to come in the middle-sized libraries with 35,000 to 100,000 nonfiction volumes. Apparently these libraries are large enough to satisfy the bulk of the users but draw from a small enough area to be convenient to them. Smaller libraries generally lack too many items and larger libraries become inconvenient. The important point for this paper is not the detail of what was found, but rather that the findings were unexpected. The findings are only useful as one examines a considerable number of libraries by the same device. Isolated figures are almost meaningless. If one knows that a certain library had 10 percent of women college graduates over twenty-five years of age visiting it, he does not get much help in evaluating it. He must have a standard of comparison. When we know that a considerable number of libraries draw more than 20 percent, the 10 percent figure takes on meaning. Therefore, it is important that user surveys be run in a defined pattern so that various types of norms can be established.

There are three important kinds of norms that should be established: (1) the median – i.e., one-half above, one-half below; (2) the upper quartile – i.e., the level at which one quarter are above and three quarters below; and (3) the highest percentage attained by any library. The median establishes what most libraries are doing. The upper quartile establishes a goal that is immediately possible, and the highest percentage attained by any library establishes an ultimate possibility that has been demonstrated as attainable by actual experience.

There are of course many other incidence measures beside the one for women, already cited. There is obviously one for men and one for students beside ones for various different political sub-divisions such as city, village, town or county. The user survey will also provide measures of the kind of service different groups want and the kind of service actually received. The measurements obtained in a user survey seem to be so important that every library should run one every few years. Measurement is essential and no other available technique comes as near to measuring the actual library product as the user survey. The expense is appreciable but the alternative ignorance is dangerously expensive. The American Library Association might logically develop a standard routine for running user surveys and gather the resulting intensity of use figures which could then be organized into standards and reported back to the members of the profession.

Somewhat similar results, with even more information on what the public thinks about libraries, can be obtained from an opinion poll. Valuable information of this type was obtained in the Public Library Inquiry made by the Social Science Research Council of the ALA almost twenty years ago.[1] This seems to be too expensive a device to use for routine measurements. The samples drawn must be large to give reliable comparisons from library to library. Occasional opinion polls are useful to gain perspective on how the total population feels about libraries, but the user survey should be part of the regular routine of library management.

A few cautions are in order concerning the design of user surveys. The period of the survey should be substantial to include a range of different kinds of days. It should be selected to be representative of normal use. The Christmas vacation is not good, for instance. Where there are main libraries, branches, and bookmobiles operating in the same political sub-division, they should all be surveyed simultaneously. The main library in a big city frequently does not draw very intensively because so many people get their service from a branch. The New York State user surveys suggest that in some of our cities branches may be too small and central libraries too large to achieve maximum intensity of use among college graduates.

Once the standards are established for each educational group, an expected total library use for a community or state can be computed by applying these standards to the educational distribution in the political sub-division under consideration. In the New York State study, an estimated number of users was computed for the total state based on the results obtained in the sample. This statewide estimate of users visiting the library in a week was 545,000. By 1985, the total population and the education level of that population is expected to increase to such a point that the weekly users will total 922,000 if there are no general improvements in library practices. If the average intensity of use improved to the effectiveness of the present upper quartile, the use would go to about 1,540,000 or an increase of 183 percent over the 1960 use. Librarians are going to have to race to keep their institutions growing fast enough to keep up with these almost automatic increases in demands.

Sample Questions. Another useful technique that is quite close to a product measure is the sample question. In this measurement device, the evaluator becomes a library user and asks a reasonable question to see if the library will actually give him a reasonable answer. This is a product measure except that the user is an artificial concept instead of a real user. A few questions of this type can be quite illuminating in showing up weak spots in a library's actual procedures. For instance, in one fine library that was obviously capable of providing good answers, the person at the information desk was not adequately trained and did not direct the inquirer to the right person. In another case, where the questions were submitted as interlibrary requests, the reviewer at the reception point was a junior librarian who thought he had the right answer but in fact did not. In another case the librarian failed to notice that part of the loose leaf *Readers' Guide* was missing. The questions that seemed to give the most trouble were simple scientific requests such as: "Where is the major breeding place for pure-bred mice to be used in medical experiments?" and "What is the maximum voltage currently bring considered for electrical transmission?"

The findings in the New York State evaluation indicated that some librarians were not well versed in scientific terminology, and that effectiveness in handling the questions was frequently dependent on the mental attitude of the librarian rather than on the amount of library training she had. One of the most startling findings was the reluctance of the librarians to refer the problems to a higher authority. Thus a local librarian would struggle with her limited resources without calling for help at the system headquarters.

Circulation. The old stand-by of available measures of library use has been circulation. The relation of circulation to library product has been seriously questioned, particularly since the increased reference and research use by students. The great advantage of circulation is the ease of getting the data and the case of definition. The serious defect is that circulation is dominated by the habits of a small proportion of library users and can be changed quickly by policy changes in the library that may not greatly change the effectiveness of the library. In the New York State User Survey, 30 percent of the users did not check out any books and 27 percent of the borrowers accounted for 72 percent of the circulation. In the Watertown experiment in regional library service, the circulation dropped in some communities when the book stock was improved. Apparently the average reader takes longer to read a non-fiction book or even a serious fiction book than to read a mystery of light love story. The evidence is overwhelming that circulation is not a reliable indicator of the libraries' product, but it still may be a reasonable indicator if used with caution. In the New York State User Survey the circulation per capita of users of the library varied from 1.5 to 2.5 in the libraries surveyed. This shows that there is fairly close relationship between circulation and number of users. If circulation changes, the measure has enough value to warrant careful exploration of the probable reasons.

The inter-relations between circulation, book stock and acquisitions are interesting and important in terms of measuring library operations. If two-tenths or one-fifth of a book per capita (one book for every five persons) is purchased in a year and if the average book is in the library for ten years, the book stock per capita would be ten times two-tenths or two books per capita. If there are 25 circulations per capita in a year and two books per capita then the books in the library would have an average circulation of 12½ (25 circulations per capita divided by two books per capita). Since each book is assumed to remain in the library for ten years the average circulation per book before withdrawal would be 125. This is an extremely high figure for circulation and if the practical limit of circulation for a book is 60 instead of 125 then the purchase of two-tenths of a book per capita would only allow 12 circulations per capita instead of the 25 originally hypothesized. This can be computed by multiplying the annual number of books per capita purchased, by the circulation of 60 for a book. In other words, .2 of a book times 60 circulations per book gives 12 circulations per person. If the purchasing policy only provided one-tenth of a book per capita the circulation would be limited to 6 per capita. Where circulation per book approaches the upper limit of the book's capacity a high proportion of the books wear out before they are obsolete and the book stock is less than the anticipated ten times annual purchases. Where many books are discarded because they are worn out, there is danger that the book stock will be deficient in the number of popular books, unless special care is taken to replace the worn out books.

Number of New Books Exposed. Among the newer measures of library effectiveness used in the New York State evaluation was the "number of new books exposed." This is a process measure and is several steps away from an actual product but it is an important measure of one of the essential processes, acquiring books. The number of books acquired has long been a measure of library operations. It assumed that the effective book supply was owned by the library. With the development of systems, a larger and larger proportion of the books available are not acquired by purchase by the local library but by borrowing from the system. The "new books exposed" measure is the sum of books purchased and books borrowed. The difference is primarily of importance in the small library. With system support, a high proportion of the New York State libraries are exposing over a thousand new volumes a year. A small library becomes a fairly satisfactory book exchange point if its readers have the opportunity of browsing in and borrowing a thousand new titles a year. This is particularly true if the titles are well selected.

Evaluation of the Book Selection Process

The attempts at evaluation of the selection process in the public library operation have established several facts but have not resulted in any fully satisfactory method of establishing standards for book selection. From the user or, more particularly, from the product point of view, one can establish certain goals for the selection process. One of the first goals is speed. Many books deal with current problems, and even novels are topics of discussion and community stimulants in the months immediately after publication. New York State studies have indicated that a high proportion of the circulation is among the new books. If the effective life of a book is two years, a delay of one month in acquisition represents the loss of about 4 percent of the value of the book. Few New York State systems deliver books to the local library within one month of publication and delays of two and three months are common. A three month delay could easily lose 12 percent of the value of the book to the users.

Another goal of the selection process is interest to the reader. There is little in the library literature to establish what the potential readers really want. Selection in the professional view seems to be an art rather than a statistical calculation. George Norvelle, formerly in the New York State Education Department, has made some extensive studies of student and adult reading interests.[2] In his published books on the interests of school children, he has reported that teacher judgments are not a good indicator of student interest. In an unpublished manuscript, he has analyzed adult interests and has established sharp differences between different groups of people and, of particular importance, differences between the judgment of the people and the judgment of literary experts. He found that the public is primarily interested in content rather than literary style. His findings suggest that objective standards of selection should be developed based on sample observations of public interest.

In the Watertown experiment, the system policy was to furnish the books the readers wanted in quantities adjusted to the demand for the books. The results seemed to be satisfactory from the user point of view, but the policy was discontinued at the end of the experiment before its advantages and disadvantages were fully established or a measure of effectiveness worked out. The policy had the clear-cut advantage of providing current books in quantity at the date of publication. Two systems are now operating programs with apparent success that approximate the Watertown process. Central buying on the basis of pre-publication data can speed up the acquisition. No one has measured whether the conspicuous errors in such a policy are really serious. When unused books revert to the central agency, the errors are very conspicuous as multiple copies accumulate on the shelves. When the buying is by individual library, the mistakes are scattered among many libraries and are not so noticeable. New York State experience suggests that this is an area demanding further study and the development of adequate measures of speed and suitability of acquisition.

In the area of suitability of acquisition, the New York State evaluation team developed a series of lists against which the library holdings could be checked. In some cases these were lists of books that almost all librarians would feel should be included in their library, and in other cases they were random selections from publication lists. These provided a standard against which the acquisition policy could be judged. There were many differences in the libraries examined, but they reflected size and adequacy of support rather than observable differences in community needs. There were, of course, some obvious librarian failures where needed books were overlooked. There was little evidence in the findings that need varied much from community to community except as the total population and educational level of the community changed. The book needs of a community with a high proportion of college graduates are quite different from one with few high school graduates. This suggests that standards for book acquisition might be set by size of community and educational level of the population.

Quality of Staff

Measuring the quality of the staff is another important but difficult part of an evaluation. One of the easy methods is to find the educational background of each staff member and assume that the higher the educational level the better. Actually this does not result in a good evaluation. If one considers the interrelation of salaries and education in terms of the labor market, one immediately sees that if an institution has a low salary scale and a high academic requirement, the people actually hired will be the leftovers among the highly educated. A high proportion of these are likely to have personality difficulties or be undesirable for some other reason. On the other hand, where salaries are high relative to educational requirements, the employing institution has lots of opportunity to employ the best. In the end, the evaluation of the staff is to a large extent subjective except as there is evidence of noticeably good or bad management, and perhaps the best way to conduct the evaluation is to measure the efficiency of the operations. Thus, if suitable books are acquired promptly, if questions are answered promptly and suitably, if interlibrary loans are prompt, the presumption is that the staff is good. A comparison of salaries paid and average salaries in the labor market for the designated types of persons is a useful evaluative tool. If salaries are below average, the quality of the staff is likely to be below average.

Estimating the Building Needs

Buildings are a key element in library service. An inadequate building can easily become jammed during student rushes and become unattractive to adults. The usual building estimates are based on population, and New York State user surveys have shown that use is not a simple function of total population but is highly differentiated by educational level. Thus, in a reasonably good library in a town of about 30,000, the incidence of use by college graduates was 19 percent, by those with 1-3 years of college about 10 percent, by high school graduates about 5 percent, by those with 9-11 years of high school less than 2 percent, and by those with below 8 grades of schooling less than 1 percent. Therefore the expected number using the library should be projected on the basis of user survey information, and the building requirements computed from expected users in a good building rather than on a per capita ratio. Obviously the building should not be designed for the number of users coming to the old building but on the intensity of use achieved in good buildings in other communities, using this measure as a standard for estimating use in the given community. This type of formula will result in larger buildings in the suburbs and generally smaller buildings in the cities than the per capita formulae.

Interlibrary Loans

The interlibrary loan is now becoming an important part of library operations in the New York State systems. Various measures are important in judging the efficiency of this operation. First of course is the simple number. Second is the average and maximum time from request to fulfillment of the loan. Third, the number of failures to find the desired item. The cost per loan is also very important as this is an expensive operation and varies widely from system to system. Statistics are also needed on the library satisfying the interlibrary loan request. If costs are to be reasonable, most requests must be filled by the primary resource, which in New York State is the central library of the regional system. This requires a highly developed acquisition policy for the central library so that the mass of interlibrary loan demands can be met. The proper design and maintenance of the interlibrary loan mechanism is difficult and demands good records to establish the nature of the problems and pitfalls. The problems are so complex and so new that professional judgment will be an inadequate basis unless supplemented with statistical reports of what actually happens.

These problems are not yet properly solved in New York State. Some systems are satisfying 80 to 90 percent of their interlibrary loan requests by local resources and some are only meeting 60 percent. The kinds of requests forwarded by the library that is meeting 90 percent of its interlibrary loan requests tend to be the really difficult ones that justify the use of a superlibrary, but many requests coming in from the 60 percent fullfillment libraries are for books that they should own. In some cases, they are for books that are available in paperbacks and it would be cheaper for the system to buy the paperback book than to forward a request to the state library.

Unit Costs

Up to this point little has been said about money, but money is one of the very important elements in library operation. There is urgent need for unit cost figures in library operation, and in the New York State studies various attempts have been made to find unit costs. No measures have been found that pleased the librarians. With present library accounting methods, unit costs are a product of gross averages and are therefore subject to many errors because of resulting poor definitions. Perhaps the most serious difficulty is the impracticability of separating research and reference expense from circulation expense. Thus there is a tendency for unit costs per book circulated to go up because the public library provides better reference facilities, and this is not fair. At the same time, one cannot think adequately about library problems without getting approximate unit costs. The competing pressures have prevented a satisfactory solution.

A regular book circulation is bound to run quite high. If the book costs $6 including cataloging, and it circulates fifty times, the cost of the book per circulation runs at 12 cents. The overhead items chargeable against the loan are at least as much. Total cost must be above 25 cents per loan. If one divides total expenditures, excluding capital, by circulation in some New York State libraries, one gets a wide range, from below 25 cents to as high as 70 cents. In other words about all we can say is that the cost of loaning a book is substantial. These rough cost figures indicate the need for improved procedures. Actually few people will work hard on improving the procedures unless unit cost figures are part of the accounting routine.

Rough calculations have indicated that interlibrary loans cost the systems from around $1 up to $3 or $4 depending on the efficiency of the library. Any cost to the local library is an addition. If the average pay of a librarian is $6,000 a year and he works 1800 hours a year, the cost of one hour of his time is a little over $3. If the requesting librarian uses fifteen minutes to place the request, and system headquarters or the central library uses fifteen minutes the total time is one-half hour or $1.50 just for the librarian's identifiable time. When a share of the cost of maintaining the central library as an interloan facility is added in, it is easy to see that the cost of an interlibrary loan is bound to be substantial.

A cost item that is seldom mentioned in the literature is the cost of selecting a book for purchase by the library. No figure is obtainable because libraries seldom keep a record of the time spent selecting books. The cost is probably quite high where a librarian actually looks at the book. Even reading and considering reviews could easily run into fifteen or twenty minutes per book purchased and twenty minutes time is $1 of salary without consideration of overhead items.

Another important cost item is the ordering and processing of books. This work is performed by the systems in New York State and costs on an average about $1.75 per book. It varies substantially from system to system, with the variations in managerial efficiency of the systems accounting for much of the difference. The $1.75 cost is a large element in library operations and needs close managerial attention. At present New York State is studying the possibility of statewide processing, which seems to offer possible savings.

In terms of unit costs, it is interesting to look at the total cost of operation of the library system in comparison to the estimated total number of persons visiting the library. In 1965 New York State spent $65,000,000 (excluding capital expenditures) on public libraries. This gave a per capita cost of $3.89. There is no good estimate of the number of users visiting the library but a crude estimate of the weekly number was made based on the results in the 39 libraries with a user survey. The estimate obtained was 545,000 per week. The week selected for the survey was, to the best of the surveyors' knowledge, a typical week so that the annual visits should be approximately 52 times 545,000 or 28,340,000. If this estimate is correct the cost per user visit was about $2.30 calculated on the basis of 1.6 visits annually per capita of the population of New York State. Even these crude estimates are valuable in planning libraries. The justification for the public library lies in the importance of its use not in the low unit cost. A large part of library expense is overhead. The expenditure has to be made if the operation is to exist. The unit costs on low volume of use are very high; if use increases, unit costs drop. With the large increase in use expected as a result of population growth and increased education, unit costs should drop.

Another cost figure that few people compute but that gives increased perspective on the nature of the library problem is the annual cost per person using the library. The highest intensity of use, found in the New York State studies, was in a small community where half as many people came into the library as there were people in the area. For this community, the annual cost per user would be twice the per capita cost. A more common figure of use is one-fifth of the number living in an area using the library. In such a community the annual cost per user would be five times the per capita cost and would be $15 for a community with a $3 per capita cost or $20 for a community with a $4 per capita cost. This measure helps one to see that the value to the user must be substantial and presumably should have transfer value beyond the immediate user. The more universal library use becomes, the nearer this figure approaches the per capita cost.

Source of Financial Support

In New York State, one of the great problems is the determination of the proper source of financial support for the library. In the past, New York State aid to libraries has been approximately 20 percent of total public library expenditures. Thus, if a community needed $4 per capita, it might hope to get about 80 cents per capita from the state. If the locality could raise $3.20, the need would be met. The critical question is, can a given community raise $3.20 for its part in maintaining a library? Actually some New York State communities do not appear to be able to raise that kind of money. In order to establish an upper limit of support, the tax support per capita was computed for a large list of central libraries and for another list of local libraries. A scattergram was made of the various per capitas relating the local tax funds per capita to the full valuation per capita. The higher the full valuation per capita the easier it is for the community to get a high per capita support. In the New York State experience, few communities raise more than .7 mills per dollar of full valuation. If this is accepted as an upper limit, then a community with a full valuation of $4,000 per capita can only be expected to raise about $2.80 per capita. Where the full valuation is $7,000 per capita, the same rate of taxation would yield $4.90. Actually many communities raise far less than the .7 mills per dollar, but few can argue that a community is not doing its share when it raises this amount. The discrepancy between the per capita full valuation times .7 mills and the needed per capita support for the desired library service is an index of need for state aid in that locality.

The relation between ability to pay and actual funds raised is an important consideration in the design of state aid and the development of cooperative library systems. Where a community refuses to tax itself but joins a cooperative system, it is likely to sponge off its neighbors and to get benefits from state aid with little or no self-help. If taxes are assessed in large units, like counties, the problem of local ability becomes less serious although it still demands attention. Figures of the type just discussed are essential to developing proper concepts of equity as library systems develop.

Managerial Efficiency

One of the interesting measures of library efficiency consists of a comparison of the proportion of the various kinds of population using the libraries and the per capita support level. In the New York State studies, some libraries with relatively low expenditures receive heavy use. Thus, a central library and branch with per capita expenditures of $2.27 had 31 percent of the women college graduates and 17 percent of the college men graduates visiting the library in one week. In the under twenty-five age group, 7 percent of the girls and 5 percent of the boys visited the library in a week. In the case of another central library with one branch with per capita expenditures of $2.29, the figures were college women 19 percent, college men 20 percent, girls 11 percent and boys 10 percent. A good central library with a branch had an expenditure of $6.06 and use intensity of college women 21 percent, college men 10 percent, girls 8 percent and boys 7 percent. The point is that there is no obvious relationship between expenditure and intensity of use. Such discrepancies between actual results and theoretically expected results call for the intensive development of measures of efficiency and the exploration of the reasons for these results. If there is no error in the figures or the assumptions, the indication is that there may be serious deficiencies of management in some of the libraries.

Wide Range of Library Purposes

One of the confusing elements in analyzing comparative library statistics is that public libraries vary in their purpose and design. In New York State, the term applies to small town libraries and also to huge central libraries such as the new central library in Buffalo. The very small town or village library, as a general rule, is lucky if it can maintain a good supply of books for circulation and seldom can provide good reference materials for students. At the other extreme, some big cities, like Buffalo, maintain central libraries that are substantial research and reference centers. The user in the small town library must generally secure whatever value he gets by borrowing and reading books. The benefits are primarily in his pleasure or his general education. The benefits to society are general rather than specific or transferable. The central library which is a good reference library may be used by some seeking general education, but its unique capacity is its ability to give critical help to persons working on difficult problems. Few inventors and research workers report the specific critical parts the library played in their research, although almost all consider the research library a necessary facility. A few cases have been reported which show the logical importance of the research library in our society. The story of insulin illustrates this principle. Banting, the developer of insulin, was an apparently unsuccessful doctor, unable to attract a lucrative practice. He supplemented his effort to start a practice by teaching medicine, and in connection with his teaching read in a small medical library. He got an idea from his reading and the end product was present-day insulin. This one discovery is estimated to benefit the residents of New York each year by more than the annual cost of all college and research libraries in the state. The New York City Public Library has been reported as a source of critical information in the development of the Xerox technique. A small royalty on all uses of Xerox would support a large research library. The little circulation library has to be judged largely on the number of users, but the large reference library may justify its existence by one or two great discoveries. There is no common method of measuring the significance of use across such a wide range in characteristics. Perhaps one should say that all indexes of library measurement must be interpreted with caution.

Proportion of Various Kinds of Users

Before closing these comments on New York State's experiments in measurement, some mention should be made of the user survey data on the proportions of different kinds of users. The discussion early in this paper dealt with the proportion of the population living in an area and using the library. This requires information on the total population as well as the visitors. No information is needed on the number living in an area to find the proportion of the users who are college graduates or the proportion who use the catalog. Many of these figures are helpful in evaluating the public libraries. Thus the proportion of children, of students using the adult library, and of other adults among the users made the "student problem" very clear. Children were 20 percent of the users, students 40 percent and adult nonstudents 40 percent. If school libraries really provided services needed by all children and students, many public libraries could not justify the maintenance of anything beyond a book exchange because the use of the reference facilities would be so limited.

College graduates were 40 percent of the users over twenty-five, those with one to three years of college were 25 percent, and high school graduates were 28 percent, leaving 8 percent for those with less than high school education. The library clearly serves the well-educated.

Of the total users in central libraries, 42 percent came to get general reading to take home, 24 percent to browse or read, 15 percent to study, and 25 percent to get material for school. The non-centrals show lower use percentages for most items but more users take general reading home. This points to the availability of reference materials as an important element in the amount of school-related use.

In the information on professional use, an interesting point is that the central libraries show 25 percent of users from this group and the non-central's 19 percent. The lowest non-central reported only 6 percent of users as professional persons and the maximum was 34 percent. The lowest of the central libraries was 18 percent professional and the maximum 37 percent. Professionals apparently use the better libraries more freely.

The distance from which users come to the library is of interest. For the central libraries, 69 percent came from within a five mile radius and 85 percent of the non-central users came from within that limit. Apparently the quality of the library has an impact on the service area.

The number of books borrowed by the users is interesting. For the central libraries, 34 percent of the users did not check any books out. Twenty-nine percent checked one or two, 16 percent checked three or four, 7 percent checked five to nine, and 2 percent checked over nine books. The figures are approximately similar for the non-centrals with some tendency for a larger proportion to borrow books.

One of the problems faced by central libraries in the New York State systems is the amount of use from outside their chartered area. If this is large it can be a serious drain on the central libraries' resources unless there is some form of re-imbursement from the system or the state. The average proportion of users from outside the chartered area was 27 percent; in one central this went to 43 percent and in several to 38 and 39 percent.

Summary

The problems of measurement cover the complete range of library activities. The result is that the many details obscure the continuing threads which tie the measurement techniques together. The following summary will attempt to bring these threads of relationship to the surface.

The first major thread is the difficulty of insuring that a measurement really defines a good library. The good library stimulates people but most of the measures merely report on a step in the process that everyone hopes stimulates people. Our measures of library use identify and quantify processes rather than end products.

The second major thread is the wide difference in use among different kinds of people. Library use is concentrated among the highly educated and students. The recognition of this fact permits large improvements in estimating probable use of libraries, including plans for new buildings, as well as providing better indices of library use and library efficiency. Because of difficulties of measuring library use without securing information on education of the user, the idea of periodic user surveys in all libraries is proposed. These should provide indices of use by type of person. National use standards should be established based on the experience of successful libraries.

The third major thread is the importance of unit costs even if they are crude. They give a perspective on the nature of the library operation.

The fourth thread is the need for new measures to reflect the new problems of systems and the resulting cooperative relationships.

The experience in New York State has shown that the careful development and consideration of the various modes of measurement can contribute materially to the success of library planning in spite of the many deficiencies and defects still existing in those modes.

REFERENCES

1. Leigh, Robert D. *The Public Library in the United States*. New York, Columbia University Press, 1950, p. 136.
2. Norvelle, George W. *The Reading Interests of Young People*. Boston, Heath, 1950 and; *What Boys and Girls Like to Read*. Morristown, N.J., Silver Burdett Co., 1958.

CHAPTER III: MEASUREMENT AND EVALUATION IN COLLEGE AND UNIVERSITY LIBRARY STUDIES: LIBRARY RESEARCH AT PURDUE UNIVERSITY

JOHN H. MORIARTY
Director of Libraries
Purdue University, Lafayette, Indiana

It would take a full-length volume to review past and current attempts at measurement and evaluation in college and university library studies. Accordingly I propose to do what I can and that is to tell the history, some of it inside history, of the various university library studies marked by a variety of scientific research techniques which have issued from Purdue in the past half dozen years. Actually our studies have ranged decently enough in type of scientific measurement used. We have produced studies of attitude and value measurement, growth measurement, work measurement, cost measurement and evaluation, usage measurement and prediction, and simulation measurement for organizational planning.

Attitude and Value Measurement. Our first scientific venture was *Purdue University Libraries Attitude Survey, 1959-1960*[1] done by our Staff Association and published in 1964. When the Council for Library Resources was established by the Ford Foundation, with Verner Clapp as its first President, the Staff Association at our libraries and Audio-Visual Center was mightily aroused. While composed of all staff personnel, it is strongly led by the professional librarians and these established in 1958 a Research Committee which in time evolved a proposal to do an attitude survey. A leader in this endeavor was Ann Belfort, a recent doctoral graduate in psychology who was head of the media research unit in our Audio-Visual Center, but also active was Abraham N. Barnett, our then social science librarian who has a doctorate in sociology. Using the "Scale for Measuring Attitudes toward Any Institution"[2] developed by Remmers and Kelly of the Purdue Psychology Department back in 1934, a 26-item Thurstone-type scale, our staff got instructors in various classes to have the libraries rated on the "Scale" by 1,843 students: graduate, all levels of undergraduate, every school group, male and female, single and married, Indiana and out-of-state. Adequate samples of all but the graduate group were obtained. Not only the attitude to the Purdue Libraries was rated but also the students' attitudes to the American library system in general and to their high school libraries. All effort up to this point was voluntary and beyond regular library or audio-visual duties, and the university computer center contributed $500 or so of its services to handle the data.

The results of the Remmers-Kelly scale are scored on a range of 1.6 for total dislike of an institution to 11.2, which expresses total enthusiasm for it. The average of attitudes to the Purdue Libraries was a score of 8.74; toward the American Library system it was 8.95; toward the high school library it was 7.44.

The staff research committee headed by Abraham Barnett worked for five years over the figures and finally and somewhat reluctantly published the results in 1964.[1] Copies were distributed and one was sent to Verner Clapp. On May 18, 1964, he wrote me as follows:

> Dear John Hellenbeck:
>
> Thanks for the copy of the "Purdue University Libraries Attitude Survey 1959-1960."
>
> I have skimmed; I shall try to read more carefully. But I gather from my skimming that the results were not world-shaking.
>
> What conclusions do you draw? Does the methodology of studies of this kind leave something to be desired, or are the initial questions formulated with insufficient insight, or what?
>
> Compare, for example, a computer program for costing information retrieval systems developed by Charles P. Bourne, reported in the current issue of *American Documentation*. Does it give one more than would an adding machine or slide-rule?
>
> All these studies leave me a little worried. Perhaps I miss their real significance.
>
> Sincerely yours,
>
> Verner W. Clapp
> President

On May 23, I replied:

> Dear Verner:
>
> Your prompt acknowledgement dated May 18, 1964, of the Purdue Libraries' staff small *Survey* is most friendly just in itself. It is also friendly in its comments, semi-critical as they are.
>
> You say the study left you worried. It certainly at the end worried our staff plenty. They started gaily to do some "research," any research. They fell into this "study" and got underway. They never liked it after the first returns were in. I'll comment formally below on the chosen instrument and methodology, but here I want to describe how almost every one of our findings bruised the staff's professional egos. Apparently the college student wants a comfortable reading room and open shelves, and these are the criteria by which he judges libraries. As the average man in a mass group, he could hardly be less sensitive about our elaborate retrieval devices, like the card catalog and reference staff. The students do, of course, use us as an information retrieval system but their perception of this is vague and tentative, certainly not critical. And this after twenty years here of most earnest deployment of materials and services for their use. So this must be generally true in large academic libraries. Any such would have trouble indeed in pinning down "pure" information output to utilize anything like the Bourne and Ford cost analysis and simulation procedures to which you refer. If you'll recall the Johns Hopkins OR report, the 3000 cases of library use collected for study proved inadequate for statistical categorization because they were so "impure."
>
> Of course this student attitude to our professional finesse in cataloging and reference services humiliates librarians, especially of the second and third echelon down, who feel hopelessly taken for granted. One of the bitterest findings was that students' grades in no way predicted their attitude to the college library. The A student gives us no credit for his success; the D student does not blame us. How are these as attitudes toward our vaunted "teaching" service? If we are "teaching" the students as we so loudly proclaim, they don't know it.
>
> You may want to note that the public library "image" came out a little better in rating than the Purdue "college" library's did. Maybe the public library with more modest goals which it more actually achieves, justifiably stands higher in these students' minds than our more pretentious services (reserve book rooms, departmental libraries, etc.) in college libraries. And certainly the school library is not so well liked, which should be of some interest to leaders in the school library movement.
>
> Your key observation that "the results were not world-shaking" is quite correct. The study does have limitations, both conceptual and methodological, but it was designed as a first exploration into an area where there are few precedents. It could be expected, therefore, that some insufficiencies of insight, or at least of foresight, would be exposed in hindsight.
>
> As a measure of attitude, we chose a readily available, easily adapted instrument. Unfortunately, it possessed neither the sensitivity nor the breadth (for our library purposes) that a more complex, multidimensional measure might have provided. Secondly, the independent variables selected were the obvious ones: school, class, library use, gross academic achievement, etc. We felt it necessary to begin with these and have at least found out for other researchers that they apparently are not so important determiners of attitude as common sense might say. Finally, the institutions with which the Purdue University Libraries were compared do not represent a diverse enough sample of the institutional images composing a student's everyday "life space." We can warn later workers that general-cultural predisposition to respond favorably to the institution of libraries may have masked subordinate, more specific effects. C. E. Osgood's Semantic Differential would probably have been a better instrument to use, though a more costly and time consuming one.

We contend, though, that this kind of survey serves a worthy purpose. Libraries play a certain, however passive, role in university education. Their contribution to instructional goals thus depends on perceived usefulness as well as actual usefulness. Especially with increasingly individualized instruction and independent study, student perceptions are part of the criteria by which college libraries must be evaluated. Such studies as this, at the very least, help us to be self-critical; to see ourselves a little more clearly as others see us.

We feel that we have profited from this study and that further investigation, if undertaken, will certainly be sharpened from the experience. We do better understand what Bernard Berelson said at Chicago last April 21, to a behavioral sciences gathering. He claimed he could summarize the findings of the nearly 1000 studies in the behaviorial sciences he had reviewed under three headings:

1) Everything is more complicated than expected;
2) Differences are not great;
3) Some do, some don't.

At one point it was strongly recommended among us that the report not be published (note the five years from the time of data gathering to imprint date). But by circulating the report, we hoped that others might also share in this first, albeit limited, experience.

Sincerely,

John H. Moriarty
Director of Libraries

Presently we have no library staff personally concerned with attitude studies, but E. A. Pessemier of our Industrial Management School and Norman R. Baker of the Industrial Engineering School are both keenly interested in such work, and some graduate student will find himself guided to undertaking a value or attitude measurement study. At the moment a graduate student in sociology, L. C. DeWeese, is writing a master's thesis on the "professional-client" relationships in libraries. The importance of such studies is probably only matched by their still shaky methodology, but badly needed they certainly are.

Cost Measurement. Our second academic library research project was sparked by a demand of our Vice-President for Finance, who gave us a small grant for a graduate student so that we might come up with the study eventually published as *The Cost of Providing Library Services to Groups in the Purdue University Community – 1961.*[3] This study was guided by our Associate Director, O. C. Dunn, in its library analyses and by W. F. Seibert, current head of our Audio-Visual Center's Instructional Media Research Unit, in its statistical planning. Known as the "Quatman Report" from the graduate student, Gerald L. Quatman, who was recipient of the Vice-President's grant, the report describes the survey made of twenty library services to undergraduate students, graduate students, faculty members and others, and the relative use of the services by these groups. A computation of the cost of the twenty services follows and then their allocation to the using groups on the basis of percentage of use. The total costs chargeable to the four groups are divided by the number of persons in each, and with this division there are computed the ratios of graduate student to undergraduate student library costs and also faculty member to undergraduate student cost. The key result is the ratio that if an undergraduate's cost is taken as one, then a graduate student's is 2.8 and a faculty member's is 2.267. In 1961 dollars the figures were $44.22 for an undergraduate, $123.80 for a graduate student and $100.25 for a faculty member.

This study was widely cited and has been replicated at least once, to my knowledge, by Stanford University, with quite similar figures. Our Vice-President for Finance has used it with government contractors with results that have satisfied him.

Growth Measurement. Out of a desire to communicate with our university administration about our own Purdue library growth problems, we decided in 1963 to investigate the growth figures annually reported by sixty-three members of the Association of Research Libraries, and finally in 1965 published *The Past and Likely Future of 58 Research Libraries, 1951-1980: A Statistical Study of Growth and Change,* by Dunn, Seibert, and Scheuneman.[4] What was done was to gather, code, key punch, and verify the statistics reported from 1950/51 through 1963/64. The annual figures treated were those for:

(1) volumes held in the collections,
(2) volumes added,
(3) money expended for materials and binding,
(4) salaries,
(5) wages,
(6) professional staff size,
(7) non-professional salary paid,
(8) lowest professional salary paid,
(9) *total* library expenditure,
(10) total reported university enrollment,
(11) total reported graduate enrollment,
(12) Ph.D. degrees granted.

When data of adequate consistency were obtained for only fifty-eight of the then sixty-three academic ARL members, the principal analyses of the study were begun. These were (1) descriptions of the past and predictions of the future of four varieties of "composite" ARL libraries; (2) rank or standing of the individual libraries on each of the several statistics *and* for each of the fourteen years spanned; and (3) the year-by-year intercorrelations among pairs of statistics which describe either the individual library or its parent university, for example, the correlation between volumes held and total expenditures, volumes acquired and Ph.D. degrees granted, expenditures for books and total enrollment, etc.

The creation of "composite" libraries enables the investigators to group the fourteen "large," the fifteen "medium-large," the fifteen "medium-small," and the fourteen "small" libraries into groups. Initially the data were used to calculate an average annual figure, 1951-1964, for each of the statistics. Then using curve fitting procedures (see, for instance, Joy P. Guilford's *Psychometric Methods,*[5]) several of these statistics were extrapolated, producing predictions of annual average figures for the years beyond 1964 up to 1980.

Further analyses consisted of fourteen annual rankings of the fifty-eight libraries on each descriptive statistic, and finally a year-by-year correlational analysis of all possible pairs of the twelve annually reported statistics. These treated each ARL library as an individual and its reported statistics for a given year as its scores. From these data, fourteen correlation matrices were developed, one for each year 1950/51 through 1963/64, with each matrix consisting of sixty-six coefficients.

Of course the predictions of growth were the real news in this study. For a second printing in March 1966, the new data for 1964/65 were available. For a third printing in February 1967, those for 1965/66 were at hand. On the whole the predictions are holding fairly close to the actual or realized growths. The predictions when first reported were widely considered too high. In fact they have proven conservative: funds and acquisitions are above predictions. The prediction was that the average ARL library in 1980 would have 2.86 million volumes. For that year now an average collection of 3.5 million seems probable.

Operations Research and the Purdue Libraries. During 1963, just as the Dunn and Seibert growth measurement study described above was settling down as a project, our then academic Vice-President, Paul F. Chenea, and I started a series of conversations about library administration and its difficulties which wound up in his allowing us a small budget, some $11,000, which permitted the libraries to serve as a laboratory for the Industrial Engineering School's graduate students, primarily under F. F. Leimkuhler's guidance. This grant of support was continued in 1964/65 and led to a successful application to the National Science Foundation for funds to support a proposal entitled "Basic Problems in the Design and Operations of University Libraries" (NSF-N-2394). NSF funds, added to our local support, amounted to a total of about $100,000 during 1966/67 and 1967/68. Almost fifty students have participated in the studies permitted. Two doctorates have been granted, two more will be completed this year; two master's thesis have been accepted; several projects by master's students have been completed; a round dozen of substantial term papers and preliminary studies have been submitted; and four or more faculty papers have been delivered and published.

The plan of academic arrangements is standard enough. Leimkuhler and his chief associate, Norman R. Baker, recruit graduate students who are planning industrial engineering graduate work to accept fellowships in our program. In the four years up to now we have kept opening up new study needs — these show up constantly in the course of projects being undertaken and there is no end of them in sight. When a student accepts a topic, after faculty and library staff counselling, he proceeds with his investigation, checking back with both groups regularly. A weekly seminar attended by twenty or so people, lasting two to two and a half hours, allows him to make a presentation, to answer questions, to ask questions, to receive faculty and library staff comment on his study, to arrange for further data gathering or treatment, and so on. These joint seminars have proven of value to professors, students and library staff in mutual adjustment by librarians to understanding of the scientific, quantitative, mathematical approach and by engineer-scientists to understanding of library service requirements.

Additional profit is added to our seminars with the occasional introduction of the point of view of other disciplines by a sociologist, industrial economist, or other expert from inside the university, and more occasionally from outside.

At this point I should express my conviction, which has evolved out of our Purdue experience, that the measurement and evaluation of our college and university libraries should be in the hands of scientists and not in the hands of the working professional librarians. I had occasion to put this conviction on record at the time of Purdue's proposal to NSF for its library problems study grant. When our preliminary proposal went to NSF, persons there raised the point that no one on the Purdue Libraries' staff was among the investigators. In the final proposal I wrote:

> The question may arise as to the propriety or need for a professional librarian to be included among investigators on the Library Design and Operation Study proposed by the Purdue University School of Industrial Engineering and the Libraries.
>
> Professional librarians have in fact raised critical voices about studies of their institutions conducted by outside investigatiors who did not consult at all or only inadequately with the library staff as to the conditions or purposes of institutional practices. They have been justified almost certainly in some instances. But any such situation between the Industrial Engineering School and the Libraries at Purdue has never arisen in over twenty years of contacts. Industrial Engineering students have done class projects in the Libraries since 1945, usually for motion and time study, sometimes for layout. The results have been interesting and on occasion resulted in Libraries' adoption of a suggested practice.
>
> While testifying to these pragmatic successes in the Purdue situation for application of engineering skills in Libraries' problems, I have a further point that has guided us from the first in our arrangements. I do not feel that it is the best scientific method for the laboratory animal itself to participate in the experiment. The librarian as experimenter in library practices is inevitably biased, probably too non-critical or sometimes too critical. I want my science to be objective and this means in regard to libraries that local, working librarians had better not be responsible for data. This does not mean any lack of librarian interest or responsiveness in furthering a scientific study. The situation here is an easy acceptance by the professional librarians of Professors Leimkuhler and Baker as a useful part of our environment. These men's professional attitude has earned this, but it also results from librarian understanding.

People at NSF have said that the reviewers ranged selectively over many points in the proposal, making their comments, but that all landed on this point, usually adversely. I am more convinced of it today than in 1965.

Cost Evaluation. The NSF grant led to several types of measurement and evaluation; one is cost evaluation. The economics of space utilization in libraries, particularly research libraries, is an old problem. The first doctorate resulting from our NSF grant was by J. Grady Cox, and his 1964 dissertation was entitled "Optimum Storage of Library Materials."[6] Cox sampled storage data at Purdue and at Auburn Universities. He constructed storage models, two-dimensional and three-dimensional, and demonstrated these for continuous and discrete size distributions. He worked out the application of these models on an unconstrained basis, and also developed three constrained models to consider restrictions of stack height, shelf thickness, shelf length, and incremental shelf adjustment; he called these the "within shelf" model, the "within stack" model and the "random shelf" model. A very interesting and practical result of all of the examples for all the models was the small number of shelf heights (from three to five) required to give a near optimal storage solution.

A second doctoral thesis was by Winston C. Lister, completed in 1967 and entitled "Least Cost Decision Rules for the Selection of Library Materials for Compact Storage."[7] Lister used two criteria for storage selection: age of the materials, and individual book usage rates. He developed models to study these and made evaluations of them using data from three departmental libraries at Purdue. Comparisons of the age policy and the usage rate policy indicate that the latter is preferred for all cases examined. But his main contribution is that his model allows us to kill forever the concept of storing a few books here or a few books there. Storing any small number of books with any retrieval possibility is always extravagant. He shows objectively that for savings to be worthwhile, a lot of books must be stored.

Both Cox and Lister demonstrate in a rigorous, modern manner what Dewey and Rider championed in an earlier era, namely that one can always improve on existing methods and achieve economies of operation. The order of magnitude of the benefits to be achieved is about a 10 percent reduction in costs, which is comparable to most industry expectations for methods improvements. Since the cost of implementing such economies is likely to be the same for small and large operations, the latter stand to gain the most.

Usage Measurement and Prediction. A doctoral candidate, A. K. Jain, has been working for three years on the problems of sampling usage of library materials based on data gathered at Purdue.[8] Jain has extraordinary mathematical skills, even for an industrial engineer. They have enabled him not only to gather his own local Purdue data with understanding of its statistical potential, but also to go back over the thirty-five years of usage study from Carnovsky's pioneer work in 1932[9] to Philip Morse of M.I.T.'s probabilistic Markov model, in 1965,[10] to use mathematical analyses (which I personally cannot follow) to show their failings. The early studies for one thing discussed only detail about the books used, not about the total library collection. Later studies and notably Morse's Markov model face up to books not used as well as those used. Morse's model of book usage is certainly the most general yet proposed but it requires three parameters for its application. Jain's advance is that he is proposing a new model which he calls "Pn model" for formula purposes (from probability distribution of the number of uses of a book). This model takes into account not only the probability distribution of use, if the book is used, but also emphasizes the probability of a book not being used at all. And Jain does this with only two parameters.

Measurement by Digital Computer Simulation. The fourth doctoral thesis, still in progress at Purdue, is fascinating as a different methodological approach to measurement and evaluation of academic libraries. This is the work under way by doctoral candidate Richard E. Nance, tentatively entitled "A Comparison of the Effects of Library Control Systems."

Nance is using the methodology of simulation technique and is adapting the theory and application of industrial dynamics — a digital simulation technique, developed by Jay W. Forrester and others at M.I.T. Industrial dynamics provides a framework within which the dynamic operations of an organization can be examined. The technique emphasizes describing the organization's dynamic behavior rather than attempting to prescribe optimal behavior. Nance's departure is to adapt this technique to simulating a service, non-profit organization such as the library, instead of to profit-motivated organizations on which it has hitherto been used. In doing this he has drawn heavily on an analytic model of the library proposed by Norman Baker of our Purdue project, which pictures the closed-loop system existing among funders, servicers, and users of the library. The central point in Baker's model, which is applied by Nance experimentally to four Purdue departmental libraries, is the statement, either implicit or explicit, of library goals which in turn dictate policies. These policies, as they are perceived by the funders and users, coupled with both the funders' and users' needs, past experiences and future expectations, determine the nature and quantity of library activity by funders and users, and their demands on its servicers. Significant in Nance's concept of his simulated model library is the amount of "control" exercised by the servicers. "Control" can be illustrated by the maintenance of open or closed stacks, the stated policies for loan and return of library materials, the enforcement of these policies, the degree to which interaction with the users is utilized in prescribing library policies, and so on. Obviously, greater control requires building costs and servicer costs in money or time which must be accepted and provided by funders. Nance's use of simulation models is certainly a unique advance in measurement and evaluation of academic libraries.

Other Studies. There have been other completed studies of merit within the NSF research group. Raffel[11] applied dynamic programming to Cox's dissertation on storage problems;[6] and Popovich[12] has applied their theoretical results to three branch libraries and obtained practical shelving recommendations and concrete estimates of the space savings attainable. O'Neill[13] demonstrated the application of statistical methods to the measurement of various characteristics of collections. Hassel* is now following up on an earlier project by Appel[14] concerning the application of work system design principles to interlibrary loan activities. More recently O'Neill* has been following up on several papers by Leimkuhler[15] which are concerned with the problems of quantitative approaches to the organization of collections for efficient information retrieval. These men are developing mathematical models which relate the likelihood of satisfying user needs with sequential search patterns applied over a collection which has been subdivided according to age and subject categories, i.e., the depository concept, the branch or departmental library concept, etc. They are seeking an analytic basis for the distribution of library resources among various user groups.

Conclusion. The varieties of measurement and evaluation described and illustrated by our local attempts do not in any way exhaust the potential and needed techniques of examining our academic libraries. I hope I have not indicated any closing of doors — the professional librarian with his service and personal contributions will have his hands full. We need other specialists too in the vineyard, we need a variety of them, with the highest capacities and on a full-time, total dedication basis. This is a matter concerning man's mind. He can only wear one pair of pants and eat a limited amount daily of food, but when it comes to books and ideas, his needs surpass anything that we dare now envision.

*E. T. O'Neill and H. P. Hassel, Jr., have had doctoral dissertation proposals accepted (1967) by the Industrial Engineering School, Purdue University.

REFERENCES

1. Purdue University. Libraries Staff Association. *Purdue University Libraries Attitude Survey, 1959-1960*. Lafayette, Ind., 1964.

2. Remmers, Hermann H., and Kelly, I. "A Scale for Measuring Attitudes Toward Any Institution," *Bulletin of Purdue University*, 35:1-36, No. 4, 1934.

3. Quatman, Gerald L. *The Cost of Providing Library Services to Groups in the Purdue University Community-1961*. Lafayette, Ind., Purdue University Libraries, 1962.

4. Dunn, O. C., et al. *The Past and Likely Future of 58 Research Libraries, 1951-1980: A Statistical Study of Growth and Change*. Lafayette, Ind., Purdue University, University Libraries and Audiovisual Center, 1965. (Second and third printings, with additions, 1966 and 1967.)

5. Guilford, Joy P. *Psychometric Methods*. 2d ed. New York, McGraw-Hill, 1954, pp. 70-71.

6. Cox, J. Grady. *Optimum Storage of Library Material*. Lafayette, Ind., Purdue University Libraries, 1964. (Purdue University Ph.D. thesis.)

7. Lister, Winston C. *Least Cost Decision Rules for the Selection of Library Materials for Compact Storage*. Purdue University Ph.D. thesis 1967. (Available as U.S. Clearinghouse Report PB 174 441.)

8. Jain, Aridaman K. "A Statistical Study of Book Use." Purdue University Ph. D. thesis, 1968. (To be published in a U.S. Clearinghouse Report.) *See also* his "Sampling and Short-Period Usage in the Purdue Library," *College & Research Libraries*, 27:211-218, May 1966.

9. Carnovsky, Leon. "Reading Needs of Typical Student Groups." Unpublished Ph.D. thesis prepared for the University of Chicago, 1932.

10. Morse, Philip M. "On the Prediction of Library Use." *In* Carl F. J. Overhage and R. Joyce Harman, eds., *Intrex; Report of a Planning Conference on Information Transfer Experiments, September 3, 1965*. Cambridge, Mass., M.I.T. Press, 1965, Appendix N, pp. 225-234.

11. Raffel, Leslie J. "Compact Book Storage Models." Unpublished thesis for M.S. in Industrial Engineering, Purdue University, 1965.

12. Popovich, John D. "Compact Book Storage." Unpublished project for M.S. in Industrial Engineering, Purdue University, 1966.

13. O'Neill, Edward T. "Sampling University Library Collections." Unpublished thesis for M.S. in Industrial Engineering, Purdue University, 1966. *See also* his "Sampling University Library Collections," *College & Research Libraries*, 27:450-454, Nov. 1966.

14. Appel, Fred A. "Personnel Utilization in Interlibrary Loan Service." Unpublished project for M.S. in Industrial Engineering, Purdue University, 1966.

15. Leimkuhler, Ferdinand F. "A Literature Search Model, Purdue University." Paper read at 31st Annual Meeting of Operations Research Society, New York, June 1967. (Available as U.S. Clearinghouse Report PB 174 390.) *See also* his "The Bradford Distribution," *Journal of Documentation*, 23:197-207, Sept. 1967.

CHAPTER IV: RECENT TRENDS IN MARKETING RESEARCH

ROBERT FERBER
Professor of Economics and of Marketing
Research Professor in the Bureau of Economic and Business Research,
Director of the Survey Research Laboratory, University of Illinois, Urbana

The purpose of this paper is to bring together and review in a relatively nontechnical fashion some recent trends in marketing research. Many of the problems which library researchers face are similar to those encountered in marketing research, and are therefore subject to much the same treatment. For example, ascertaining what sort of people make use of a library is conceptually much the same kind of problem that media researchers face in ascertaining what sort of people subscribe to a particular publication. Hence, it is hoped that this review of developments in the field of marketing research will suggest means of dealing with problems that are encountered in library research.

This paper is divided into three parts. The first part provides a general overview of the principal trends of thought in marketing research, focusing primarily on the basic rational governing much of the current work in this field. The second part is more detailed, presenting a broad but brief summary of the analytical tools which are most popular in marketing research, indicating possible future uses of these techniques. A final part outlines a few simple rules on how *not* to do research, applicable primarily to marketing but with much more general implications.

GENERAL FRAMES OF REFERENCE

The first, and perhaps most important, concept underlying much of current marketing analysis is the relatively simple one that a knowledge of marketing is not sufficient to solve marketing problems. In its broadest sense, marketing can be said to relate either to human behavior or to problems of logistics (such as the optimum number and location of warehouses). In either case, the solutions of such problems necessitate a knowledge of other subject areas besides marketing. In problems of logistics, this may entail a knowledge of only one other area, such as operations research, whereas the study of human behavior may require knowledge of theories and techniques from many other social sciences.

In either event, the fact remains that a competent and well-trained market researcher of today has to acquire a broad interdisciplinary knowledge of other fields, especially of the social sciences and of quantitative methods.[1] Thus, the marketing researcher has to be acquainted with theories of group behavior from sociology, of personality tests from psychology, of theories of consumer behavior from economics, of numerical methods of analysis from statistics, and of means of constructing and testing models of business behavior from operations research and mathematics.

This is not to say that the marketing researcher has to be an expert in all areas. Rather, he has to know enough of these areas to recognize when that type of information is needed or may be useful, and when an expert in one of those areas should be consulted. As a rule, a marketing researcher will try to specialize in one of these areas, although there are generalists who have a good working knowledge of all of them.

A partial corollary to this first point, and a second major point in itself, is that marketing activity cannot be viewed in the abstract but must be considered within a broader framework of human and social behavior. What this means is that any particular activity, such as the purchase of a specific product, is best interpreted within the broader system of which it is a part. For example, rather than seeking an explanation for the purchase of the product in terms of the circumstances under which the purchase was made, an examination might be attempted of the considerations entering into the felt need for the product in relation to other purchases that might have been made during the same period.

In effect, the analysis of the purchase is then made within the context of a system of purchase behavior. Such a systems approach serves to place the analysis in proper perspective in addition to possibly bringing to light factors affecting the purchase decision that would not be immediately obvious. Thus, in analyzing the factors which enter into a consumer's decision process, a systems approach might take into account not only the factors entering into that particular purchase but also the socio-economic background of the consumer, the inventory of that product in the household, the means used by the household to consider alternative products, and even some of the attributes of the manufacturer of the product. In this way it may be found for example, that the favorable image of the manufacturer was a major factor in inducing the household to make the purchase.

A third general frame of reference, which in a sense follows from the first two, is that the analysis of marketing behavior has to be undertaken within a multivariate framework. Any particular type of action is influenced by many factors, some of which might interrelate with each other, and it is only by carrying out some type of analysis which allows for the joint effect of these different factors acting simultaneously that it is possible to isolate the effect of any one of them; hence the term, multivariate analysis.

Utilization of a multivariate framework means that if one is interested, for example, in finding out the influence of family income on the purchase of books and magazines, it is not possible to do so simply by relating such purchases to income level. Rather, it is necessary also to take into account other factors which may influence such purchases — such as education of family members, occupation, family size, perhaps the presence of children — and then to try to estimate the influence of income level while simultaneously taking into consideration these other factors. If such a multivariate approach is not followed, and if say income effects are highly correlated with education effects (as is often true), spuriously high indications of the effect of income on purchases will be obtained.

The fourth general frame of reference, and the last one which will be mentioned here, is that to be most effective, the analysis of marketing behavior should be carried out within a formal framework or model of that behavior. Again, in many ways this statement represents but a further extension of the earlier frames of reference. For if we are to study the interdisciplinary aspects of marketing behavior, which imply a systems approach and multivariate analysis, exactly how will such analysis be carried out? For example, in estimating the effect of family income on purchases of books and magazines, exactly how do we take into account the effects of such other factors as occupation, education, and family size? The answer lies in the construction of an analytical model that seeks to incorporate all of these factors and can then be subjected to empirical analysis. Thus, in ascertaining the influence of family income on book purchases, the model may consist of nothing more than a multiple correlation equation, in linear arithmetic form, with purchases as the dependent variable, and with income, education, occupation, and other factors as the independent variables.

In other examples, the model used may be graphic representation showing interdependencies and causal flows; while in still other cases the model may lead to a system of equations which includes a large number of variables, ranging from overt behavior to expressed attitudes and preferences.[2]

These general frames of reference are reflected in the types of analytical methods being used in modern marketing research. Indeed, they have influenced the development of these methods, as will become clear as we turn now to a brief summary of analytical tools popular in current marketing research.

ANALYTICAL TOOLS IN MARKETING RESEARCH

Six types of analytical methods will be covered in this review. Although these are not the only methods, they are among the most important and should give a good idea of the range and diversity of methods used to deal with marketing problems.

1. Behavioral Methods. Marketing researchers have been borrowing many new tools from the behavioral sciences, principally from economics, psychology and sociology. One example will be cited from each of these fields to illustrate what methods are being used and how.

From economics, marketing researchers have borrowed the idea of the consumption function, namely, the search for a relationship between consumption and income while holding other factors constant. However, marketing people recognize clearly that other factors cannot be held constant, and hence a major part of their efforts is to identify these other factors and to measure their relative importance in consumption. Rather than focusing on the search for relations between aggregate consumption expenditures and aggregate income, marketing people use the idea of the consumption function as a basis for searching for relationships between purchases of particular products on the one hand, and the characteristics of the family as well as their past purchase behavior on the other hand.[3] Similar ideas have been used recently in brand loyalty studies, in attempting to ascertain why some families tend to purchase the same brand of a product while other families keep switching from one brand to another.[4]

From psychology, marketing people have borrowed the theory of cognitive dissonance. In brief and oversimplified form, this theory states that people strive to establish conformance between what they expect and what actually happens.[5] As a result, if a person buys a car, and doubts whether he made the right choice, he will consciously or unconsciously look for evidence to support his decision. In line with this theory, for example, it has been found that some of the most avid readers of automobile advertisements are people who have recently purchased that very same brand. From a marketing point of view, this suggests that to retain brand loyalty and future purchasers, continual advertising is desirable, not only to attract new customers but to reassure old ones.

From sociology, marketing people have borrowed ideas about leadership behavior and the theory of innovation. Along these lines, a number of marketing studies have been undertaken to identify the opinion leaders in product purchases, for previous findings indicate that a new product is first accepted by a very small group with distinctive characteristics and that this group then transmits its information and influence to the rest of the population. Obviously, if the characteristics of this group can be pinpointed and the members identified, the future success or failure of a new product can be gauged much more accurately and much more inexpensively. This economic gauging would be no mean feat considering that over 90 percent of new products turn out to be failures.

2. Mathematical Methods. The pressure for more rigorous formulation and testing of marketing theories, plus the trend toward formalistic representation of marketing behavior, has led to the increasing use of mathematical methods in marketing analysis. From the viewpoint of a mathematician, these methods are rarely very sophisticated. However, it is surprising how much can be accomplished with even a little mathematics (as well as how easily most people can be frightened by a few algebraic symbols).

The three branches of mathematics perhaps used most frequently in marketing, as well as in many of the social sciences, are calculus, algebra (including matrix algebra), and probability theory. Thus, calculus may be used to analyze the characteristics of mathematical models, such as ascertaining marketing strategies that will maximize market share or perhaps profits under different market conditions.

Algebra, especially matrix algebra, underlies virtually all of multivariate analysis, and serves as the basis for deriving and analyzing multiple correlation equations and other multivariate forms.

Probability methods have been used with increasing frequency in recent years to obtain models of consumer purchases, of brand choice, and of means of predicting success of new products. These methods have also been used to derive general relationships between purchase rates and buying patterns in past periods. Thus, using these methods it has been found possible to explain to a large extent future purchases of the same brand of a product as a function of the frequency with which the product was purchased in the past.[6]

3. Statistics. The use of statistics in marketing research is of course not new. However, some of the directions which these uses are taking are novel and deserve mention. One tendency is toward increasing skepticism of the reliability of data. Thus, survey data are more and more being examined not only for sampling errors but also for biases and other forms of nonsampling errors. In some cases, these biases have been found to be so large that the usual measures of sampling error are meaningless for all practical purposes. In effect, the focus is more on a concept of total error in a set of data, of which sampling errors may represent only one part.[7]

Another tendency is toward greater sophistication and is manifested in the increasing use of multivariate methods, as already mentioned. Simple tabulations are still widely used, however, in part for exploratory purposes and in part for illustrating the net relations between two variables after the effects of other factors are held constant.[8]

The concept of Bayesian statistics has also invaded marketing analysis to a large extent. By this is meant the use of Bayes' Theorem, a theorem from probability theory, as a device for bringing together all the information on a particular subject as a basis for decision making by statistics. For example, by this method it is possible in deciding whether to undertake a particular promotional campaign, to include in the estimates informed guesses that the campaign might be successful. This approach makes it possible to compare the costs and benefits of alternative courses of action and to come up with single estimates (or ranges of estimates) for each action, which would then indicate which is likely to be superior.[9]

4. Computers. The advent of the computer enables researchers to collect more data and to do more analyses and more complex analyses with these data. It also enables researchers to make more mistakes and to do so more quickly!

The fact remains, however, that computers have pretty much taken over empirical work in marketing. A market research department is simply not accepted socially these days if it does not either have or have access to a large or small computer; and no self-respecting marketing research director would dare to show his face on the golf course without first being prepared to talk about his department's computer.

Yet computers can be tremendously useful and are used extensively in marketing as well as in other research. In part, they are used to store large amounts of data and have them easily accessible. This is particularly true in the case of panel surveys, where the same families are reinterviewed many times. In such cases, data storage by computer tape greatly facilitates comparisons of the replies for a particular family at a certain date with both the replies of other families at the same date and with the replies of the same family at earlier dates.

For analysis, the computer makes available a much wider range of possibilities than would exist by desk calculator. For one thing, many more computations can be made. Computer manufacturers claim that their machines will multiply something like two 46-digit numbers in a fraction of a second. What they do not say, is that it may sometimes take many weeks, if not months, for a computer to be programmed for the necessary computations, so that for a one-time operation a person could have done the computations on a desk calculator and be loafing for several weeks by the time the computer is ready to do the job.

For repetitive operations, however, the computer is ideal, as well as for a large amount of testing. For example, if one is not sure which particular set of variables best explains variations in the purchase of books, various combinations can be tested by the computer and the best one selected.

It should be stressed, nevertheless, that the very ease with which computations are carried out on a computer can also be a major drawback. At times, there is an almost irresistible tendency to relay on the computer and on empirical results to answer any problems that may arise. As a result, theoretical considerations may be disregarded and nonsense results obtained. Computers, and computer programmers, like to pressure researchers into doing the type of analysis for which programs are already available rather than to do analyses most suitable for the particular problem. If one is not careful, the computer and its programmers can take over the direction of research, and a type of negative serendipity results, namely, right answers are obtained — but to the wrong problems.

5. Simulation. Simulation is a formalistic means of representing a human or nonhuman activity which has the wonderful feature, in the minds of most people, of requiring virtually no mathematics. However, the method can deal with problems which cannot be dealt with by the present-day mathematics, or at least not easily so.

In effect, simulation involves outlining every step in a particular process, assigning a procedure for dealing with that step, and then putting the entire thing together into an integrated model. As a rule, simulation is applied to individual units of a system, with aggregates obtained by summing the end-results. The following example illustrates what is involved in a simulation.

Suppose we are interested in finding out how many people might visit a library under different types of conditions. As possible determining factors, we might postulate that a person will visit the library depending on whether or not he is a college student, on the educational background of the individual, on the weather conditions that day, on whether he has visited the library in the past two weeks, and on the condition of his health. Based on past information, we assign probabilities or determining factors of their own to each of these variables. Thus, we may say that a student has a 32 percent probability of visiting a library on any particular day, while other people have a probability of doing so of only .06 percent. From other data, we may be able to assign probabilities of visiting the library by educational background, and by whether the person has visited the library in the past two weeks. In the case of weather, data would also be available for determining the probabilities of visiting a library on a clear day or on a rainy day, while health can be represented as a so-called dummy variable, taking the value one if the person is walking around, and zero otherwise.

These probabilities cannot be exact, and to allow for deviations we introduce random elements into each variable by adding a random number in every computation for every individual. On the average, however, we assume that these are the probabilities which will prevail.

The next step is to take the characteristics for each individual in the population and combine these characteristics, one at a time, with these values. Here a computer is virtually essential, because there would obviously be as many sets of calculations as there are individuals. In practice, therefore, the simulation procedure will be programmed on a computer. Once this is done, the characteristics of each individual are fed into the computer, with random numbers to reflect deviations from the average probabilities that might arise in actual practice, and the computer generates a prediction as to whether or not that individual is likely to go to the library that day under those conditions. After doing so for all individuals, the computer sums the results and gives us an aggregate figure of how many individuals go to the library on that particular day.

The beauty of this procedure is that very complicated relationships can be introduced and results obtained very easily, at least without high-powered statistics or mathematics. Also, one can repeat the procedure many times to estimate the likely range of the number of people visiting the library on any particular day. Moreover, the values of the probabilities can be manipulated so that estimates can be made of how the number of visits per day might be altered as conditions change, for example, if it is rainy rather than sunny, or if the number of students in the area increases by say 30 percent in the next ten years.

The disadvantage of the method is that a full-scale simulation can require large amounts of computer time. Also, the simulation, to be valid, requires prior knowledge of the relevant factors as well as information on the necessary probabilities and on what type of random elements are to be introduced. Yet simulation is a very intriguing as well as powerful and simple method, and in the study of human behavior its full potentialities have yet to be explored.[10]

6. Laboratory and Experimental Methods. The experimental methods of statistics and of psychology are being used increasingly in marketing to study human behavior. From statistics, marketing people have borrowed the principles of experimental design. For example, to find out the extent to which extra shelf space for a product will generate more sales, a frequent practice is to select a sample of stores, classify them in groups, and assign that product a different amount of shelf space in each group. To correct for possible bias in the initial sample selection, the amount of shelf space given that product for any particular group may be altered from one week to another.

Many forms of these experimental designs exist, some of them very complicated and others extremely simple. Perhaps the simplest of all is the split-run method, which is particularly useful in survey work. As an example, suppose that on a mail survey asking people for their ranking of the popularity of different types of books, there is some fear that the ranking might be influenced by which types of books are listed first. In that case, two forms of the mail questionnaire can be prepared, one form with one listing and the other form with the same listing of books in reverse, and these two forms of the questionnaire would then be rotated systematically among the sample members.

The use of the laboratory as a means of ascertaining the influence of particular factors is also becoming increasingly popular.[11] As an example, in one recent study, one group of people was shown a depressing movie while being given a new brand of soft drink, while another group at a later time was shown a very entertaining movie and given the same brand of soft drink. Reactions obtained after the movie showed that people's reactions to the soft drink were influenced markedly by the type of movie they had seen, thus providing clear evidence that product acceptance can be influenced by the type of environment in which the product is introduced.

In other circumstances, the laboratory may be used for probing interviews to ascertain what factors really influence product preferences. Thus, in one other recent study, on male students' attitudes toward men's cosmetics, it was found, not surprisingly to some, that reactions of coeds to these cosmetics had substantial effect on the male students' purchase of these products, although various other reasons were first given for their purchases.

7. Survey Methods. Surveys are still the mainstay of marketing research, as of many other areas of human behavior, and there is no indication that they are likely to be any less important in the future. Some tendencies would seem worth mentioning, however, especially in view of their implication for library work.

First, there is the tendency already mentioned to view survey data with increasing skepticism and not to accept estimates of sampling variation automatically as indications of the total error in the data. More time is being devoted to consideration of possible biases in survey work and to means of measuring these biases.[12]

Second, there is a related tendency not to accept attitudes and preferences at face value but to relate these statements to actual behavior. Partly for this reason, panel methods have assumed growing importance in marketing work. Through their use, it is possible to study the attitudes, preferences and behavior of the same families over a period of time, and thereby to relate attitudes to what the people actually do. By this means it has been found, for example, that although the over-all proportion of people using particular products or particular brands is fairly constant over time, nevertheless substantial changes are taking place among individual families, with perhaps as much as one-third of the purchases in one period differing from the purchases in a previous period. Similar results are found for opinions, i.e., while attitudes in the aggregate may be constant, many changes in attitudes are going on among individual families.

A third tendency is to utilize survey methods in conjunction with fairly sophisticated methods of analysis. Thus, before a survey is undertaken, or even planned, an analytical model may be developed of the problem to be solved (often within a multivariate framework) the relevant variables and other factors are spelled out, and then the survey is designed to yield the necessary information. Although these surveys do not always work out as planned, and relevant variables may still be overlooked, they are more likely to yield a coherent set of results.

HOW NOT TO DO RESEARCH

These remarks complete the overview of analytical tools popular in marketing research. This review does not pretend to cover all the methods used in marketing analysis nor does it pretend to present each one thoroughly. However, it should at least give some idea of the kind of thinking in a field which, from a research point of view, has essentially the same sort of problems that are found in the study of library use.

To conclude, I would like to outline very briefly a few simple rules on how *not* to do research. The basis for this list is the various studies and dissertations that I have had to review over the years in one capacity or another. The sad fact is that many of these mistakes are still being perpetrated, and it would therefore seem most desirable that the same "diseases" are not transmitted to others. Here are the rules:

1. Begin the study without any clear purpose or objective. In this way you are more likely to confuse everybody, including yourself.

2. Do not prepare an operational budget or time schedule. You never can tell what surprises may pop up along the way.

3. If you have to make up your own questionnaire, be sure to phrase the questions in such a way that they will yield expected answers, and be careful not to make any pre-test. By the former procedure, you will be all the more sure to get the answers you want, while by avoiding a pre-test you will save money, and are also not likely to be bothered by having to rework questions just because some silly respondents cannot answer them.

4. If you are doing a mail survey, be sure not to follow up the nonrespondents by telephone or personal interview. You can always assume that the nonrespondent would have given the same answers as the respondents, and if you should be wrong, nobody is ever likely to find out about it anyway.

5. In analyzing the data, do not bother to make any significance tests. If people do not want to accept your word on the reliability of the data, that is simply too bad.

6. If you are investigating whether some particular characteristic influences the variable which you are studying, do so by a two-way comparison leaving out other possibly relevant variables. This makes it virtually certain that you will find the particular characteristic to be a major influencing factor, as you had predicted all along.

7. If the data are to be analyzed by computer, find out first what is the simplest form of analysis available from the computer and twist your study around so that the objective fits the type of output obtained from the computer. This will leave the computer more time to rest its tired transistors and will also free computer programmers to spend more time on programming new and more powerful methods of playing tic-tac-toe.

8. When you prepare a report on the study, be very brief in giving details of the study or in discussing methodology. The more information you give, the more embarrassing questions people are likely to ask anyway, and the more likely they might be to find a mistake. For these reasons, be sure also not to give sample sizes or base figures as in the percentage tables. You know that your work is correct, so why should anybody bother checking it?

These rules, carefully followed, will at least shorten considerably the time that one assigns to research.

REFERENCES

1. *See e.g.*, Nicosia, Francesco M. *Consumer Decision Processes; Marketing and Advertising Implications.* Englewood Cliffs, N.J., Prentice-Hall, 1967.

2. *See* Barton, Samuel G. "A Marketing Model for Short-Term Prediction of Consumer Sales," *Journal of Marketing,* 29:19-29, July 1965; *see also* Nicosia, *op. cit.*

3. *See e.g.*, Frank, Ronald E., *et al.* "Correlates of Grocery Product Consumption Rates," *Journal of Marketing Research,* 4:184-190, May 1967.

4. Kuehn, A. A. "Consumer Brand Choice as a Learning Process," *Journal of Advertising Research,* 2:10-17, Dec. 1962.

5. *See e.g.*, Anderson, Lee K., *et al.* "The Consumer and his Alternatives: An Experimental Approach," *Journal of Marketing Research,* 3:62-67, Feb. 1966.

6. Lipstein, Benjamin. "A Mathematical Model of Consumer Behavior," *Journal of Marketing Research,* 2:259-265, August 1965. Some of the problems involved in applying probability methods to marketing problems are discussed in A.S.C. Ehrenberg, "An Appraisal of Markov Brand-Switching Models," *Journal of Marketing Research,* 2:347-363, Nov. 1965.

7. Brown, Rex V. "Evaluation of Total Survey Error," *Journal of Marketing Research,* 4:117-128, May 1967.

8. For a number of examples, *see* Frank, Ronald E., *et al.*, eds. *Quantitative Techniques in Marketing Analysis: Text and Readings.* Homewood, Illinois, Richard D. Irwin, 1962, Part IV.

9. Schlaifer, Robert. *Introduction to Statistics for Business Decisions.* New York, McGraw-Hill, 1961.

10. For further readings in this area, *see* Frank, *Quantitative Techniques, op. cit.*, Part V; *see also* Morgenroth, William M. "A Method for Understanding Price Determinants," *Journal of Marketing Research,* 1:17-26, Aug. 1964.

11. Examples will be found in Frank, *Quantitative Techniques, op. cit.*, Part III; *see also* Venkatesan, M. "Laboratory Experiments in Marketing: The Experimenter Effect," *Journal of Marketing Research,* 4:142-147, May 1967.

12. For an interesting reverse approach, *see* Tortolani, Ray. "Introducing Bias Intentionally into Survey Techniques," *Journal of Marketing Research,* 2:51-55, Feb. 1965.

CHAPTER V: TRENDS IN THE ACCREDITATION OF HIGHER INSTITUTIONS

CHARLES M. ALLEN
Associate Dean, College of Education
University of Illinois, Urbana

The question, "Is your college accredited?" is asked so often that colleges no longer wait for it; they print an answer on an early page of the college catalog. They ordinarily print only a part of the answer, however — the part that answers the question of the parent who is helping his child select an appropriate college. The parent is asking, "Is the college a member of (and thus accredited by) its regional accrediting association? — the North Central Association, the Southern Association, or the Western Association?" If the questioner is a member of one of the professional groups ordinarily represented on college faculties, he is likely to mean, "Is this institution accredited by my professional group — the American Library Association, the American Chemical Society, or the American Veterinary Medical Association?" The student completing a junior college may be asking, "Is this institution sufficiently accredited that its graduates will be accepted by graduate schools in my specialty?" If the questioner is from an agency dispensing state or Federal funds, he may have in mind the question whether the institution is approved by its own state department of education and thus is eligible for the funds.

All of these interpretations of the question relate to the approval of the college or university by some formal action of a regional accrediting association, a professional association or an agency of the individual state. Before considering in more detail the problems of such formal means of accreditation, it should be noted that higher institutions are subject to many kinds of less formal approval. We are all familiar with the fact that the American Association of University Women accepts as members the graduates of colleges shown on a restricted list. The determination of what colleges are and are not on this list constitutes a form of accreditation, of course. The American Association of University Professors not only supports the formal accreditation of colleges and universities, but also maintains its own list of "Censured Administrations." While the AAUP does not urge its members to refuse appointment to any university appearing on this list, it does suggest that the policies of the listed institutions regarding academic freedom and tenure be carefully examined before offers of employment are accepted. The American Association of Collegiate Registrars and Admissions Officers publishes an annual "Report of Credit Given by Educational Institutions" which indicates whether institutions are or are not members of their regional association, which professional associations accredit elements of their programs, and whether the reporting institution in each state (usually the state university) accepts credit from the institution in question. At the bottom of each of its introductory pages is the statement, "This Report is an exchange of information among members of the Association and is not the report of an accrediting agency"[1], but the report does provide information on acceptance of college credit by major universities and thus is a form of accreditation.

The above are cited as examples of less formal types of accrediting activities which are certainly not the central purpose of the organizations and are often entirely disclaimed by them. Even less formal accreditation occurs through the general press, through the activities of high school counselors and private counseling services, and through the selection of institutions, usually by panels of specialists, to receive foundation or Federal grants. While these less formal means of accreditation may be highly effective, they will be considered here only so far as they are a part of the social context in which the formalized accrediting agencies work.

Formal accreditation of higher education institutions, represented by the formation of the regional accrediting association, originated during the period between 1890 and 1910. Up to that time, and indeed for some time after, since the regional associations were not well-established by the end of the period, individual colleges and universities had investigated and approved the high schools from which they would accept beginning students and the colleges from which they would accept transfers. Two major characteristics of the period were associated with the formation of accrediting agencies.

The first of these is emphasized by William K. Selden, for many years Director of the National Commission on Accrediting:

Historically, this country was developed and has thrived in the past on the philosophy of *laissez faire*. The forests were felled, the land cultivated, the mineral resources explored, and business and industrial enterprises created through individual initiative seldom restricted until near the end of the past century by governmental regulations and legal controls. It was only after flagrant abuses of the public welfare became widespread that the United States Congress officially recognized the situation and adopted legislation providing for some governmental regulations.

After describing some of the Federal regulatory agencies created, Selden continues:

The abolition of those agencies of the Federal government that assist in the governance of our society is unthinkable despite the fact that there is widespread yearning for the simple and readily comprehended days of the past untrammeled by governmental controls.[2]

The use of organizations to help avoid abuses in our *laissez faire* society was not lost on college and university people who, close to the turn of the century, also organized their own regulatory agencies.

A second aspect of the American scene associated with the development of accrediting agencies was the rapid increase in school and college attendance. It was in 1890 that the doubling of the high school population every decade began in the United States. This doubling every ten years was to continue until 1950 when attendance in high schools in the United States was universal — except, that is, for a large number of culturally unassimilated youth who, because of their group membership or because of their own capacities or goals, were alienated from the main stream of the youthful culture of America. During the same period (1890 to 1910), there was a great increase in the number of post-high-school institutions — colleges and normal schools — operating at state expense. The new institutions did not themselves appear to be particularly concerned over accreditation as a means for controlling their own admissions. They did add greatly, however, to the problems of the well-established colleges and universities which, up to that time, had been approving individually the colleges and high schools from which they would accept students. The effect was to add emphasis to the movement toward the formation of accrediting agencies and the development of standards.

Further development of the accreditation movement is described by Hefferlin:

The years following the turn of the century saw the development of...standards. Several of the regional associations began to define standards for the admission of colleges to membership; the Association of American Universities initiated a committee "for the standardization of American colleges"; and a National Conference Committee on Standards sought agreement on criteria for institutions and for institutional quality in higher education. At the same time, the established professions of law and medicine renewed their efforts to raise professional standards and established criteria for education in their respective professional schools. During the 1920's, other occupational groups followed their examples. By the 1930's, with support in some cases from foundations and state licensing agencies, many of these groups had adopted the process of accreditation, complete with questionnaires, visiting teams, and lists of approved institutions, as a major device in their own professionalization.[3]

As this new means of professionalization (and of seeing to it that the interests of one's own discipline were not overlooked in the academic scuffle) was expanded to more and more groups, and sometimes to competing groups in the same profession or discipline, it was not long before the objections of presidents were heard. Departments in some institutions were being visited and accredited or not, without the knowledge of the president. In other cases, pressures were being put upon the institution by competing accreditation groups in the same profession. In many institutions, it seemed that inspections were being planned for some aspect or other of the institution's program with intolerable frequency. As increasing numbers of college and university presidents came to think of themselves as victimized by the practices of accrediting agencies over which they had no control (largely the professional agencies rather than the regional associations), a movement was started to organize the presidents into an association which would approve or refuse to approve the accrediting agencies themselves.

An early step was the appointment of a joint committee on accreditation by several associations of colleges and universities in 1938, and by 1949 the independent National Commission on Accrediting was formed. The Commission "has worked as the agent of the nation's colleges and universities in granting recognition to qualified accrediting agencies, helping to improve accrediting standards and practices, fostering increased cooperation among accrediting agencies, and recommending action concerning accreditation to its member institutions."[4] As of last March, almost 1400 institutions — junior colleges, colleges, and universities — held membership. In the eighteen years of its existence, the National Commission on Accrediting has been successful in avoiding proliferation and overlapping of accrediting activities, in reducing some duplications which existed at the time of its formation, in helping to clarify definitions of function for various accrediting organizations, and in developing criteria which make accrediting agencies acceptable to college administrators.

The accrediting agencies approved by the National Commission on Accrediting are of two types: first, the professional accrediting associations, and second, the regional. One additional development which should be noted is that the regional associations, a few years ago, formed the Federation of Regional Accrediting Commissions of Higher Education in order to achieve greater unity among their programs. Accreditation of higher institutions by state agencies is so generous in most of the states that it has little effect.

At the top of the ladder for accreditation of higher institutions is the Commission on Accrediting — a Commission which not only assists with the communication problems among accrediting organizations, but which also takes responsibility for improving the operations of accrediting groups, and which recognizes (or refuses to recognize) the accrediting groups themselves. The Commission approves, in general, two types of groups. First, the six regional associations which cover the entire United States, and second, professional organizations accrediting college and university programs in twenty-eight fields. These accrediting organizations deal with college and university undergraduate, graduate, and professional programs; there are a number of other accrediting organizations which deal with post-high-school educational institutions not of college grade. Since these institutions include a wide variety of technical and other vocational programs, and thus are of immediate concern when questions of manpower or programs for the underpriviledged are considered, the accreditation of such programs in itself constitutes an issue of major concern.

A COMPARISON OF THE NORTH CENTRAL ASSOCIATION AND THE NATIONAL COUNCIL FOR ACCREDITATION FOR TEACHER EDUCATION

In order to illustrate some of the issues associated with accreditation, I will turn now to a description of the accreditation practices of two of the agencies with which I am most familiar: the Commission of Colleges and Universities of the North Central Association of Colleges and Secondary Schools (which will hereafter be referred to as the North Central Association itself, although the Association has at least equal concern with the activities of its Commission on Secondary Schools) and the National Council for Accreditation for Teacher Education.

Both the North Central Association and the National Council for Accreditation for Teacher Education are controlled by representatives of colleges. This is in conformity with one of the "Criteria for Recognized Accrediting Agencies" of the National Commission on Accrediting which says, "In the agency's process of recognition for accreditation there shall be adequate representation from the staffs of institutions offering programs of study in the fields to be accredited."[4] The Commission on Colleges and Universities of the North Central Association is entirely selected by and from representatives of colleges. In the case of NCATE, although the controlling representation on the Council comes from colleges, part comes from professional organizations of teachers and administrators, and part represents the chief state school officers.

Both the North Central Association and NCATE are often described as "voluntary" associations, in contrast to the vesting of complete accrediting authority in a central governmental agency such as a ministry of education. "Voluntary" does not mean, however, what it did in the early days of accrediting, for if an institution does not participate "voluntarily," not only will students transferring from it be denied admission to other institutions, but the college will have difficulty in attracting students and will be denied access to many kinds of Federal grants. The freedom of institutional choice in seeking accreditation is still further limited by the fact that a number of the professional accrediting associations require accreditation by a regional association before the professional group will give consideration to the institution.

Both the North Central Association and NCATE have a central purpose, accreditation, but the North Central Association interprets this to mean, for most of the collegiate institutions which are already its members (and almost three quarters of its total possible constituency are accredited), that its job is to help its member institutions to improve by means of its re-accreditation procedures. NCATE, on the other hand, regards its function as solely accreditation and is obliged to leave the improvement of programs for teachers to its major constituent organization, the American Association of Colleges for Teacher Education.

Both accrediting agencies have published standards which serve as guides to the institutions seeking accreditation and to the representatives of the accrediting agency who visit and inspect it. Both also have printed statements supplementing the standards and find that these supplementary statements actually become standards in themselves. For example, NCATE suggests that the institution use standardized test data to indicate how its teacher education students compare with other students in the institution. The North Central Association furnishes forms on which it is suggested that the institution report on such matters as its sources of financial income and the nature of its expenditures. The classifications used in each case, although they are clearly labeled as suggestions from which the institution may deviate, are taken seriously by institutions seeking accreditation.

The North Central Association asks the institutions themselves and the examiners to consider seven questions in evaluating institutions. These, as printed in its *Guide for the Evaluation of Institutions of Higher Learning*, form "a guide — not a manual which sets forth the standards to be employed in assessing the quality of an institution."[5]

The chapter headings in the table of contents include the following questions:
1. What is the Educational Task of the Institution?
2. Are the Necessary Resources Available for Carrying Out the Task of the Institution?
3. Is the Institution Well Organized for Carrying Out Its Educational Task?
4. Are the Programs of Instruction Adequate in Kind and Quality to Serve the Purposes of the Institution?
5. Are the Institution's Policies and Practices Such as to Foster High Faculty Morale?
6. Is Student Life on Campus Relevant to the Institution's Educational Task?
7. Is Student Achievement Consistent with the Purposes of the Institution?[6]

It can be seen that, in the above list, each of the questions after the first relates to the educational task of the institution. The materials published by the Association might appear to indicate that any purposes which are accepted by the institution are accepted by the Association as adequate bases for judging it. In practice, this is not true, for those taking action on accreditation matters generally assure themselves that the definition of its task given by the institution being evaluated is really appropriate for an institution of college grade.

Parenthetically, evaluation of the library and its operation appears primarily under question two, which is concerned with the availability of resources for carrying out the tasks of the institution. Under this general heading, the major sub-heads are: "Faculty Resources," "Financial Resources," "Plant and Equipment Resources," and "Library Resources and Other Instructional Facilities." Under the last heading, the sub-heads are: books and periodicals, usage, staff, librarian-faculty relationships, expenditures, and relation to other libraries[7].

NCATE standards also are seven in number and are organized under these headings:
1. Objectives of Teacher Education
2. Organization and Administration of Teacher Education
3. Student Personnel Programs and Services for Teacher Education
4. Faculty for Professional Education
5. Curricula for Teacher Education
6. Professional Laboratory Experiences for School Personnel
7. Facilities and Instructional Materials for Teacher Education[8]

In connection with the NCATE standards, it should be remembered that, to be considered, institutions must have been accredited by the appropriate regional association. NCATE relies on the regional association for evaluation of the general quality of the institution and for the evaluation of the effectiveness of the subject matter or courses in teaching fields offered to all students, including prospective teachers.

Both the North Central Association and NCATE ask the institution to be visited to engage in a self-study and report its findings in terms of the criteria used by the agency in judging the quality of institutions. When this task is carried on thoroughly, the preparation and use of the self-study by the institution under consideration is reported to be one of the most valuable activities of the accreditation process. Both of the accrediting organizations allow the institution to deviate from the suggested forms, if it wishes, and thus permit the institution to develop its own method of reporting and, to some extent, the criteria upon which it wishes to be judged. It must be admitted, however, that few institutions take advantage of these offers.

The appropriate regional association is informed each time NCATE is scheduling a visit, and the institution is asked if it would like to have an individual representing the regional association on the NCATE team, a person who is a general administrator in a member college or university.

Both of the organizations have visiting committees who examine the institution for two to four days, depending on the size and complexity of the college or university, after the members of the committee have read the reports and catalogs furnished by the institution. The two types of agencies have quite different methods of preparing members of visiting committees. The North Central Association has an elaborate program of internships in which people recommended by their home institutions and willing to serve as examiners and consultants over a period of years are provided with special materials and a workshop, and are sent, during a year of internship, on two or three visits under selected chairmen who will assist in their training. In this process, as well as in the formation of the visiting committees, there is the understanding that members of the consultant-examiners group may serve as consultants for some institutions and examiners for others, but one may never, of course, serve as examiner for an institution for which he has been a consultant. The North Central Association conducts a two-day training meeting each year for all members of its consultant-examiners group. NCATE has no such training program but ordinarily assigns a few novices to each visiting team and always uses an experienced chairman. The chairman also attends special conferences which train him for his duties.

The nature of the visits differ somewhat in that, as suggested earlier, the chief function of the visiting team sent by NCATE is to audit the accuracy of the institution's report and to supplement it in any way deemed necessary. The examiners from the North Central Association give less emphasis to the auditing function and more to exploring what they believe to be the major strengths and weaknesses of the institution. North Central Association examiners are encouraged to make recommendations to the administration of the institution during the visit, while the visiting teams from NCATE are asked not to do so.

At the conclusion of the visit, the chairman of the committee in each of the organizations makes a written report. The chairman for the North Central Association reports rather briefly the strengths and weaknesses of the institution with some supporting data, and at the close of the report, on a separate page, makes a recommendation for action to the North Central Association itself. All of the report except the recommendation is sent to the institution. The report of the NCATE team is much more voluminous and includes a statement of relevant facts, but not opinions, as to whether the institution qualifies for accreditation. The institution receives a copy of the entire report. The fact is often stressed that NCATE reports include descriptive data and statements validating the data given in the institution's own report, but do not give the judgments of visiting team members. It is evident, however, that team members do use judgment in selecting the facts to be reported and, through the exercise of these judgments, may exert considerable influence on on the final decision regarding accreditation.

In both accrediting agencies, the final decision as to accreditation is made by the controlling body, the Commission on Colleges and Universities for the North Central Association and the National Council for Accreditation of Teacher Education, in the case of NCATE. These are the people elected by representatives of member colleges or, in the case of NCATE, by the representatives of colleges and other professional groups. In both cases, there are, between the visiting teams and the Commission or Council, intermediate committees which study the visitors' reports, hear representatives of the institutions under consideration, and make a recommendation to the overhead body regarding the action to be taken.

RECENT DEVELOPMENTS IN ACCREDITATION

As one takes part in the work of two accrediting associations, helps to plan for an accreditation visit to his own institution, reads in this controversial area, and speculates at odd hours with his professional acquaintances on accreditation, it becomes apparent that there is no lack of problems. It may be useful to examine some of them which may serve as a basis for later generalizations.

As a result of a widespread criticism of its activities for the last few years, NCATE is now subjecting its standards to an elaborate review and has a national committee appointed to propose new criteria. In the course of the discussions thus far, there are a number of recurring issues which may be of interest, for some of them seem to apply to other organizations as well as to NCATE.

1. Several of those taking part in the revision process say that the only criterion which gives an adequate basis for judgment of an institution's quality is the product of the institution — that, in a professional program, the performance of the person who is produced is decisive. The actual method of accreditation used until now, however, has been to evaluate the process by which people were educated: the institutional organization, the estimated quality of the faculty, the resources available, the nature of the prescribed sequence of courses. There is no doubt that the final purpose of a professional program is to turn out an acceptable performer, and there is also no doubt that the inferences one draws concerning the product by looking at the process by which the graduate was prepared may be subject to gross error. It is also true that we do not know how to measure the merit of the product. It appears that not only NCATE but most accreditation agencies will continue to look at factors related to the process by which students are educated, rather than at the graduates themselves in evaluating colleges.

2. It has been mentioned before that there is a difference of opinion as to the purpose of accreditation. Is accreditation primarily to establish a floor below which institutions will not be approved if they are preparing teachers, or is it expected to stimulate improvement in institutions whose programs are well above the floor? In answer to this question, those responsible for the discussion seem to be accepting the notion that initial accreditation should involve the rigorous application of minimum requirements, and that re-accreditation should place emphasis upon the stimulation of improvement.

3. Should there be a single set of criteria applicable to all institutions, or should the criteria vary, depending on the nature of the institution? If the standards applied to a multipurpose university are also used in judging a small independent college, the small college may be expected to have difficulty in meeting criteria which depend upon resources and the diversity of staffing, while it may excel in the accessibility of faculty to students. Should standards on these matters be fully applicable to both, or should there be some means devised for getting at a general balance of strengths and weaknesses?

4. Everyone seems to agree that the proper preparation of a teacher includes preparation in what he is to teach, and that the accreditation process should include examination of the preparation of prospective teachers in their teaching fields. There is some question, however, as to the nature of the involvement of specialists in the teaching fields (often called subject matter specialists in contrast to the faculty members in professional education). Some believe that teaching field specialists should be members of all visiting teams, while others believe that only teaching field specialists who have a thorough knowledge of the public schools and the demands of public school teaching should be used. Still others think that the use of specialists tends to divert the energies of the team from the examination of the college in relation to the accepted standards and to favor the specialists' own fields.

5. The question of the generality of standards has also been much debated. Should the standards be so specific that misinterpretation is unlikely? If so, the standards may interfere to an objectionable degree with the institution's freedom to develop its own programs. Should the standards be stated in terms of broad generalities, and thus permit application to a wide variety of institutions, even though their interpretation may not be clear?

The North Central Association, although it is not engaged in a major revision of its criteria for accreditation, has been giving considerable attention to the question of approving emerging institutions — those which constitute the large number of junior colleges just beginning their programs and the institutions which are expanding their operations into upper-division and graduate work. The junior or community colleges provide unusual accreditation problems because of their necessary emphasis on technical training, some of which is not at the college level. The institutions initiating graduate programs face the accrediting agencies with a dilemma: How can the standards of graduate scholarship be maintained in the face of the obvious need for large numbers of college teachers with advanced graduate preparation?

Another interesting recent development has been the "Periodic Membership Review Program" under which each college is asked to report and is visited once every ten years for two purposes: to maintain the standards of the Association and to stimulate the institution by means of a re-study of its problems. As a part of the Periodic Membership Review Program, the question of how to examine the large, complex universities was given special attention. Evaluating all the aspects of the large university's activity would be difficult, so an alternative has been proposed, concentrating attention on the processes by which decisions are made in the several areas of the institution's activities. A statement from the Association on this matter says:

> This type of inquiry would have the advantage of relieving the visiting team of the task of attempting to analyze large amounts of factual data pertaining to the status of the institution which may or may not have implications for the quality of the institution. Rather, it would permit the visitors to concentrate their attention primarily on the dynamics of the institution, referring only to such factual data as the ongoing inquiry suggested might be important.
>
> The decision-making process permeates every area of the institution's activities. For this reason, this kind of inquiry, together with the raising of questions suggested by the Basic Institutional Data and the Institutional Profile, should provide a vehicle through which the institution's major strengths and weaknesses could be discovered.
>
> As the examination proceeded, it would be important that the team be continually alert to the possible need for redirecting the inquiry or probing more deeply in certain areas on the basis of discoveries made during the course of the examination. Though the initial approach to the institution would be through the decision-making process, the team would of course be prepared to depart from that line of inquiry as soon as questions began to be raised which would seem to call for such departure.
>
> The report of the examination would deal only with the outstanding characteristics of of the institution — the notable strengths and the major weaknesses.[9]

This proposal seems to me to have much promise, both for encouraging institutions to examine their own decision-making processes, and for providing a more efficient approach in the initial stages of the inspection.

The National Commission on Accrediting is faced by some fundamental decisions as it considers the maintenance of institutional freedoms as against their usurpation by state and Federal agencies distributing funds. Frank G. Dickey, the present Executive Director of the Commission said in his last annual report:

> Probably no issue in American education poses a greater problem than that produced by the juxtaposition of the tradition of freedom for institutions and the availability of funds through state and federal agencies. Our institutions of higher education have consistently resisted domination by the various publics with which they deal, but the question arises as to how we can best establish a position of cooperative interaction with the political agencies and at the same time retain the independence and autonomy which have characterized American education through the years.
>
> It is in this context that the National Commission on Accrediting is seeking answers to various questions bearing upon the future direction of accrediting.
>
> In attempting to strike a balance between federal and institutional powers, at least three alternatives in accrediting have become discernible.[10]

"*Alternative One: A Separation of Function Between Voluntary Accrediting and Governmental Eligibility.*" Dickey goes on to point out that for fifteen years Federal funds for veterans' training were tied closely to the approval of institutions by generally accepted accrediting agencies. Problems continue to arise, however, because the usual accrediting agencies do not attempt to accredit institutions providing post-high-school training which is not of college grade. The problem is given increasing importance, of course, by the addition of curricula which are designed to provide vocational and other types of education for the poverty programs.

Accepting this alternative, says Dickey, would leave accreditation very much where it is now. He does not give sufficient emphasis, perhaps, to the possibility that it would put the Federal government much more heavily into the accreditation business and would associate governmental accreditation with major financial rewards, many of which might be expected to go directly to the institutions accredited.

"*Alternative Two: Institutional Accreditation by the Regional Associations.*" This activity would necessarily be accomplished through the Federation of Regional Accrediting Commissions of higher education, a new organization mentioned earlier. Action would have to be taken speedily, as Dickey points out, and would include provisions for accrediting non-collegiate as well as college-grade, post-high-school institutions. Such institutions include a host of proprietary technical schools and business colleges, and some which engage largely in provisions for home study.

"*Alternative Three: Recognition of All Valid Accrediting Agencies by the National Commission on Accrediting.*" This presents the possibility of "retaining the control of accrediting in the voluntary sector rather than ceding such control to various federal agencies".[11] The acceptance of this alternative would require major and speedy changes in the criteria presently in use by the National Commission on Accrediting for determining what accrediting organizations it will accept.

After considerable discussion of the pros and cons of these three alternatives in his annual report, Dickey suggests the following:

> that the National Commission on Accrediting consider reorganizing in such a way that our Commission would be composed of two divisions: a Council of Colleges and Universities and a Council of Specialized Institutions. The former division or council would be composed of essentially the same institutions that now make up the National Commission on Accrediting and would concern itself with the professional program accrediting activities and agencies which now are recognized by the Commission.
>
> The second division or council would be composed of institutions which are post-secondary in nature and which now work in the field of technical or vocational education and in professional areas not ordinarily included in the usual or traditional college or university pattern.[12]

The alternatives presented by Dickey were considered by the governing body of the National Commission on Accrediting in April and again September 1967.* The Commission has rejected the alternative of "separation of function between voluntary accreditation and governmental eligibility." It will continue to support recognition of two-year institutions by the regional accrediting associations and, in addition, will approve specialized accrediting groups as "auxiliary accrediting associations." The Commission points out that,

> Associations on the "List of Recognized Auxiliary Accrediting Associations" will be recognized to (1) grant formal program accreditation at the associate degree level when institutions request such accreditation and when programs meet approved standards of the association; (2) work cooperatively with the various regional accrediting associations in establishing federal funding eligibility for associate degree programs in institutions which elect to secure eligibility through means of the institutional review offered by regional accrediting associations ....
>
> A specialized accrediting association will agree to furnish the regional accrediting associations with appropriate guidelines which will be used in the examination of associate degree programs and will provide the regional associations with lists of specialists who are qualified to serve on regional accrediting teams and from which lists representatives will be selected.[13]

This arrangement was in force with a number of auxiliary associations during 1967-68 and conversations with others were continuing.

MAJOR ISSUES IN ACCREDITATION

The first of the major issues associated with the accreditation of collegiate institutions may be described as political and is simply stated by the question: Who shall control the accreditation of colleges? The analysis given earlier from the most recent annual report of the National Commission on Accrediting clearly

---

*This paragraph was revised after review of the minutes of the September Commission meeting, held after the date of the conference whose proceedings are printed here.

sets forth the problem, but perhaps does not give it sufficient emphasis. The National Commission on Accrediting is concerned with keeping the control of the formal accreditation of colleges in the hands of the college themselves, and sees as a major danger the possibility that increasing responsibility for accreditation may be placed in the hands of the Federal government. But there are other dangers, less obvious, but perhaps just as important.

In maintaining the control of college accreditation in the hands of the colleges, one method under consideration by the National Commission is to set up a separate organization — under its auspices to be sure, but still separate — for the accreditation of non-college, post-high-school, formal education institutions. If this procedure is followed (and it may be the best of the available alternatives), then the question becomes even more important: How can a college be distinguished from other kinds of institutions? Maintaining appropriate standards for liberal arts colleges which are frankly and openly profit-making may be comparatively simple compared to the task of deciding whether a non-profit, post-high-school institution preparing technical specialists should be classified as a college for accreditation.

A second type of question arises from the fact that the emphasis up to now has been on *formal* accreditation, although there is a probability that *informal* means of accreditation are of increasing importance. The interest of major corporations in the field of education, the probability that such a major business has long experience with effective techniques for persuading people to accept its products, and the increasing practice of college counseling by private individuals as a means of livelihood are all examples of informal forces of accreditation which should be considered as one examines the process.

A third element in the question of control is the probability that as the number of institutions increases, the problems which families have in choosing among them also increase, and thus questions of accreditation become of greater importance. The possibility that colleges can be operated at a profit may be expected still further to add to the pressures for formal and informal accreditation. Whatever process of accreditation is used will be more frequently subject to vigorous criticism. The problem of control of accreditation may take on new dimensions as social forces encourage even more effective criticism.

A second general issue arises from a philosophic conflict inherent in accreditation itself. The fundamental purpose of any accreditation activity is to protect the public from poor institutions. If it is needed at all, accreditation must say about some institutions, "These are not acceptable places to send the children of the public," and about other institutions, "These are acceptable." In its operation, accreditation goes even farther and tells institutions what they must do to become acceptable. Thus, the fundamental purpose of accreditation is to interfere with an institution's freedom — the freedom to be inferior.

In conflict with this purpose is the desire of most institutions of higher learning to maintain their freedom to be whatever they want to be — always good, of course. But if an institution is not free to deviate from the pattern adhered to by the majority, how then is progress made? And the freedom to be different must include the freedom to be worse in the eyes of the majority. The conflict between the fundamental nature of accreditation to regulate and the desire of institutions to maintain their freedom is basically irreconcilable, but accrediting organizations resort to a number of different means of reducing the area of conflict.

One that was mentioned earlier is to state the criteria so generally that they can mean anything to anyone and, therefore, leave the entire matter of judgment of individual institutions up to the acquired knowledge and prejudices of the judges — the visiting committees or the intermediate and final committees who pass upon the institution's acceptability. Associated with this method of reconciling the conflict is the acceptance of almost all institutions as worthy. By such an arrangement, the number of institutions rejected, and thus the number likely to be vocal in their criticism, is very small, and the "in's" have the great preponderance of respected opinion on their side.

Still another means of attempting to reduce this conflict is to place emphasis on the processes used by the institution for reaching its decisions, rather than on the outcomes of these decisions. This has been illustrated earlier in the discussion of a proposal by the North Central Association for examining multipurpose institutions. Another procedure commonly used among accrediting groups is to say to the institution: "These are our standards, but if you wish to do so, please feel free to describe your institution along other dimensions which you feel will enable us to judge it more accurately." This is intended, of course, to provide an opportunity for an institution to report on its own terms if it believes that the standards do not do it justice.

Most accrediting agencies use a combination of these methods of reconciling the conflict between the necessity for regulating institutional behavior and allowing for the kind of institutional freedom which will develop unusual strengths.

A third kind of major issue in accrediting may be called technical and arises from the fact that the art and science of judging or measuring the quality of a college are not well established. It is this problem about which many of the other papers here are also concerned. As I have attempted to show, in describing some of the problems of the two accrediting agencies I know best, the question of what criteria to use in judging the merit of an institution is difficult and far from settled. The question of whether the product of education (the teacher, the businessman, the lawyer, or the liberally educated person), or the process by which he was educated, should furnish the basis for our criteria is presently under debate. Some have proposed that standardized tests could be used as means of judging the quality of the graduates of an educational institution. More people, however, doubt whether any combination of our present tests will furnish adequate measures of the product of college education. The question of the judging of the institution by its product becomes even more difficult when one considers institutional aims such as "the development of habits of critical inquiry." In any case, the development of external criteria, against which institutional accomplishment can be measured, is one of the major problems in all accreditation activity. People engaged in higher education do not agree on the nature of the changes they wish to induce in their students. They do not even appear to agree as to what changes are distinctive features of colleges as opposed to other educational institutions such as high schools.

This discussion, has pointed out that there is a useful distinction between formal and informal accreditation, described in brief the development of some of the agencies engaged in formal accreditation of institutions of higher learning, and compared in more detail the workings and some of the problems of two accrediting agencies.

All this has led to consideration of three issues associated with the accreditation of colleges — issues likely to be with us for some time. Stated as questions, these issues are:

1. Who shall control the accreditation of colleges?
2. How can the essential regulatory nature of accreditation be applied so as not to stultify institutional development?
3. How can the accomplishments of an institution be measured?

REFERENCES

1. American Association of Collegiate Registrars and Admissions Officers. *Report of Credit Given by Educational Institutions.* 1967, pp. 3-6.
2. Selden, William K., "Nationwide Standards and Accreditation," *American Association of University Professors Bulletin,* 50:311, Dec. 1964.
3. Hefferlin, J. B. Lon. "The Past — A Historical Sketch." In *The Past and the Future.* National Commission on Accrediting, Washington, D.C., 1965, p. 2.
4. "Facts About The Commission." National Commission on Accrediting, Washington, D.C.
5. *Guide for the Evaluation of Institutions of Higher Learning.* Chicago, Illinois, North Central Association of Colleges and Secondary Schools, Commission on Colleges and Universities, 1966, p. iii.
6. *Ibid.,* p. i.
7. *Ibid.,* pp. 6, 7.
8. "Standards for Accreditation of Teacher Education," In *Evaluative Criteria for Accrediting Teacher Education.* American Association of Colleges for Teacher Education, Washington, D.C., 1967, pp. 107-119.
9. "Suggested Procedure for Membership Review Visit to A Complex University." Chicago, Illinois, North Central Association of Colleges and Secondary Schools, Commission on Colleges and Universities, 1966, pp. 1, 3. (Mimeographed.)
10. Dickey, Frank G. "Change, Crisis and Challenge." *In* National Commission on Accrediting, *Annual Report of the Executive Director,* March 1967, p. 3.
11. *Ibid.,* p. 9.
12. *Ibid.,* p. 10.
13. From "Reports" (Minutes) of the National Commission on Accrediting, September, 1967. (The Commission, 1785 Massachusetts Avenue, N.W., Washington, D.C. 20036.)

CHAPTER VI: A REVIEW OF RESEARCH IN SCHOOL LIBRARIANSHIP

JEAN E. LOWRIE
Professor and Head, Department of Librarianship
Western Michigan University

An examination of research in the field of school librarianship since the early 1950's reveals a very small number of studies for a period of nearly twenty years. The early 1950's were arbitrarily chosen as a beginning point for this survey, since this was the period following World War II when the emphasis on school library service at all levels began to be evident. It was also the time when the need to expand library resources to include materials other than the traditional printed aids became recognized.

This paper will attempt to categorize topically the studies which have been produced, will explore the predominant methods of research and will discuss in detail some of the studies and their implications. In addition, some indication of trends and areas for future research will be touched upon.

The decision was made to explore primarily the research which has been carried on at the doctoral level. This is the level at which the majority of librarians doing research are concentrating their efforts, with the notable exception of such studies as Gaver's, under the auspices of a research grant from the Office of Education, the Lohrer study under an NDEA contract and, of course, the specific work (particularly statistical surveys) carried on by the USOE Library Services Branch. The decision to omit most of the work at the master's level was made for two reasons: (1) the subjects explored are generally minute, relating very specifically to a problem in a narrow or limited environment, or they are bibliographic in nature and (2) few library schools are requiring a master's thesis as a part of the fifth year program.

DOCTORAL RESEARCH

A search for doctoral dissertations related directly to school library service reveals some fifty completed since 1950. Of these, twenty-nine were carried on in universities offering accredited library school programs though the studies were not always done in the library school; in fact the greater part of the research has been carried out under the auspices of schools or departments of education. Whether the writers have been practicing librarians cannot be accurately determined, but the research obviously has been conducted by people concerned with the administration of, the resources in, and the services available through school libraries. One could hardly construe from this that the existence of an accredited library school on the campus influences school librarianship as a topic for research; indeed, quite the opposite seems evident, and schools of education have been more forward in implementing research in this area.

The dissertations fall into fairly definite subject categories with some inevitable overlapping: (1) historical studies, including legislation, (2) readers' services (reference, reading guidance techniques, etc.), (3) resources (materials, evaluation, dissemination, organization, etc.), (4) library skills and instruction, (5) development of elementary school libraries, (6) development of secondary and junior high school libraries, and (7) analysis of state, regional or city services.

An examination of the majority of these doctoral studies (listed in the bibliography) indicates that about 50 percent use a combination of research techniques. Most of the researchers employ questionnaires, combining these with interviews and field observations or with data derived from local system or state reports. These questionnaires tend toward orthodox groupings to determine the number of staff (professional and clerical), size and type of collection, and make-up of school community, budgets, and so on, to show growth or present status. A few studies are found which analyze articles in periodicals related to certain subjects such as reviews in selection aids or library articles in school-oriented journals. One piece of research analyzed two state surveys nearly ten years apart, to determine growth patterns and then related these to national school library standards.[47] One piece of historical research appears[1], a study of the legislation in Ohio which affected public school libraries' development from 1785 to the early 1950's. The variety of approach is illustrated by two studies[28,23], of which one is concerned with socio-economic environment and its effect on library service to students, while the other assumes that there is a relationship between qualification and experience of the teacher which has a bearing on library service.

As can be seen, these studies are almost without question designed to show growth patterns or trends or to present the current status in a specific locale. All of them emphasize readings in the literature of the field. In addition use is made of the questions in the *Evaluative Criteria*[90], and the *Elementary Evaluative Criteria*[71], of the recommendations from regional accrediting associations, and the 1960 *Standards*[70] prepared by the American Association of School Librarians. The questionnaires have generally been pretested by a jury of experts or by a seminar class. A few studies include the use of a standardized test such as the Iowa Work Study Skills Test or Watson Glaser Critical Thinking Appraisal Test or, in two cases, measurement devices tested by the Gaver study. The material is generally presented in narrative form frequently employing case studies, and using statistical tables of a survey type. Not all of the studies cited in the bibliography could be included in this review – but they are of value in the total overview of developments in the field.

Historical and Legislative Studies. Aldrich's survey of the development of Ohio public school libraries as seen through state legislation[1] constitutes the only study employing historical research. His primary sources were the laws themselves, to which he added his own educational and political background. He points up the growth of urban versus rural school library service stimulated by legislation, and also indicates the changes in educational philosophy which were evidenced in the laws and which ultimately influenced the type of materials to be added to school libraries. The legal framework responsible for the establishment of the school library either directly by boards of education or by contracts with public libraries is carefully explained. This is a good case history of one state, and similar historical studies would be valuable. Indeed little has been done to collect and evaluate the many patterns which were established early in educational history to develop vehicles for school library service.

Readers' Services. There is some difficulty in distinguishing the studies intended to show the development of elementary, secondary and junior high libraries or instructional materials centers, since readers' services often are included in the overall development patterns. However, for purposes of this paper, those studies which relate only to readers' services, such as curriculum improvement or enrichment, reading guidance techniques and reference will be considered. Among this group are those studies by Hagrasy, M. Jones, Lowrie, S. Smith, Voisard, and Warner. [23, 28, 33, 50, 55, 56]

Voisard[55] attempts to ascertain what high schools with enrollments of over one thousand are doing to assist curriculum improvement programs and how this can be done more effectively. Through the use of a questionnaire he concludes that as the number of students increases the adequacy of library staffing diminishes; librarians are most likely to participate in programs for modification of subject curricula, and are frequently included in committees established to solve specific curriculum problems but rarely participate. A similar study by Smith[50] of the role of school librarians in curriculum improvement in New York state schools having central libraries analyzes questionnaires sent to professional librarians. The writer reports the most frequent activity to be providing guidance materials and guidance fiction; the least frequently reported activity was participation in curriculum improvement meetings.

The role of the librarian as a co-worker was studied from the point of view of guidance workers by Warner[56]. The questionnaires contained nine situational cases used to elicit reactions of guidance workers based upon their personal experience, and also questions to elicit judgment and opinions related to the effectiveness of the librarian as a co-worker in guidance and recommendations for increasing his effectiveness. The evaluative summary was designed to include statements which could be correlated with the *Evaluative Criteria*. The study indicates that librarians will need to come nearer to meeting present-day standards for school libraries if the librarian is to become effective in working with guidance personnel. In turn guidance workers will need to have a greater awareness of the contribution other staff members can make. Further research is needed to develop new approaches, instruments and procedures for testing similar types of co-worker services. A study of programs in elementary schools in the areas of curriculum enrichment and reading guidance[33] uses the techniques of interview and observation. Primarily a series of case studies, the examples are intended to show the methods by which both teachers and librarians make use of library facilities and materials to enrich the total educational program in the elementary schools. Measurement evaluation of the experiences is not attempted.

Two interesting studies with overtones directly related to reading guidance are those by Hagrasy and M. Jones. [23, 28] Hagrasy has assumed that an exact relationship between qualification and experiences of teachers which have a bearing on library service on the one hand, and services given to pupils and their gains from these services on the other, is yet to be established. His hypothesis was that "there should be a measurable relationship between (1) teacher's reading habits and library backgrounds (as predicators) and (2) pupils' reading and library skills (as criteria)." He used both school-centered and class-centered data, devised questionnaires to measure teachers' understanding of the library and their reading habits, and used some measures for pupil understanding from the Gaver study. The thesis was substantiated in that (a) when a teacher's reading habits and library background are significantly low, then his class's reading and library skills are also low; and (b) when a class's reading and library skills are significantly high, then the teacher's reading habits and library backgrounds must have been at least relatively high.

The study by Jones[28] relates socio-economic factors and library service to students. It tests the hypothesis that provision for library service in both school and public libraries for twelfth grade students varies according to the socio-economic level of the neighborhood. Data were collected on the socio-economic characteristics of six communities and a ten percent sample of the twelfth grade pupils from each of the eight schools. School districts were ranked on the basis of median incomes. Data were also collected on the libraries, space, staff, accessibility, use, and so on and compared in terms of socio-economic ranks established. The hypothesis is substantiated for the branches of one large city and the school library collections: more services by school and public libraries are provided by agencies with larger staffs and the larger staffs are generally in better neighborhoods; schools in upper socio-economic neighborhoods possessed newer quarters, more space, and other advantages.

Resources. Accessibility, characteristics of organization, evaluation of materials, and administration of resources have been examined from many aspects. Studies by Barrilleaux, Becker, Cianciolo, Coburn, Corbacho, Donnelly, Farley, Galloway, Grassmeyer, Hall, N.L. Jones, McCusker, MacWilliam, Mehit, Monagan, Prostano, Schmitz, and Sheriff fall in this category. Donnelly and Grassmeyer[25, 21] carried on studies at selected senior and junior high schools of the organization and administration of instructional materials centers. Staffing, facilities, services and utilization of materials were examined. In both studies, schools were identified by representative state departments of education and questionnaires were sent. Donnelly also visited the centers. Conclusions from both studies indicated that state departments of education have not been exceptionally active in disseminating information, guidelines, etc., on the development of materials centers. The centers studied tended to be library-oriented. Few fulfilled ALA standards. Among high schools, teachers with more experience and advanced degrees tended to use the center more often; in junior high schools, teachers utilizing the service most were those with less than ten years of teaching experience and under thirty-nine years of age. In-service training needs were emphasized in both studies.

A study in acquisition and distribution of material in Pennsylvania of regional centers[6] and a plan for centralized cataloging the elementary school libraries of New York City[11] assessed current practices and made recommendations for procedures which will facilitate and speed up technical services. Again questionnaires, interviews and direct observations were used to gather data. The Becker study utilized a rating scale to reflect the degree to which practices of each regional center fulfilled principles stated in the criteria. Coburn analyzed work procedures and staff organization, and compared duplicating equipment and costs to determine plans for centralized cataloging. In both instances a jury panel was used to pre-evaluate proposals or criteria employed. Recommendations in the Becker study emphasize, among others, the need for active participation of all members within a district in planning and evaluating procedures and changes. Materials should be directed toward representing teacher's needs, correlation with curriculum, and incorporating technical production excellence.

Other studies in this area tend to establish criteria for selection and use,[10, 48] to discuss censorship tendencies,[18] to analyze the nature of reviews of juvenile books in periodicals[19] and to survey resources in general and specific subject areas[29, 46, 45, 38]. Among the findings are the following:

(1) The need was established for criteria for the use of trade books in the elementary school program, for the selection of trade books that are to be used in schools, for the accessibility of trade books, and for the provision of learning experiences in which trade books are involved.[10]

(2) The quality of library book selection in elementary schools (in Pennsylvania) is higher in schools using centralized libraries having a full-time certificated librarian. There is no significant difference in quality of selection where there is a part-time certificated librarian compared with schools where there is

no librarian (chi square test applied). There is a significant difference in quality of selection when related to per pupil allocation of funds[6].

(3) Book censorship in the senior high school libraries of Nassau County, N.Y., is evident in voluntary form. All librarians differ about books to be censored. There are many small external pressures which affect decisions in each community. This study could not reduce data to statistical form or treatment and inevitably the conclusions, despite the sincere efforts of the researcher, are subjective[18].

(4) More descriptive and critical reviews of juvenile books are needed. Reviewers need to be more aware of the increasingly vast and diverse audience which relies on assessment of reviews. Other media besides journals and newspapers should be studied for their usefulness in reviewing juvenile books.[19]

(5) From two studies which surveyed collections in the biological sciences and in the math and physical science areas in fifty-four Michigan high schools, it was concluded that NDEA was beginning to help build school library collections although it had not had any great impact on collections at the time of the study. Collections were rated good rather than excellent or fair, although the percentage of the average collection devoted to biological science was less than that recommended in the standard bibliographies used in the study. There was evidence that some biology teachers were using methods of teaching which require pupils to use library materials; more than 50 percent were not [29, 46].

(6) Inadequacy of expenditures by most public high schools for developing and maintaining effective library collections in California is attributed to deficient professional preparation of librarians[38].

(7) In Connecticut, in every area where specific comparisons of library resources were made to national criteria, not only were the percentages of schools meeting the standard exceedingly low, but the percentages of schools actually providing the resources suggested a rather dark picture[45].

Hall's study[24] sought to determine which of two types of administrative organization of instructional materials centers provides the greater accessibility of instructional materials to the elementary school classroom, and obtained data from a status study of system type and individual elementary building types. Eight crucial factors affecting accessibility and utilization were identified, and teachers in school systems supporting either type were randomly selected to give their reactions. Among the findings were the following: (1) the concept of the IMC varies in school systems; (2) provision for pupil utilization is not evident in system types and seldom exists in individual building centers; (3) accessibility is the most crucial factor; (4) staff should be qualified in A-V and librarianship and have classroom teaching experience; and (5) pre-service and in-service training for teaching should be provided to a much greater degree.

In addition three studies discuss special phases of utilization. One of these was a controlled experiment to test the effects of instruction on achievement and learning activities of students in eighth and ninth grade science classes with and without the use of an issued basic textbook[4]. A second tested the effect of library service upon the utilization of books by sixth grade pupils in selected elementary schools[39]. The third investigated the selection and acquisition of resources other than textbooks and supplementary texts and the scope of classroom book collections in rural and elementary schools without libraries during 1956-57 in Iowa[35]. These three studies are related here in greater depth because of the research procedures employed and the conclusions drawn.

Barrileaux[4] compared the effects of instruction on achievement and learning activities of students in eighth and ninth grade science classes with and without the use of an issued basic textbook. School library facilities were available to all students; thus, the contribution or influence of the textbook was sought. Fifty-six eighth grade students in 1962-63 at the Malcolm Price Laboratory School, State University of Iowa, constituted the sample; of these students, forty-two were studied an additional year (1963-64) while enrolled in the ninth grade. Two instructional groups were matched with reference to mental ability and preference for science. For the experimental and control sections, the investigator served as teacher; instruction was based on the same content outline and centered about activities prepared by the teacher. The variation in treatments resulted from the use of different reading and reference materials; both sections were encouraged to use library materials, but only the control group was issued with a textbook. Hypothesis concerning differences were tested by the method of analysis of variance and the F-test at the .05 level of significance. The findings were as follows:

    1. Growth in science achievement. As measured on the I.T.E.D. (Iowa Test of Educational
       Development), Test 2 (Background in the Natural Sciences) and the I.T.E.D., Test 6
       (Ability to Interpret Reading Materials in the Natural Sciences), achievement in the class

using school library materials without a text was, on the average, about the same as in the class using a textbook. On Test 2 of the I.T.E.D. for students of high ability and on Test 6 of the I.T.E.D. for students of average ability, the library materials approach resulted in significantly higher mean scores, after two years, over the use of an issued text.

With the S.T.E.P. (Sequential Tests of Educational Progress) science, as the criterion measure, the library materials procedure was statistically superior in overall effectiveness, after two years, to the use of an issued textbook. The interaction of treatments with levels was not statistically significant.

2. Critical thinking. On the Watson-Glaser Critical Thinking Appraisal test, the library-nontext approach resulted in superior student achievement to the use of a textbook, but not to a statistically significant degree. There was no statistically significant interaction of treatments with levels.

3. Science attitudes. As measured by the Test On Understanding Science, the class using school library materials without a text, after one and after two years, achieved significantly higher scores than the class using a text. There was no significant interaction of treatments with levels.

4. Writing in science. The evaluation of writing on science problems during the second year of the treatments showed that mean scores for students without a text and who used library materials were, on the average, significantly higher than mean scores for the students who used an issued text. There was also a statistically significant interaction revealing that students of average ability profited more from the library materials procedure.

5. Library utilization. When student utilization of the library was observed during the second year, the experimental (library-nontext) group scored significantly higher mean ratings than the control (textbook) group in total number of library visits, time devoted to library activities related to science classes, and time devoted to all library activities.

The use of library materials without a text in science was, on the average, more effective than the use of an issued text when measured by frequency of students pursuing related interest (unassigned) areas, participation in free reading, extent of locating and using library materials for science and nonscience classes, and number of library items checked out in interest, science, and nonscience areas.

The purposes of Mehit's study[39] were (1) to survey the elementary school library services offered in the thirteen counties of northeastern Ohio, (2) to describe the three types of library service available to elementary school pupils of selected county elementary schools of northeastern Ohio, (3) to determine whether a significant difference exists among the means of the utilization of school library books by sixth grade pupils of the sample schools in each of the three types of service (classroom, central, combination), (4) to determine whether a significant difference exists among the means of the utilization of school library and outside reading source books by sixth grade pupils of the sample schools in each of the three types of library service (classroom, central, combination), and (5) to determine whether proximity to a city with a population of ten thousand has an effect on results of utilization of school library and outside reading source books by sixth grade pupils of the sample schools.

To select the eighteen schools for the sample, the 233 county elementary schools of northeastern Ohio were compared to selective criteria. In order to be selected for the stratified population, schools had to satisfy the criteria by being within one standard deviation (+ and -) of the mean of the county elementary schools of northeastern Ohio in each of the following areas: tax valuation per pupil, size of school population, number of pupils per teacher, and number of book titles available. Data for these four items were obtained from the State of Ohio Education Department. The fifth area called for a checklist of twenty selected book titles to indicate the quality of titles available. This was accomplished through a questionnaire submitted to the principal of each county elementary school in the region. Responses to the questionnaire were received from 178 (76 percent) of the county elementary schools of northeastern Ohio. Fifty-four schools satisfied the selective criteria and were divided into three categories: schools with classroom libraries, schools with central libraries, and schools with combination libraries. To determine whether proximity to a city with a 10,000 population has an effect on results of utilization of school library and outside reading source books by sixth grade pupils of the sample schools, these three categories were then divided into two subgroups: schools within five miles of a city with at least 10,000 population, and schools not within five miles of a city with at least 10,000 population. A random sample of three schools was drawn from each subgroup. This action resulted in each category having six schools; three in each category within five miles of a city of at least 10,000 population and three in each category not within five miles of a city of at least 10,000 population.

Observations, interviews, and available printed materials provided the needed information to describe the three types of library service available to the school pupils of the eighteen schools of the selected sample.

To obtain the data pertinent to the testing of the null hypotheses, sixth grade teachers of the sample schools tabulated the number of library books and outside reading source books, excluding dictionaries and encyclopedias, utilized by their pupils for a period of twenty consecutive school days. The mean number of school library books per pupil utilized by the schools of each category was determined, as was the mean number of school library books per pupil and outside reading source books per pupil utilized by schools of each category, and the mean of school library books per pupil and outside reading source books per pupil utilized by schools of each subgroup. Assumptions of normality and homogeneity of the fifty-four schools in the stratified population were tested, and the null hypotheses were then tested using the F statistic with a critical region of .05, with no significant differences. Average library expenditures surpass the state minimum standards although the number of titles available is below state minimum standards.

The hypothesis tested by McCusker[35] was that Iowa elementary schools without school libraries do not have well-rounded and well-selected book collections to meet the needs of the modern elementary school's teaching program and its pupils. Sub-hypotheses which contributed to the testing of the major hypothesis were concerned with book selection policies and procedures of the new teachers and superintendents in the elementary school. Case studies were made by visiting all schools and public libraries in one representative county, two schools and public libraries in a city, and one school and public library in a town.

The median per pupil expenditure for books was $1.31; only six school districts spent as much as $3.00 per pupil. The county superintendent did most of the selection of books for the county superintendent's collection, which was the primary source of books for the rural schools. No one of the case schools evaluated had aggregate collections which met state or national recommendations for size of collection. The quality and variety of the classroom book collections, as reported by teachers, were inadequate to satisfy the reading needs of pupils. Findings from the study showed that in all but three of the schools books of fiction made up 70 percent or more of the school's collection. The range of approved books in the schools' total collections ranged from 9.1 to 31.5 percent. Teachers recorded a higher opinion of the adequacy and quality of their collections than was supported by the findings on size and quality of these collections.

Library Skills and Instruction. The field of library instruction as it applies to the use of the library, development of problem-solving techniques, influence on extent of reading for individual purposes or pleasure, and similar topic possibilities have barely been explored. Studies by Gengler[20], Harmer[25], and Stull[51] have resulted in some interesting findings which should stimulate further research. Gengler's primary purpose was to answer the question, "What differences exist in the ability to apply selected problem solving skills between sixth grade pupils who are instructed by a classroom teacher and those who receive additional instruction from an elementary school librarian?" Subsidiary questions in the investigation were:

    1. What responsibility do librarians assume for instructing children to utilize the selected problem-solving skills?

    2. How extensively are the selected skills developed by students upon termination of six years of elementary school?

    3. What qualifications do the participating librarians possess for instructing students?

    4. What effects do librarians have upon the quantity and quality of basic reference materials in the elementary school libraries?

The instruments utilized in gathering data consisted of a Problem Solving Skills Examination and two questionnaires. The examination consisted of two parts. Part I was an oral examination and evaluated students individually in eleven basic abilities needed to solve problems. Examinees were verbally presented with a problem situation in the school library, then asked to locate or acquire information which would solve the problem. All oral testing was done by the investigator. Students were assigned a score on the basis of action taken to solve the problem, and answers given orally to the examination administrator. All orally presented problems were individual testing situations. Part II was a written examination, and evaluated students in nine additional basic skills by means of a paper-and-pencil test. Students were assigned scores by the number of correct responses made to the questions and problems. Two "mailback" questionnaires collected data concerning personal information about and instructional responsibilities of librarians, and materials and resources of the libraries. Treatment of the data compared the teacher-instructed group with the librarian-teacher instructed group by determining the statistical significance of the difference between means at the .01 and .05 levels of confidence. Major findings of the study were as follows:

    1. Elementary schools operating library instructional classes obtained a significantly higher mean than the schools not operating such a program. The difference between means was significant at the .01 level of confidence.

    2. Librarians regarded the eleven tested locational skills either as major or supplementary instructional responsibilities. Librarians also considered the nine skills involving acquiring, recording, organizing, summarizing, and evaluating as supplementary or as sole responsibility of the classroom teacher.

    3. The selected librarians had an average of 12.3 years in classroom teaching experience. Library Science training averaged approximately five courses per librarian.

The study by Harmer[25] is somewhat on the periphery of the topic of this paper but would appear to have some significance for school librarians. Even though the occurrence of losses and gains in children's reading ability during summer vacation has been recognized by researchers as well as classroom teachers for many years, few attempts have been made to explain or describe these changes. The most common theory, though unsubstantiated by research, is that children simply do not engage in enough reading during vacation periods to prevent a loss from taking place. Since children's reading during the summer must usually be of a voluntary nature and since the public library becomes the most readily available source of books for children while schools are closed, it was believed that a library training program might influence the amount of recreational reading done by elementary school children during this vacation period.

The Lorge-Thorndike Intelligence Test, Non-Verbal Battery, and Form A of the Developmental Reading Tests for the Intermediate Grades were administered to all pupils approximately two weeks before the end of the school year. The entire sample of pupils was stratified into two levels of reading ability on the basis of the total score achieved on the five sections of the Developmental Reading Text. Form B of the reading test was administered to all pupils during the first week of school in the fall. All pupils of the experimental group participated in a ten day training period which included several visits to their branch library. Increased attention was focused upon recreational reading and the branch librarians visited each class with a collection of books that were especially appealing to children of this age.

Each set of data — pre- and post-scores on the five sub-tests of reading ability, the total reading score, and the single test of intelligence — was inspected through the use of the analysis of variance and, where appropriate, the analysis of covariance. In each case, differences were sought between experimental and control groups, between high and low reading groups, and between sexes. Differences in interactions of any two or all three of these sources of variation were also sought. The level of significance was placed at .05.

No differences were found to exist on Part I — Basic Vocabulary, when the effects of pre-test differences were controlled. On Part II — Reading to Retain Information, a difference favoring the experimental group existed at the .01 level even when differences in intelligence and pre-test scores were controlled. Girls were found to be significantly better than boys on Part III — Reading to Organize, and also on the total score when the effects of differences in intelligence and in pre-test scores were removed. On Part IV — Reading to Evaluate and Interpret, no pre-test differences existed and the girls again excelled the boys on the post-tests. A difference on Part V — Reading to Appreciate, favoring experimental classes was found when pre-test scores were controlled. No differences, however, existed on this test when the effects of intelligence and pre-test scores were removed.

A summarization of the findings lends further support to existing evidence of the general reading superiority of girls in the elementary school. The superiority of the experimental group in reading to retain information and for appreciation indicates the importance of providing more rigorous training in the use of the library.

Development of Elementary School Libraries. Overlapping of categories is inevitable, but the following studies primarily emphasize the development of elementary school libraries even though resources and services are included to some degree. Two of these studies[43, 37] analyze elementary school library programs in Ohio; both use ALA standards as the basis and survey questionnaires as a procedure technique. Both studies agree that the minimums specified by the Ohio State Department of Education were met or exceeded and both concluded that less than 50 percent conformed to ALA criteria. There is an apparent lack of strong leadership at all levels by librarians and other school personnel. In addition, McMillens' analysis of academic achievement reveals that schools with good libraries were superior to schools with minimal libraries or no library service in the area of reading comprehension, and knowledge and use of reference materials. There was little significant difference in the area of vocabulary.

A similar study of selected elementary schools in North Carolina [44] showed that the majority of the schools met the North Carolina standards but very few met the national standards in 1962. Helfert's appraisal in Wisconsin[26] likewise presents similar conclusions. The implication from these studies certainly would seem to be a need for revision of state or regional standards.

Two studies by Kaye[31] and Leonard[32] survey the role of the principal or school superintendent and the development of elementary school libraries, and a third, by Coryell[13] compares effects of the roles of the county library and the county superintendent of schools in developing potential services. All three reaffirm that better programs are derived from strong school administrative support rather than public library support. In addition, Coryell develops a pattern for development based on supervision by the county superintendent. Leonard shows that in virtually all areas of administration, actual practice does not correspond to the convictions of school superintendents. For example, although 89 percent recommend centralized libraries, only 44 percent have them in their own schools; 71 percent recommend a full-time librarian in schools over five hundred while only 20 percent employ a full-time librarian.

The Tolman study[52] based on a checklist survey, attempts to discover high appeal activities and plans for promoting elementary school library service. A wide variety is suggested, but no research has been done to indicate the specific value of any one or combination of plans.

The identification of valuable learning experiences in centralized elementary school libraries and the analysis of these experiences to determine which facilitated and which retarded learning is the purpose in the Bishop dissertation[7]. The critical incident technique was used to gather the data from two school systems (Oak Park, Illinois, and Arlington County, Virginia). This technique consisted essentially of obtaining descriptions of specific incidents during personal interviews. The behaviors involved determined whether the children's experiences were good or bad. Similar behaviors were classified in categories and related categories were grouped to form three major areas, viz., pupils' descriptions of good and bad experiences, ways in which pupils received help in the library, and reasons why pupils did not receive help in the library. As a result, it was found that there were seven critical elements which influenced the outcome of the incidents: the librarian, materials and equipment, activities and privileges, conduct of persons in library, atmosphere of library, other pupils, and the library as a separate entity. There were two critical elements which emerged in each of three major areas: the librarian and the library materials. The librarian's influence on the outcomes of the library experience were due to: her ability and willingness to help children locate materials, her efforts toward helping children to learn efficient library usage, her reactions to and methods of controlling children's conduct, her efforts to inform children of the contents of the library, and her interest in children's personal needs and problems. The influence of materials and equipment was largely due to their availability, accessibility, utility and organization.

Development of Secondary and Junior High School Libraries. A parallel grouping of junior high and secondary school libraries reveals a similar breakdown of subjects and methodology. Cyphert[14] and Sisson[49] have attempted to analyze junior high school library practices. Sisson found that a national survey gave no evidence of any planning for the "unique needs" of the junior high library. The quantitative standards in state regulations are far below those now recommended nationally and show little or no inclination in recent years to reflect economic or education changes. Cyphert's study[14] attempts to identify current practices in instruction in library skills in junior highs in Pennsylvania. It was concerned with purpose and interest in use of materials, teaching practices in various subject areas, working relationship to teachers, library physical aspects and personnel of the library. All junior highs give some type of preplanned library instruction, with emphasis at grade 7. The librarian usually conducts the instruction, which follows routine formal patterns and topics. Creative methods are rarely used. More research is needed in this field for there is little scientific evidence or reliable information concerning the values of library instruction or methods of imparting it. Again the lack of pre-service or in-service training for teachers is pointed out.

The Ducat study[17] on student and faculty use of the library in three secondary parochial schools was based on the assumption that the contribution of the school library to the total school program is conditioned to a great extent by the importance which teachers assign library resources in achieving the teaching objectives of their courses, and by use made of the materials in their teaching. Data were obtained from three co-educational parochial secondary schools in the Midwest and from one school for a depth study of the characteristics of students in relation to their use of school and public library facilities. Some of the findings provide little evidence that the school library plays a vital role in the total school program of the schools investigated. Significant in relation to this was the evidence of lack of leadership at higher levels of administration, and within various departmental subject areas in providing the necessary motivation to use the school library as a source of materials in the teaching program, and in developing programs which require the use of varied materials.

Batchelor[5] considers the improvement of the school library program in Philadelphia secondary schools; Meyer[41] evaluates library facilities and services in Nebraska; and Sheil[47] compares comprehensive surveys of 1956 and 1963 in secondary schools of Ohio. All three related the criteria in their questionnaires to the national school library standards in existence at the time of the study.

Facilities. Herald[27] and Trotter[53] have carried out studies of facilities for secondary school libraries. Herald compares existing facilities of twenty-five recently constructed secondary school libraries against the standards recommended by the ALA to determine which standards have proven most difficult for these schools to meet. The study proposes a procedure for using standards for the planning of secondary school library facilities. The point by point analysis reviewed certain basic weaknesses, notably insufficient flexibility in initial planning, poor spatial relationships, slighting of functional details, and little consideration given to expanded types of materials. Herald concluded that despite limiting financial support, standards could have been met had the initial planning been more complete through the development of educational specifications for the library center. Library standards can be a vital resource and are most effective in the hands of teachers, librarians, administrators and architects in a cooperative team planning effort.

Trotter's study[53] not only ascertained desirable quantitative standards but then developed a Fortran computer program which will enable these standards to be adapted to public secondary schools with an enrollment of two hundred or more. He concluded that instructional materials centers are on the increase and no optimum design has yet been decided. Each situation presents different problems. He, too, emphasized that the most feasible procedure for developing adequate centers is through well planned educational specifications. The quantitative standards presented in this study must be adapted to local conditions.

There are a few other doctoral studies which should be identified because of the particular subjects explored. One is Mack's 1957 analysis[36] of the contents of representative educational periodicals to determine the nature and amount of school library information contained therein, particularly as the library contributes to the total educational program of the school. At the time, several conclusions were drawn, among which were: (1) school libraries have assumed little responsibility for contributing to the dissemination of school library information through writing, (2) the scant attention to the school library's contribution to a number of curriculum areas and to co-curricular activities is inconsistent with the modern concept of the library as a teaching and service agency for the entire school, (3) information about the library's relationship to other special services and agencies is uneven in emphasis and inadequate in coverage, and (4) administrators do not find adequate information about administrative provision for school library service. Although this study does not truly qualify as research, it does point up areas where research is needed in order to help school administrators and librarians plan and promote better services.

The role of state departments of education in providing library services is of real significance. Burke[8] has investigated the states in the Southern Association of Colleges and Secondary Schools, and found that (1) school library supervision by the state permits long range planning, (2) legislation fails to provide for contractual and cooperative services among school libraries and other library agencies in the state, (3) state assistance stimulates local interest in school libraries, (4) certification requirements stimulate establishment of training centers for school librarians, (5) the greatest weakness in school library service in these states is the lack of adequately prepared librarians. More research is needed to determine the role which these departments could play in the future, and to bring this study up to date by showing the effects of NDEA and ESEA.

The professional status of school librarians in Michigan public secondary schools of five hundred enrollment or more is investigated by Vance[54]. Data show that significant advances have been made in regard to the professional status of school librarians during the past thirty years. The increase in the number of full-time librarians, the attainment of a better formal education with substantial library science training, the meeting of certification requirements and the increased amount of professional experience and librarianship are areas of improvement. Vance suggests changes needed if effective school library programs are to be attained, and implications for recruitment and school library education. Paralleling the above is McCreedy's attempt[34] to identify those factors which influenced practicing and prospective school librarians to select school library work as a career. Practicing librarians, accredited library schools, and selected undergraduate library school students were surveyed. A wide range of factors contributed to choosing school librarianship as a career. The typical responses were love of books, good school libraries in teaching situations, student assistants in school libraries, and school libraries staffed by full-time librarians.

From the group of doctoral studies presented, it may be concluded first that the majority are survey studies, often of local significance; second, that there are a few studies which present an hypothesis followed by a controlled experiment, with devices for measuring which substantiate or disprove the hypothesis; and third, that more experiments need to be conducted which will develop a body of knowledge which may be used in solving future problems in the expansion of school librarianship. Almost all the studies draw the following conclusions, and thus fundamentally substantiate facts known: (a) collections assembled or selected by persons not qualifed in book selection are inadequate; (b) better direction by local, regional and state consultants or supervisors is needed; (c) educational institutions should make a greater effort to coordinate the efforts of teachers and administrators and to improve their understanding of their role in relationship to the school library and utilization of its materials; (d) national standards now play a significant role in the development of criteria for most status studies; (e) in-service training programs for teachers should be developed in some form in all libraries or materials centers, since the role of the classroom teacher is crucial in promoting and expanding library services; and (f) lack of adequate personnel and insufficient funds are continuing hindrances to developing services.

RESEARCH OUTSIDE THE DOCTORAL FIELD

Cognizance must be given to the research efforts outside the doctoral field. Two types are evident, those supported by grants or other funds, including USOE and NDEA studies, and master's studies of some significance.

Two outstanding studies by Gaver[75, 76] are in the first group. *Effectiveness of Centralized Library Service in Elementary Schools* (Phase I) was produced under the auspices of a contract from the U.S. Office of Education. An abstract in *Library Quarterly*[75] by Gaver gives a report of this in depth as does her article in *Library Trends*[77]. Publication of the second edition of the report in book form[72] has made the whole study available. A quotation from her conclusions will recall the study to mind:

> This investigation has been primarily of an exploratory nature, designed (1) to develop measures which differentiate among three methods of library provision in elementary schools, and (2) to study the relationship of these measures to the socio-economic status of parents and educational gain made by sixth-grade pupils between fourth and sixth grades.
>
> The measures have differentiated in favor of the school library category in most, though not all cases, for the sample of six schools. Differentiation in favor of the school library was found by the measure for evaluation of collections, by the measure of accessibility of services and facilities, by the measure of extent of library-related activities, by the test of library skills, and by the measure of amount of reading. Only qualified differentiation was found in favor of the school library category for the measure of depth of library-related activities and the measure of quality of reading. For this sample, the measure of educational gain between fourth and sixth grades was found to be associated with

the school library category. It seems likely, from the schools in this sample, that resources and educational purposes of the community as a whole may be more significant for differentiation among library categories than socio-economic status of the specific school neighborhood.

Only brief identification has been made of additional variables which may be related to library provision, although the staff believes that among these one of the most important for further research is the factor of administrator-teacher relationships.

Finally, the statistical procedure applied in this study has pointed out the need for the application of all measures to a sufficiently large sample of the accessible population to secure mean scores for schools which can then be handled by analyses for prediction of the relationship to library category of all measures — that is, for both school and pupil variables as identified in the present study. The importance of the provision of library materials and services for the education of boys and girls, adequate to meet the demands they face in the world today and the identification of the best method for doing so, indicate a need for more intensive research in this problem.

The measures developed and the statistical procedures applied have, for the limited population used in this study, indicated that definite advantages accrue in schools that have school libraries manned by professional library staff[75].

This is probably the most significant piece of research in the field of school librarianship today and can well serve as a model for the type of study which needs to be undertaken in design, measurement devices, and so on. In addition Gaver has done two surveys on elementary school library development based on the Encyclopaedia Britannica award applications, which provide interesting statistical studies of growth patterns in staff, budget, support, space and program[76].

The well known work by Fiske, *Book Selection and Censorship; a Study of School and Public Libraries in California*[74] has also been reviewed at length. The implications for school librarians need to be examined regularly and devices designed to test some of these in view of today's school library relationships. Humphry's study of university-school-community library coordination[82] goes beyond the immediate confines of this paper, but is mentioned because of the significance of the subject. A design for measuring the values of this type of cooperative effort should be attempted and many library communities should be studied.

A regional study of importance is the second volume of the Pacific Northwest Library Association Library Development Project[92]. The studies here relate to the role of the school library in the schools of the region, the school library standards of the region, the school administrators' concept of the role of the school librarian, supervision of public school library programs in the area and school-public library relations. Pre-tested questionnaires, observations and interviews, and planned sampling of schools were employed. Many of the findings on supervision, status and standards concur with previous studies cited. One interesting finding was that "a divergence of viewpoints between the librarian and the school administrator does exist...the survey turned up very little agreement among the superintendents themselves on numerous points of school library policy." In addition, there was revealed "a failure to communicate" between school and public library personnel.

A study for which an official report has not yet been published is the project sponsored by the Ford Foundation to develop work-study skills and independent study capabilities in elementary schools in Shaker Heights[81, 97]. This is a three year study in grades 4, 5, 6 in two elementary schools. The project was planned around large group lessons on (1) orientation to the Learning Center; (2) what study is, how to organize, where to study; (3) the Dewey Decimal system; (4) the card catalog, index to the Learning Center; (5) using the audio-visual section; and (6) techniques of reporting, use of many sources, note-taking, bibliographies, etc. All classes of one grade level are taught at one time in the auditorium by one of the three librarians. Classroom teachers observe these sessions. Children use the learning center individually and in groups on an unscheduled basis. Emphasis shifted from the teaching process to the learning process. The Iowa Work Study Skills Test and the Educational Stimuli Library Skills examinations were to be given in the project school and in the two control schools.

Although the Knapp School Library Project was not set up primarily as a research program, the report of the director and the evaluations made should be of value in determining criteria for other research studies. New editions of *Evaluative Criteria, Elementary Evaluative Criteria Planning Guide for High School Libraries* and the ALA Standards will likewise affect research.

A research monograph produced by the NEA Research Division in 1958[89] entitled *The Secondary School Teacher and Library Services* was a fruitful investigation which developed statistically the actual use of library services made by subject area classroom teachers. This should be brought up to date. A similar study of elementary teachers and their use of library facilities would be valuable.

Statistics related to school libraries are regularly collected and evaluated by the U.S. Office of Education and present information on current status; e.g. *Survey of Centralized School Libraries and School Librarians, 1958-1959, Public School Library Statistics for 1960-61 and for 1962-63*[87, 71], and *State Department of Education Responsibilities for School Libraries*[86].

The *Standards for School Library Programs* used in so many of these studies is based on survey data collected by Henne and her committee:

> Various procedures were used for the compilation of the quantitative standards: the judgments of a panel of experts consisting of members of the Committee and the advisory consultants; information obtained from questionnaires sent to schools characterized as having very good school library facilities and resources; and the subsequent appraisal of the standards in conferences with specialists in the field. In the questionnaires that were sent to established school libraries, the respondents were asked for facts about the library budget, staff, materials collections, and quarters. They were also requested to make estimates about what the libraries needed if the current provisions for funds, staff, and collections were inadequate. This last request was made in order to avoid perpetuating in the standards a *status quo* that reflected any prevailing conditions which failed to provide for the facilities and resources known to be essential for very good school library programs[70].

Two studies by Lohrer are relevant: one is authorized by the Indianapolis Public Library to develop and test a method for the evaluation of the effectiveness of a program of school library service administered by a public library, and to determine the relationship between IQ and reading levels to adequacy of reading material in a school in order to recommend types of library collections needed. The second deals with "Identification and Role of School Libraries which Function as Instructional Materials Centers, with Implications for Training." Progress reports on the latter have appeared at intervals[83, 84], and the implication is that school libraries of tomorrow will have the characteristics of multimedia centers for individual, small group or large group learning processes.

Recognition must be given at this point to the continuing review and evaluation of research conducted by Mary Gaver not only in the field of school libraries per se, but also in peripheral but relevant areas. From October 1959 to March 1966 she edited the column "Current Research" in *School Libraries*, the only regularly appearing source related specifically to this field of research. Her articles in the *ALA Bulletin* ("Research on Elementary School Libraries"[78]) and in *Reading Teacher* ("What Research Says about the Teaching of Reading and the Library"[79]) have already been noted; she has produced more research in this area in recent years than any other single person and has stimulated some of the more creative pieces of research produced by others.

At this point I shall review a sampling of the master's theses or predoctoral studies which seem to be as creative in approach as any of the doctoral ones, or of special significance, though on a small scale, and so worthy of study on a broader level. One such is James's study of the use of the public library by students in fourth through eighth grades, in the Phoenix, Arizona, elementary schools[60]. Little evaluative study has been done in this field. The reading program as it relates to the school library was explored by Masterton[65], Monahan[66], J. H. Smith[68], and Lennon[63]. Masterton indicates that the activity of a library program as opposed to mere book exposure can be a strong factor in a reading program. Higher scores on reading tests were evidenced in schools with centralized school libraries and full time librarians. Socio-economic factors were recognized as possible factors since the students were from a well-to-do, high level community.

Monahan[66] found that "children with a school library read more and, except for seventh grade girls, read more high quality books than children with only classroom collections...and, made higher scores on standardized reading tests." Smith discusses an experimental high school freshman reading program designed by a school librarian[68]. These first two studies[65, 66] were mentioned by Gaver in her background chapter for developing measures of evaluation, although they were decidedly limited in scope, community background and sampling. Furthermore "the relationship to educational achievement is not established by these studies and there is no conclusive evidence of relationship to skill in the use of libraries and reference tools" in either of them. Lennon[63] evaluated techniques which were used in a junior high school library to serve a gifted and a slow learning class having the same grade level, same instructor and same subject matter. Variety of materials, and basic teacher-librarian planning were essential for growth. Creative processes of the gifted were stimulated; communication skills of slow learners were improved. Library skills can be developed with understanding when integrated with needs of students and curriculum.

New developments in educational programs and technology obviously affect the school library. In this area Blakely[58], Larson[61], and Washington[69] have done some probing which should be followed up on a broader but more definitive basis. Blakely[58] has attempted to show the effect of consolidation on the materials collection of consolidated high school libraries in North Carolina. Larson[61] has explored the use of the punched card to program all materials available in one school in the area of the social studies which related to the fifth grade social studies guide. The material was coded to correspond with the units in the guide and a dictionary was amassed. Ultimately two other school collections were similarly coded and key-punched to ascertain the feasibility of quick interlibrary loans as well as total bibliographies by subject. The very small sampling appears worthy of further investigation and evaluation.

Washington[69] studied the use that librarians in selected schools in North Carolina have made of the newer media of education. Branyan's study[59], again only a small sample, begins to probe the type of services given, the activities required of, and the time spent on extra-curricular professional areas by the professional librarian at the junior high level. The studies by Lunnon[64] of the program for centralized cataloging in Dade County (Florida) school libraries and by Nicholson[67] for Chicago school libraries were used extensively in the doctoral study cited earlier, conducted by Coburn[11]. Two pieces of student research in progress might be mentioned as examples which hopefully will contribute to our understanding of school library needs. A doctoral study at Wisconsin, by Woodworth, is based on a series of detailed questionnaires, and attempts to determine from school librarians on the national level the areas in which they believe research needs to be carried on. This should be of assistance in guiding future research efforts. A sixth-year study at Western Michigan University by McKinney is an attempt to determine whether the use of National Science Foundation packaged instructional programs tends to increase or decrease the need for a school library program at the secondary level in the area of science instruction. Nine high schools of 900 to 1500 students in Indiana, Michigan and Illinois are being evaluated.

TOPICS FOR FURTHER RESEARCH

Topics for further research have been suggested throughout this paper. They are listed here indiscriminately, together with additional important topics:

Impact of NDEA and ESEA funds on secondary and elementary school libraries with an eye to forecasting the most relevant and advantageous methods for using these funds, as well as being able to make constructive suggestions with regard to legislative changes.

Effect of the addition of a librarian in the elementary school upon the utilization of school library books regardless of library structure.

An analysis of school library structure patterns to see if there is any one, or combination of types of, organization offering greater service strength to the school program.

Formulation of measures to determine successful motivating methods to encourage use of elementary or secondary school library books or other media.

A study of the variables which make an established centralized library an effective instrument in the educational program.

Additional research on the role of the teacher and the utilization of library services and materials.

Identification of various means by which materials may be made accessible throughout the school, and an evaluation of these techniques (if such an instrument for measurement can be designed).

Testing library instruction methods at all levels as they relate to skills in learning.

Further study of evaluation and selection methods for both print and non-print materials.

Value of pre-service and in-service training for teachers in the use of all media.

The impact of full elementary school library service on the secondary school instructional program.

The whole area of supervision and its concomitant responsibilities, role, and value to program expansion.

Exploration of computer use for organizing and disseminating information in the school library.

The effect of methods of reading guidance, as practiced by school librarians, on learning patterns.

Evaluation of state plans for school library expansion such as the Pennsylvania program; also related historical developments.

Cooperative studies in education and sociology, which make use of grant support, to study in greater depth the socio-economic factors, and the educational trends which inevitably affect school library services.

School-public library relationship, especially the development of regional public library systems.

Only a few members of our profession will become truly research-oriented, but in the field of school librarianship there is a need to establish a core of professional research workers who will understand the importance of indirect approaches to the solution of educational problems, who will be interested in experimental study (not just the survey, observation, and interview techniques, important as they may be), and who will test theories and probe for those guidelines needed to develop the yet unknown possibilities in school librarianship.

REFERENCES

DOCTORAL STUDIES

1. Aldrich, Frederic D. "History of Ohio Public School Library Legislation." Unpublished Ph.D. dissertation, Western Reserve University, 1952.

2. Autio, Andrew William. "A Study of Library Practices and Facilities Provided in Selected Elementary Schools of Nebraska." Unpublished Ph.D. dissertation, University of Nebraska Teachers College, 1958.

3. Barnes, Virginia Cooper. "The Organization and Administration of the Instructional Materials Center in Medium-sized School Districts." Unpublished Ph.D. dissertation, Stanford University, 1960.

4. Barrilleaux, Louis E. "An Experimental Investigation of the Effects of Multiple Library Sources as Compared to the Use of a Basic Textbook on Student Achievement and Learning Activity in Junior High School Science." Unpublished Ph.D. dissertation, University of Iowa, 1965.

5. Batchelor, Lillian L. "The Improvement of the School Library Program in Philadelphia Secondary Schools." Unpublished Ph.D. dissertation, Columbia University, Teachers College, 1953.

6. Becker, Earl Arthur. "An Appraisal of Administrative Practices for the Acquisition and Distribution of Materials in the Regional Instructional Materials Centers of Pennsylvania." Unpublished Ph.D. dissertation, Lehigh University, 1965.

7. Bishop, Martha Dell. "Identification of Valuable Learning Experiences in Centralized Elementary School Libraries." Unpublished Ph.D. dissertation, George Peabody College for Teachers, 1963.

8. Burke, John Emmett. "State Department of Education Library Services in States of the Southern Association of Colleges and Secondary Schools." Unpublished Ed.D. dissertation, University of Denver, 1957.

9. Chen, Cecilia. "Library Personnel of Catholic Diocesan Secondary Schools in the U.S." Unpublished Ph.D. dissertation, Fordham University, 1960.

10. Cianciolo, Patricia Jean. "Criteria for the Use of Trade Books in the Elementary School Program." Unpublished Ph.D. dissertation, Ohio State University, 1963.

11. Coburn, Louis. "A Plan for Centralized Cataloging in the Elementary School Libraries of New York City." Unpublished Ph.D. dissertation, New York University, 1961.

12. Corbacho, Henry Francis. "An Analysis of the Administrative Organization of Selected System Instructional Materials Center Programs." Unpublished Ph.D. dissertation, Wayne State University, 1963.

13. Coryell, Gladys A. "Emerging Patterns of Elementary School Library Service in California." Unpublished Ph.D. dissertation, University of California at Los Angeles, 1953.

14. Cyphert, F. R. "Current Practice in the Use of the Library in Selected Junior High Schools in Pennsylvania." Unpublished Ph.D. dissertation, University of Pittsburgh, 1957.

15. Donnelly, Edward Joseph. "The Organization and Administration of Instructional Materials Centers in Selected High Schools." Unpublished Ph.D. dissertation, University of Nebraska Teachers College, 1965.

16. Dorin, Alex. "Current Practices in Vocational High School Libraries of New York City." Unpublished Ph.D. dissertation, New York University, 1960.

17. Ducat, O.P., Sister Mary Peter Claver. "Student and Faculty Use of the Library in Three Secondary Schools." Unpublished Ph.D. dissertation, Columbia University, 1960.

18. Farley, John J. "Book Censorship in the Senior High School Libraries of Nassau County, New York." Unpublished Ph.D. dissertation, New York University, 1964.

19. Galloway, Mabel Louise. "An Analytical Study of the Extent and Nature of the Reviewing of Juvenile Books in Eight Journals and Newspapers with Special Regard to their Usefulness as Selection Aids for School Libraries." Unpublished Ph.D. dissertation, Columbia University, 1965.

20. Gengler, Charles Richard. "A Study of Selected Problem Solving Skills Comparing Teacher Instructed Students with Librarian-Teacher Instructed Students." Unpublished Ph.D. dissertation, University of Oregon, 1965.

21. Grassmeyer, Donald Leroy. "The Organization and Administration of Instructional Materials Centers in Selected Junior High Schools." Unpublished Ph.D. dissertation, University of Nebraska Teachers College, 1966.

22. Grunau, Allen R. "An Investigation of Existing Approaches to the Problem of Providing Library Service in the Rural Kansas Community: A Study of the Interrelationships of the Public Library and the Public School Library in Selected Rural Communities of Kansas." Unpublished Ph.D. dissertation, University of Kansas, 1965.

23. El-Hagrasy, Saad Mohammed. "The Teacher's Role in Library Service; An Investigation and Its Devices." Unpublished Ph.D. dissertation, Rutgers University, 1961.

24. Hall, Sedley Duane. "A Comparative Study of Two Types of Organization of Instructional Materials Centers." Unpublished Ph.D. dissertation, University of Nebraska Teachers College, 1963.

25. Harmer, William Richard. "The Effect of a Library Training Program on Summer Loss or Gain in Reading Abilities." Unpublished Ph.D. dissertation, University of Minnesota, 1959.

26. Helfert, Byron Alois. "An Appraisal of Elementary School Library Practices in Wisconsin." Unpublished Ph.D. dissertation, University of Wisconsin, 1957.

27. Herald, Homer Wayne. "Planning Library Facilities for the Secondary School." Unpublished Ph.D. dissertation, Stanford University, 1957.

28. Jones, Milbrey Lunceford. "Socio-economic Factors and Library Service to Students." Unpublished Ph.D. dissertation, Rutgers University, 1964.

29. Jones, Norma Louise. "A Study of the Library Book Collections in the Biological Sciences in Fifty-four Michigan High Schools Accredited by the North Central Association of Colleges and Secondary Schools." Unpublished Ph.D. dissertation, University of Michigan, 1965.

30. Jones, Ruth Merrell. "Selection and Use of Books in the Elementary School Library." Unpublished Ph.D. dissertation, Stanford University, 1953.

31. Kaye, Bernard William. "The Role of the Principal in Relation to Library Service in Public Elementary Schools." Unpublished Ph.D. dissertation, Columbia University, Teachers College, 1954.

32. Leonard, Lloyd Leo. "Practices Followed in Administering Elementary School Libraries in the State of Iowa and the Opinions of the School Superintendents in these Cities Concerning those and other such Practices." Unpublished Ph.D. dissertation, Colorado State College of Education, 1955.

33. Lowrie, Jean Elizabeth. "Elementary School Libraries: A Study of the Programs in Ten School Systems in the Areas of Curriculum Enrichment and Reading Guidance with Emphasis on Fourth, Fifth, and Sixth Grades." Unpublished Ph.D. dissertation, Western Reserve University, 1959.

34. McCreedy, Sister Mary Lucille. "The Selection of School Librarianship as a Career." Unpublished Ph.D. dissertation, Columbia University, 1963.

35. McCusker, Sister Mary Girolama. "The Accessibility of Books in Elementary Schools without Libraries." Unpublished Ph.D. dissertation, Columbia University, 1963.

36. Mack, Edna Ballard. "The School Library's Contribution to the Total Educational Program of the School: A Content Analysis of Selected Periodicals in the Field of Education." Unpublished Ph.D. dissertation, University of Michigan, 1957.

37. McMillen, Ralph Donnelly. "An Analysis of Library Programs and a Determination of the Educational Justification of these Programs in Selected Elementary Schools of Ohio." Unpublished Ph.D. dissertation, Western Reserve University, 1965.

38. MacWilliam, Mary. "A Survey of the Library Resources in the California Public High Schools." Unpublished Ph.D. dissertation, University of California at Berkeley, 1956.

39. Mehit, George. "Effects of Type of Library Service upon Utilization of Books by Sixth Grade Pupils in Selected County Elementary Schools of Northeastern Ohio." Unpublished Ph.D. dissertation, Western Reserve University, 1965.

40. Melvin, Sister M. Constance. "History of Public School Libraries in Pennsylvania." Unpublished Ph.D. dissertation, University of Chicago, 1962.

41. Meyer, Floyd Raymond. "Library Facilities and Services in Nebraska Secondary Schools Accredited by the North Central Association." Unpublished Ph.D. dissertation, University of Nebraska Teachers College, 1957.

42. Monagan, Rogers Thomas. "A Study of the Administration of Libraries in the Public Elementary Schools of St. Louis." Unpublished Ph.D. dissertation, University of Missouri, 1950.

43. Moyer, Alan Keith. "Conformance of Ohio Elementary School Libraries to Regulations and Standards." Unpublished Ph.D. dissertation, Ohio State University, 1963.

44. Parker, Johnny Robert. "An Analysis of Library Services in Elementary Grades of Selected Classified Schools in North Carolina." Unpublished Ph.D. dissertation, University of North Carolina, 1962.

45. Prostano, Emanuel Theodore. "An Analysis of School Library Resources in Connecticut as Compared to National Standards, 1960-61." Unpublished Ph.D. dissertation, University of Connecticut, 1962.

46. Schmitz, Eugenia E. "A Study of the Library Book Collections in Mathematics and the Physical Sciences in Fifty-four Michigan High Schools Accredited by the North Central Association of Colleges and Secondary Schools." Unpublished Ph.D. dissertation, University of Michigan, 1966.

47. Sheil, Marion Dorinda. "Library Services in Public Secondary Schools of Ohio, 1955-1963." Unpublished Ph.D. dissertation, Western Reserve University, 1965.

48. Sheriff, Ralph William. "A Study of the Level of Quality used in Selecting Library Books in Elementary Schools in Pennsylvania." Unpublished Ph.D. dissertation, Pennsylvania State University, 1965.

49. Sisson, Silvanus Hull. "Planning the Junior High School Library Program." Unpublished Ph.D. dissertation, University of Nebraska Teachers College, 1961.

50. Smith, Susan S. "The Role of the School Librarian in Curriculum Improvement." Unpublished Ph.D. dissertation, Columbia University, Teachers College, 1957.

51. Stull, Edith G. "A Proposal for the Teaching of Reference Reading in the Elementary School (with) Handbook for Teachers and Librarians Guiding Reference Reading in the Elementary School or Guiding Detection, Discovery, and Development through Reference Reading in the Elementary School." Unpublished Ph.D. dissertation, Columbia University, 1962.

52. Tolman, Lorraine Enid. "Initiation of Elementary School Library Service." Unpublished Ph.D. dissertation, Boston University, School of Education, 1957.

53. Trotter, Charles Earl. "A Fortran Computer Program Designed to Identify the Physical Facilities for Public Secondary School Instructional Materials Centers." Unpublished Ph.D. dissertation, University of Tennessee, 1964.

54. Vance, Kenneth E. "The Professional Status of School Librarians in Michigan Public Secondary Schools Enrolling 500 or more Students." Unpublished Ph.D. dissertation, University of Michigan, 1962.

55. Voisard, Boyer Warren. "Librarian Participation in High School Programs of Curriculum Improvement." Unpublished Ph.D. dissertation, University of Southern California, 1955.

56. Warner, John Ellsworth. "The Role of the Librarian as a Co-worker in Guidance from the Viewpoint of the Guidance Worker." Unpublished Ph.D. dissertation, Columbia University, 1963.

57. Woodring, Wiley Fletcher. "A Study of Library Facilities Provided in Selected Elementary Schools in Southwest Missouri." Unpublished Ph.D. dissertation, University of Missouri, 1964.

MASTERS PAPERS

58. Blakely, H.B. "Effect of Consolidation on the Materials Collection of Consolidated High School Libraries of North Carolina." Unpublished Master's dissertation, University of North Carolina, 1965.

59. Branyan, Brenda May. "The Junior High School Librarian and Requirements beyond the Library Daily Schedule." Unpublished Master's dissertation, Western Michigan University, 1967.

60. James, Gertrude. "Use of the Public Library Agencies by Students in Grades IV through VIII of the Phoenix Elementary Schools, Phoenix, Arizona." Unpublished Master's dissertation, University of Chicago, 1952.

61. Larson, Maxine. "Data Processing in Vine School Library with Fifth Grade Social Studies Materials." Unpublished research paper, Western Michigan University, 1964.

62. Leavitt, M. G. M. "Effect of School Library Facilities on Fifth and Sixth Grade Reading Habits." Unpublished Master's dissertation, Drexel Institute, 1954.

63. Lennon, Joan. "A Library Program for Seventh Grade Gifted and Slow Learners at Otto Junior High School." Unpublished Master's dissertation, Western Michigan University, 1962.

64. Lunnon, Betty J. "Development of Centralized Cataloging for the Dade County School Library." Unpublished Master's dissertation, Appalachian State Teachers College, 1959.

65. Masterton, Elizabeth. "An Evaluation of the School Library in the Reading Program of the School." Unpublished Master's dissertation, University of Chicago, 1963.

66. Monahan, Marietta. "A Comparison of Student Reading in Elementary Schools With and Without a Central Library." Unpublished Master's dissertation, University of Chicago, 1956.

67. Nicholson, C.F. "Proposal for Centralized Processing for School Libraries in Chicago Area." Unpublished Master's dissertation, University of Chicago, 1950.

68. Smith, J. H. "Experimental Reading Program for High School Freshmen Designed by a School Librarian." Unpublished Master's dissertation, University of Chicago, 1964.

69. Washington, C.W. "Study of the Use that Librarians in Selected Schools of North Carolina make of the Newer Media of Education." Unpublished Master's dissertation, University of North Carolina, 1964.

BOOKS AND ARTICLES

70. American Association of School Librarians. School Library Standards Committee. *Standards for School Library Programs*. ALA, 1960, pp. vi-vii.

71. Boston University School of Education. *Elementary Evaluative Criteria*. Boston, 1953.

72. Darling, Richard. U.S. Department of Health, Education and Welfare, Office of Education. *Public School Library Statistics, 1962-1963*. Washington, D.C., U.S.G.P.O., 1964.

73. Darling, Richard. *Survey of School Library Standards*. Washington, D.C., U.S. Department of Health, Education and Welfare, Office of Education, 1964.

74. Fiske, Marjorie. *Book Selection and Censorship: A Study of School and Public Libraries in California*. Berkeley, University of California Press, 1959.

75. Gaver, Mary V. *Effectiveness of Centralized Library Service in Elementary Schools* (SAE-8132). 2nd ed. New Brunswick, N.J., Rutgers University Press, 1963, p. 127. Abstract in *Library Quarterly*, 31:245-256, July 1961.

76. Gaver, Mary V. *Patterns of Development in Elementary School Libraries Today*. 2nd ed. Encyclopaedia Britannica, Inc., 1965.

77. Gaver, Mary V. "Research on Effectiveness of Elementary School Libraries," *Library Trends*, 13:103-116, July 1964.

78. Gaver, Mary V. "Research on Elementary School Libraries," *ALA Bulletin*, 56:117-126, Feb. 1962.

79. Gaver, Mary V. "What Research Says about the Teaching of Reading and the Library," *Reading Teacher*, 17:184-191, Dec. 1963.

80. Gaver, Mary V., and Scott, Marian. *Evaluating Library Resources for Elementary School Libraries*. New Brunswick, N.J., 1962.

81. Krohn, Mildred L. " 'Learning Center' Experiment at Shaker Heights," *School Libraries*, 12:27-31, May 1963.

82. Humphry, John A. *Library Cooperation: The Brown University Study of University-School-Community Library Coordination in the State of Rhode Island*. Providence, R.I., Brown University Press, 1963.

83. Lohrer, Alice. "Future Possibilities in the Development of the School Library Materials Center." In *The School Library Materials Center: Its Resources and their Utilization* (Allerton Park Institute No. 10). Urbana, Illinois, University of Illinois Graduate School of Library Science, 1964, pp. 101-107.

84. Lohrer, Alice. "Identification and Role of School Libraries Which Function as Instructional Materials Centers with Implication for Training." (NDEA Title VII, Part B, Contract B-144, July 1961-June 1962). Urbana, Illinois, 1963.

85. Mahar, Mary Helen, ed. *The School Library as a Materials Center*. Washington, D.C., U.S. Department of Health, Education and Welfare, Office of Education, 1963.

86. Mahar, Mary Helen, ed. *State Department of Education Responsibilities for School Libraries*. Washington, D.C., U.S. Department of Health, Education and Welfare, Office of Education, 1960.

87. Mahar, Mary Helen, and Holladay, Doris C. U.S. Department of Health, Education and Welfare, Office of Education. *Statistics of Public School Libraries, 1960-61*. Washington, D.C., U.S.G.P.O., 1964.

88. Martin, Lowell. *Students and the Pratt Library: Challenge and Opportunity* (The Deiches Fund Studies of Library Services, No. 1). Baltimore, Enoch Pratt Free Library, 1963.

89. National Education Association, Research Division. *The Secondary-School Teacher and Library Services* (Research Monograph 1958-MI). Washington, D.C., 1958.

90. National Study of Secondary School Evaluation. *Evaluative Criteria....* 1960 ed. Washington, D.C., 1960.

91. National Study of Secondary School Evaluation. *Evaluative Criteria for Junior High Schools.* Washington, D.C., 1963.

92. Pacific Northwest Library Association. *Library Development Project Reports.* Vol. II: "Elementary and Secondary School Libraries of the Pacific Northwest," by R.L. Darling, *et al.* Seattle, University of Washington Press, 1960, pp. 307-311.

93. Southern Association of Colleges and Schools. *Evaluating the Elementary School Library Program.* Atlanta, 1964.

94. Taylor, James L., *et al. Library Facilities for Elementary and Secondary Schools.* Washington, D.C., U.S. Dept. of Health, Education and Welfare, Office of Education, 1965.

95. Travers, Robert M. W. *An Introduction to Educational Research.* 2d ed. New York, Macmillan, 1964.

96. Wisconsin Free Library Commission. *The Idea in Action: A Report on the Door-Kewaunee Regional Library Demonstration.* Madison, Wis., The Commission, 1953.

97. Emery, Donald G. "Third Year Report and Final Summary of an Experiment Program in Work-Study Skills and Independent Study." (Grades IV, V, VI, Lomand and Ludlow Schools). Shaker Heights, Ohio, Shaker Heights City School District, 1964-65 (Mimeographed, unpublished).

CHAPTER VII: MEASUREMENT AND EVALUATION IN SPECIAL LIBRARIES*

EUGENE B. JACKSON
Director, Information Retrieval and Library Services
International Business Machines Corporation, Armonk, New York

Special libraries are said to be most alike in their differences, whether they are located in a legal firm, a newspaper, a museum, an industrial firm or in a governmental agency. They exist primarily to advance the interests of their host organization through the provision of dynamic information service. Their goals must be the goals of their host organization and they are inseparable. Somewhat more formally, a special library has been defined as being "engaged in activities serving the technical information needs of a special clientele which departs from standard library procedures and uses non-conventional sources and methods as necessary to fill those needs."[1] It is similar to documentation in being an active rather than a passive service, but it normally requires a lesser level of subject matter competence than does documentation. It may also have a tendency to use existing literature and sources. I have stated elsewhere that it will be impossible to distinguish, however, between special librarianship and documentation services in 1980.

Many of today's practitioners are members of the Special Libraries Association which describes itself as "an international association of 6700 professional librarians and information experts who provide specialized library service to banks, manufacturing concerns, newspapers, research organizations, advertising and Government agencies, hospitals, transportation and insurance companies, museums, business, technical and other specialized departments of public and university libraries, professional and trade associations and other organizations in the fields of business, science, technology and social sciences."[2] Other associations of special libraries include the Music Library Association, Theatre Library Association, American Association of Law Libraries, and the Medical Library Association.

The size of the special library universe is subject to some controversy, depending on the definition used of a special library. Havlik estimated that there were 6,086 as of 1965; however, this figure excludes all special libraries in college, university or public libraries. It does include those serving state governments, the Federal government, municipalities, commerce and industry, associations and non-profit institutions. He estimated that the 6,086 libraries had 171,152,000 volumes, that they received 1,277,890 periodicals, that they had 12,000 professional positions, and that they spent nearly $190 million. His complete table is given here as Table 1.[3]

TABLE 1
Estimates of Special Library Expenditures and Resources, 1965

Type of Special Library	State Government	Federal Government & National Libraries**	Other Governmental Libraries	Commerce & Industry	Associations & Non-Profit Institutions	Total
Estimated total number of libraries	433	848	82	2,163	2,560	6,086
Estimated total number of volumes in these libraries	23,208,000	85,800,000	444,000	19,100,000	42,600,000	171,152,000
Estimated total number of periodicals received	88,390	295,000	28,500	456,000	410,000	1,277,890
Estimated total number of professional positions	975	3,640	335	3,470	3,580	12,000
Estimated total number annual expenditures	$18,307,000	$83,248,000	$1,600,000	$45,000,000	$41,000,000	$189,155,000

*The literature search and annotation were prepared by Ruth L. Jackson, using the facilities of the Thomas J. Watson Research Center Library, IBM, Yorktown Heights, New York, The Engineering Societies Library, New York, N.Y., and the New York State Library, Albany, New York. Appreciation is extended to Gordon E. Randall, Manager, the Thomas J. Watson Research Center Library, for presenting these remarks at the Conference in my necessary absence.
**Library of Congress, National Agricultural Library, and National Library of Medicine
Source: Havlik, Robert J. "The Role of Special Libraries in the United States," *Special Libraries* 57: 236-237, April 1966

Comparable U.S. Office of Education estimates for other types of libraries were: 2,140 college and university libraries, with 12,000 full-time professionals (the same number in special libraries), 7,200 public library systems employing 21,200 full-time professional librarians, and 49,000 public school libraries employing some 31,500 school librarians.

The Havlik figures are appreciated and are the most authoritative known. It is regretted that they perpetuate the concept of excluding the departmental libraries in colleges, universities and public libraries which seems to have originated in organizational problems in the U.S. Office of Education rather than in library practice.

The best directory of special libraries available is Kruzas',[4] the second edition of which is about to appear. The statistical tables from his first edition show the breakdown of 8,758 special libraries in 1962 as follows:[5]

College and university departmental libraries	25.8%
Company	25.3%
Government agency	14.3%
Public library departmental libraries	4.6%
Other organizations	30.0%

Of all libraries, 28.4 percent were devoted to science and technology, 11.8 percent to medicine, and 10.8 percent to law. Just over 30 percent had been founded since 1949, and geographical concentration is striking: of the total 17.8 percent for New York State, 16 percent are to be found in the New York metropolitan area; another 7.1 percent are to be found in the Baltimore-D.C. area, while 8.5 percent of the remainder are in California. The model response was 10,000-19,000 for books and 100-199 for periodical subscriptions. The average staff consisted of 2.2 professionals and 3.1 non-professionals.

While grand totals of the number of special libraries, size of the collections, number of professional positions, and annual expenditures are interesting, special libraries tend to be such individualistic entities that profiles take on an exceptional meaning. At the instigation of the SLA Professional Standards Committee, Ruth S. Leonard of Simmons College, prepared six profiles of the following libraries:[6]

(1) the research library in the ABC Manufacturing Corporation,
(2) the library for the Research & Development Div. of the DEF Industrial Corporation
(3) the library for the GHI Public Utilities Corporation,
(4) the library for the JKL Bank,
(5) the MNOP Advertising Agency Library, and
(6) the library for the Research & Development Division of the QRS Chemical Manufacturing Company.

They are summarized here in Table 2, and it is suggested that these profiles be kept in mind as typifying the size of patronage, staff, resources and equipment currently employed in their operations. The question might well be raised as to the differences between these libraries and information centers of the most advanced nature. A spectrum of literature and data service centers does indeed exist that goes from the most conservative of traditional libraries to supplementary services for the technical population of an international industrial firm. There are many examples of the former; of the latter, it might be pointed out that one centralized industrial document retrieval and dissemination center sent out 901,870 notifications based on 24,552 documents to an average of 1,221 users over a two-year period. If one were to take the degree of mechanization as a criterion of where on the spectrum most of the special libraries are, the results of the SLA/LTP survey of data processing show that 348 out of Havlik's total of 6,086 special libraries are using basic unit record (electronic accounting machine) equipment, the beginning form of mechanization. This amounts to 5.7 percent. It is thus clear that the majority of special libraries are on the side of the spectrum shaded conventional libraries, rather than the opposite.[7]

Bonn points out that there is not much solid information available either about or from special libraries, including evaluative, comparative, cooperative, economic and experimental information: "To be sure there are many good descriptive articles on library plans, practices, personnel, and a need for performance standards, for example. And there are more or less theoretical papers on all sorts of esoteric terms, machines, concepts and processes.... But solid special library break-through studies are indeed rare."[8]

Presumably special library studies would be of greatest value if they were related to the major problems facing them at this time. In a recent communication, Bill M. Woods, for eight years Executive Director of the

TABLE 2

Profiles Of Six Special Libraries

	Research Library ABC Mfg. Corp.	Library for R&D Division DEF Indus. Corp.	Library for GHI Public Utility Firm	Library for JKL Bank	MNOP Advertising Agency Library	Library for R&D Division QRS Chemical Mfg. Co.
Probable Users	200	800	6,000	6,000	400	150
Staff						
Professional	1	5	3	4	3	2
Clerical	1	9	4	5	4	3
Collection						
Books	4,250	18,500	8,150	6,500	2,800	6,000
Government documents				6,000		
Periodical volumes	900	8,350	2,100	2,650	840	2,550
Pamphlets	2,500	2,000	8,500	16,000	3,000	8,000
Internal reports	500	5,000		2,000	4,000	1,500
Technical reports		30,000				
Specifications & standards			2,000			
Slides			6,000			
Clippings					8,000	
Pictures					8,000	
Competitive advertising file items					5,000	
Patents						10,000
Technical correspondence						5,000
Equipment						
Shelves	320	2,310	740	700	195	600
File drawers	60	35	120	340	200	140
Space						
(sq. ft.)	1,530	8,375 (incl. vault)	3,580	4,130	2,225	3,020
Budget ratios						
Salaries	70%	69%	69%	72%	HAVE NO SEPARATE BUDGET	67%
Acquisitions	25%	26%	27%	25%		32.5%
Photocopies						
Binding	3%	3%	3%	2.5%		
Travel	2%	2%	1%	0.5%		0.5%

Source: "Profiles of Special Libraries," *Special Libraries*, 57: 179-184, March 1966.

Special Libraries Association, suggested that the problem areas for special libraries would fall under the following heads: role, personnel, equipment and facilities, resources and services, standards and statistics, cooperation, association, government, and other.[9] (See Appendix)

Under these headings, he raises such questions as the possible misunderstanding about the role of the special library in its host organization: How does it relate to other information sources in the organization? Is the shortage of personnel crucial, and in what areas? Is there a chronic lack of space? Is there a lag in the development of photocopy and communication equipment, particularly for the small libraries? Is the special library a parasite on other libraries? Does it offer too great a variety of services? Should there be consolidations of special libraries within an organization or of similar libraries in a common subject field and located in a geographic area for efficiency reasons? Is copyright a major problem? Is a lack of comparable special library statistics a significant matter? If so, what kinds are most needed? How essential is development of quantitative standards? What research is most needed at once, within the year, within five years? What kinds of cooperation and how much may be anticipated from and among special libraries? Are customary patterns of cooperation outmoded or obsolete? How should the professional library associations help solve this problem? What is the role of subject-based associations in the information/library field? What joint efforts are needed between the libraries and the subject interest association? What is the proper role of the Federal, state and municipal governments in the solution of the special library problems? What legislation is needed to ensure the ability of special libraries to achieve their full potential? While all of Woods's questions do not call for measurement and evaluation in their replies, it is clear that many do. Though Wasserman admits that it is difficult to measure the industrial special libraries, he says that the problem is not unique to them because it is also faced by the public relations department, by the advertising department, and by other functions in industry that do not end in a concrete product. He sees first the need for the special library to determine its purpose, i.e., "a clearly conceived rationale for its existence."[10] This is the first problem area as seen by Woods nine years later, and, stated another way, calls for the drafting and promulgation of a "library charter" that is mutually agreeable to the library management and that of the host organization to which it is attached. (Examples have been seen that occupy only one page of typing, yet seem to fill the bill.) If no objection is made to the draft as submitted to management, the possibilities exist that the latter does not know all the services it might require of the library (or should be prepared to support with resources), or that the library was too modest in its aspirations for service. Wasserman continues,

> It is only after this very difficult process of determining goals and their hierarchy has been concluded that it becomes possible to consider the instruments with which to accomplish the objectives.... Ultimately, in measurement, there is the problem of determining what change or advantage accrues from the service.... As it becomes more possible to sharpen definitions of objectives in very specific terms and as statistical facts governing activity become available, standards evolve to more exact specifications.... The real problem of measurement is less one of attaining the right answers than it is of asking the right questions.... It is virtually impossible to treat measurement without alluding to standards.... The real question here is that of determining what change or advantage accrues to the organizations due to the library program.... The librarian applies his skills, knowledge and technology to accomplish the results and achieve the objectives which are tied to the organization's goals and needs.[10]

Wasserman's article merits reading in full.

Rothstein agrees generally with these concepts of measurement and evaluation[11] and quotes Hutchins on a key point as decrying the gathering of statistics previous to the determination of what are the truly significant data. Hutchins emphasizes the need for clear statements of objectives and criteria before materials, personnel, and organization are assessed.[12]

To this point we have considered the definition of a special library, the size and composition of the special library universe, profiles of typical examples, some of the problems they face, and their need for measurement and evaluation. What research methods may be most effectively used in approaching the special libraries' problem areas? An approach via the matrix system was taken to match the problem areas with the methods and devices cited by Tauber for surveys,[13] with inconclusive results. This means that documentary analyses, statistical analyses, questionnaires, checklists, visits, interviews, observations and specialized data compilations must all be considered on their merits, whether historical, descriptive, or experimental research is undertaken.

There is no need to belabor the difficulties a researcher faces due to poor statistics, sketchy records, and a pragmatic attitude on the part of special librarians. These may be traced largely to too few people trying to do an important job so quickly with inadequate resources. "The phone won't stop ringing long enough for us to count reference questions" has been heard many times. However, those of us who have been involved in conducting orientation seminars in the last few years for the American Management Association on the organization and management of the company library (at a substantial registration fee, but they have been invariably oversubscribed), have seen an increasing awareness of the need to secure better data for presentation to company management. Participants have seized eagerly on Leonard's "Profiles" mentioned earlier,[6] and on the 1967 salary survey covering 4,000 SLA members.[14]

It has not been too many years since Shaw's pioneering diary studies on use of technical information by patrons, but by now many studies are available.[15, 16, 17] They are mentioned because research results can be uncomfortable, and these studies contain implications that the library is *not* the main source of information for scientific engineering users, which point is made more emphatically by the in-depth interview results for the Department of Defense by the Auerbach Corporation and the North American Aviation Company from hundreds of government facility and government contractor staff respectively.

The Rosenbloom and Wolek study provides a contrast in procedures but similar results.[18] Their study of 1,735 scientists and engineers in four major corporations shows that their sources of information differed, with the scientists favoring sources *outside* the corporation, while engineers favored sources inside the corporation. Their search strategies agreed in favoring personal collections of documents and interpersonal contacts over formal information services. (The report includes a very useful bibliography.)

The evaluation of the role played by the library in a given organization is complicated on the one hand by the existence of other information services in the company that may have library-like functions, and on the other hand by deposit stations for materials which may be labelled as "libraries" but are not worthy of the name. There are cases where the library, near-library, and non-library information functions are all elements in an institution's over-all technical information center. It may include a unit for production of company technical reports or even company-sponsored technical periodicals, and possibly analysis centers for evaluation of information of use to the organization, varying from a commercial intelligence activity in a chemical company to a data evaluation center operated under government contract.

The Battelle Memorial Institute Library, for example, has complex relations with the dozen or so data centers conducted under various contract auspices at that Institute. The internal relationship problem becomes more complicated in a multi-location, multi-division company, and in one such company the standard used for representation of a "library" on a company committee on technical literature activities was that the unit in question possessed a rubber stamp bearing the legend "library."

After the internal relationships have been sorted out via documentary analyses, questionnaires or visits, it is then necessary to sort out the external relationships of the library. We have by this time determined where the company information is acquired that is utilized by the library. The open literature would come into it via the bibliographic centers of major public or university libraries in a geographic area or via a major discipline-related library such as the Engineering Societies Library, Linda Hall Library, John Crerar Library, Chemists Club Library, and the like.

The next step outward is the abstract-service-related facility offered by professional societies, for example, the Technical Information Service of the American Institute of Aeronautics and Astronautics, and the various services of the imaginatively conducted Chemical Abstracts Service. The next stage is the government contract or trade association sources. A diagram of information sources for a major corporation appeared recently in *Library Trends*.[19] As most librarians are not in the fortunate position of the present writer, who can make the omnibus statement that his staff responsibility is to insure that all the information needed by IBM staff is made available to them on a reasonable basis for the performance of their assigned tasks, the development of an adequate checklist of the possible relationships of a given library to all of the possible internal and external information sources would be source material for the formulation of the role statement for that library. (The latter is Research Need A — see Appendix.)

The next problem we consider is personnel. The conduct of adequate personnel audits in special libraries is complicated by the very large number of one-man operations revealed by the Kruzas study mentioned earlier;[4] 52 percent of company libraries have but one professional, and 19 percent have no non-professionals. Special libraries under civil service procedures normally have better position descriptions and more orderly promotion procedures than industrial libraries, although there are exceptions such as the John Deere Company with carefully constructed descriptions and career path forecasts. Other industrial concerns find libraries to be numerically too small a group to be concerned with, and one major industrial corporation contents itself with equating librarians with statisticians for job levels and pay.

A devoted group of Washington, D.C., SLA Chapter members has continued to press for realistic librarian-documentalist progressions, and there are now separate but equal series. The chapter has also conducted training programs in data processing procedures and has persuaded the General Services Administration to provide management training institutes. On the "up-training" of members, the medical and legal library associations have taken the lead. Closed circuit TV and other experimental procedures need to be considered to bring instruction to the small, dispersed special libraries to help make them viable and effective. Limited manpower resources make it essential that special libraries extend their competences and sophistication. An authoritative survey of the manpower requirements of special libraries is urgently needed.

The number of individuals involved in special libraries will be shown in the new edition of the Kruzas directory, which will also state that the profession will be a long way from the goal of 30,000 special libraries for 1970 as set by the SLA Goals for 1970 Committee and as promulgated by Miss Winifred Sewell, SLA President 1960-61, in her chapter presentations. That there is and has been for some time a shortage can be testified to personally by the writer, as he has had a steady stream of inquiries for more than ten years for people of excellence needed to fill jobs of great opportunity. It is a frustrating experience to "sell" management on the need for a professional special librarian and then not be able to provide more than a single name of a suitable candidate for interview, and in some cases to have no name to suggest at all. The weekly advertisements appearing in the *New York Times* for librarians are perhaps the most dramatic evidence of the special libraries' manpower requirements and intensified efforts to fulfill them. (This is Research Need B.) The SLA personnel survey has been mentioned here as one of the very few definitive works in this field for special libraries. It is noteworthy that the actual survey was conducted by an independent research firm rather than by volunteer membership effort, as was true of many Special Library Association projects in the past. Woods's question about those areas in which the special library shortages are the most critical would seem to be answered by pointing to the cataloging and subject analysis areas. The trend toward consortiums of special libraries, mentioned earlier, has tremendous implications on the utilization of personnel, especially in the "housekeeping" areas.

To take up next the questions on equipment and facilities, we are still somewhat at the stage of development in which organizations have libraries because it is a part of the folklore that a library lends them prestige and distinction. That this concept is still current is evidenced by the illustrations on the covers of business magazines depicting executives with book shelves displayed in the background. Special library facilities can be highly ornate mausoleums intended to impress — or just emancipated broom closets. Surveys, questionnaires, checklists, visits and observation may all be employed to determine the presence of needed equipment and facilities and their absence. An internal company survey uncovered one complication in that floor space was reported by some of its European libraries in square *meters*. This instance demonstrates the need for compatibility of information and sources, as management tends to compare the equipment, facilities and personnel assigned to serve a given clientele with those employed by other arms of the company in other geographic locations.

Special libraries are very much the prisoners of their host organizations in regard to equipment and facilities. Hence they will range in different elements from being unconscionably short or Spartan to being rich almost beyond belief. For example, the special library on the one hand might be so bound by company regulations as to have standard office equipment in the library rather than regular library furniture.

As far as data processing facilities are concerned, the special library will use the facilities of its host, as documented by the Special Libraries Association-Library Technology Project's survey of data processing activities. Other evidence shows that special libraries tend to congregate in metropolitan areas, and observation indicates that these libraries tend to be in the high rent districts. It is plausible to assume that they will be short of space. This is also a consequence of the profit-minded management of private business or of the economy-minded management that non-profit or trade associations must foster in order to exist. Most industrial special libraries are rich in communications possibilities. Tie-lines connecting the industrial organization with other metropolitan areas are commonplace, as are teletype nets and some private mail systems (one electrical manufacturer distributes company mail in its own vehicles from the Atlantic coast to as far west as Fort Wayne, Indiana). When with a previous industrial firm, the writer was able to use the cable facilities of the corporation to any address in all countries in the free world. Further, tie-lines with the Atlantic seaboard cities made it possible to administer the library as if it were located in the midst of their bibliographic resources. In his present organization one library provides central processing for those of three other laboratories, one located thirty miles distant, another two hundred, and another about six hundred miles distant. In the case of the nearby library, there is real-time communication by means of typewriter keyboarded terminals, while in the cases of the other libraries, it is by data link calling for transmission of bibliographic information during the night at tremendous speeds over telephone lines.

Every industrial librarian should have intimate familiarity with the equipment and facilities available to the library, as an integral part of the host organization, and should use them to the hilt for library purposes. Often imagination is the only limit on the effective use of these devices. The efforts of the Library Technology Program of the American Library Association are of great assistance in equipment decisions, and the Special Libraries Association has been represented on its Advisory Committee for some time. This portion of librarianship is being considered in several studies underway, such as that of the U.S. National Advisory Commission on Libraries on special libraries and on technology and industry. It would seem that almost as important as the findings reported by the Commission will be consideration of the procedures used to arrive at these conclusions, i.e., a research critique. (These are Research Needs C and D.)

Resources and services may be identified by virtually all the research techniques mentioned by Tauber.[20] Russell Shank's ongoing study of the science library facilities of the New York metropolitan area includes a section relating to this sub-field.[21] Resources of special libraries tend to be highly oriented toward the prime objective of their host organization. For example the General Motors Research Laboratory's main interests are in fuel-air mixtures, engines, semiconductors, and mechanisms, and the National Advisory Committee for Aeronautics specializes in airfoils and structural analysis. Typically the special library collects exhaustively in its specific field and with increasing casualness as one retreats from the prime area of interest. The desirability of keeping collections up to date is so great that every volume weeded should be counted as two in comparing special libraries. Under this philosophy, a collection of 5,000 books that has been severely weeded would be more than the equivalent of a 10,000 book collection in the same subject area that had "just growed."

The resources required for a special library are directly affected by the physical proximity of major public or other libraries, as discussed in the January 1966 issue of *Library Trends* devoted to library service to industry. Various studies have been undertaken of the usefulness of the materials in special library collections, partly because of space limitations mentioned earlier. The writer's article in the above issue shows that interlibrary loan requests at the G.M. Research Library were 60 percent to references of the past five years with another 24 percent to the preceding ten years. These 577 interlibrary loan requests were composed of samples taken at two different times — one in 1964 and another one in 1965 — and showed that 84 percent of needed materials were borrowed from the Detroit Public Library, 15 percent from the Wayne State Library, and 1 percent from other local sources. This of course did not include the several hundred photocopies secured from the Engineering Societies Library, New York Public Library, and the John Crerar Library during those periods.[19]

Paula Strain has studied the usage and retention of technical periodicals[22] and found considerable differences between usage in her electronics systems library and those earlier reported by Bonn for the New York Public Library[23] and by Keenan and Atherton for *Physics Abstracts*.[24] Extensive studies based on recorded use of biomedical journals have been reported by Fleming and Kilgour.[25, 26] As might be expected, British researchers tend to use a broader spectrum of journals and those of greater age. Among the studies reporting this is that by Hogg and Smith for atomic energy installations.[27] Resources and services were carefully considered by C.W. Hanson in his survey of the information library units in British industrial and commercial organizations, published in 1960.[28] Aitchison at the same time reported on a survey of nearly fifty British libraries in aircraft and guided weapons units.[29] (This is Research Need E.) The Herner study of about the same era on atomic energy reference questions was based on 4,696 questions, with 82 percent being technical. One-quarter were on a process, method and procedure; another quarter were on physical, chemical and engineering properties and substances; and 17 percent were on description of apparatus or equipment. Most reference questions had two concepts included in them, though nearly one-third had three. The advantages of reference services offered on the basis of actual inquiry experience was emphasized.[30] The National Science Foundation pioneered the concept that a proportion of the funds devoted to research should be reserved for the publication of the results of that research. The IBM Advanced Systems Development Division Library at Los Gatos, California, has followed this precept in reporting regularly on the results of their mechanized services and procedures. Marjorie Griffin has for some time worked on the assumption that the library there has the dual purpose of providing a test-bed for experimental procedures as any other section within the laboratory would, and also of maintaining service to Division personnel. The culmination of the project on mechanized record keeping procedures through keyboard terminals (the so-called Administrative Terminal System) was recently described with full flow charts and sufficient details for other libraries to copy if they are so inclined.[31] The Army Technical Library Improvement Studies are available from the Federal Clearinghouse, Springfield, Virginia, and are in this same tradition of making library study results widely available. For example, Report 12 is entitled *An Approach to Cost Effectiveness of a Selective Mechanized Document Processing System.*[32] Surveys are being undertaken of equipment and service provided by small and medium military libraries as well as the better known large defense library installations.

As has been mentioned, special libraries are strongly dependent on services from the outside. For many of the libraries in science and technology, the services provided by the Defense Documentation Center, National Aeronautics and Space Administration, Clearinghouse for Federal Scientific and Technical Information, and the Atomic Energy Commission, plus specialized information centers, data centers and government-supported information centers, are crucial to the performance of reference work at the frontiers of technology and under severe time constraints. Here, the SLA Government Information Services Committee has served as a "prod" for the last several years, and the Committee's program presentations are always among the best attended at the SLA Annual Conferences. In 1965 the Committee surveyed the current services of the libraries, forty-two of which replied to the questionnaire. While generally the services were found to be improving, there was still a feeling that the non-defense portions of the government were not accustomed to reacting on the time scale required for efficient service by government contractors, with the Government Printing Office coming in for pointed criticism. The value of this kind of survey is determined by the actions taken to correct deficiencies. Some of the services mentioned are supplied without specific cost to contractors as support for their contract efforts. This does not temper the criticism of less-than-adequate support for the special libraries to get their job done.[33] (Research Need F.)

Consideration of resources and services leads logically to the consideration of the information actually needed and used by patrons. Bernal made one of the classic statements on scientific information and its users in 1960 when he said: "I anticipate the building up of an information service in the future on a logical basis as a piece of communications engineering.... The functions of the information officer and the specialized libraries will be transformed in the process. The storage system will become relatively subsidiary and the communications system will become dominant."[34] (Professor Bernal is probably better known for his revolutionary proposal that scientific periodicals be abolished and that distribution of reprints or preprints of individual articles be substituted. His proposal is somewhat related to the present concept of selective dissemination of information with hard copies supplied on the basis of stated interest.) Among Fishenden's findings[35] in the user area are the following: (1) substantial losses of time and expenditures occur because of pertinent information found after the project started; (2) the resources of existing libraries and staff are not fully used; (3) there is a need for better training for scientists in the use of information; (4) in some circumstances lists of titles are as good as abstracts; and (5) there is a need for more reviews of the state-of-the-art. Barnes[16] points out the difference between new studies that are based on examination of the primary sources of information and others that consider the means by which these primary sources are discovered.

A thoughtful paper by Alan Rees suggests that "librarianship and information science will be substantially advanced if we were to approach the information problem via the user and his needs."[36] He mentions the fact that user needs are too complex to be met by documents or document representations alone, and that there have to be other means of transferring information, e.g., informal information networks. He also recognizes the existence of "stars" or "cosmopolitans" which is a similar concept to that of Rosenbloom[37] (these are the transfer agents — sort of Typhoid Maxes — who "infect" others with information from the outside.)

There is evidence that the conducting of user studies in special libraries is a complicated undertaking. Bare advocates a combination of questionnaire, a diary and an interview to secure the needed information. She advocates the prompt referral back of findings to the respondent so as to preserve his interest and facilitate successor surveys.[38] A vote for the diary and interview techniques in evaluating selective dissemination procedures is offered by Resnick and Hensley. Their main finding was that individuals subjected to active dissemination programs do not read more material; they just read more important materials.[39]

There is a bridge to the next Woods's question— the one on standards and statistics, via the procedure used to develop comparable figures for probable users among the several IBM Laboratories which vary in intent from pure research facilities to prosaic industrial engineering endeavors on through to economic and marketing activities. (We should remember the previous assertion that comparisons may be odious but they are a management habit; hence the necessity on the part of the library administrator to assure that apples are being compared with apples, rather than with oranges.)

In examining detailed records on the backgrounds of the persons classified in research and engineering specialties at IBM, a wide divergence was noted in educational level, in subject specialization and in administrative assignment. First, the persons were divided into some twenty-five subject specializations and some ten administrative technical specialties. There resulted a total of the maximum possible users of the respective libraries, with sub-tabulations by division and by geographic location. These numbers were duced to "most probable users" by removing from the totals persons with administrative non-technical assignments, even though they had technical degrees; furthermore on the assumption that technicians did not use the library as much as fully professional employees, only one-third of them were counted, while all the persons on professional assignments were counted in the "fold." The resulting figures for "most probable users" were 65 percent of the maximum possible users, with the results showing graphically which facilities were weighted with more than average density of technicians and hence could afford somewhat less library support. It also showed that laboratories toward the pure research end of the spectrum had "most probable users" totals approaching the maximum possible users.

This point was felt to be so important that an additional classification was made of the population by educational level and what was termed "equivalent usage units." The pragmatic weights used to calculate the latter were: (1) persons with bachelor's degrees were later counted as *one* equivalent usage unit; (2) those with master's degrees were each counted as *two;* (3) those with doctor's degrees were each counted as *three;* (4) those counted as technicians were calculated as one-third of a unit; and (5) those with no degree but a professional rating were counted as two-thirds of a unit. (There was a fairly large group of the latter category, mostly individuals who had advanced to professional classification via the drafting board route and were a reminder of the electro-mechanical content of the company's original products. Using this 3-2-1-1/3-2/3 weighting on equivalent usage units, the dichotomy between library service required by the research and advanced development activities and by the production facilities was brought into even sharper focus. Not everyone will agree with the pragmatic weights assigned in this calculation of uses that people with differing education will probably make of the library, but at least it has the virtue of consistency and gives statistical support for some intuitive feelings. It has the further virtue of identifying rather completely the populations in the various facilities and of being comprehended immediately by management personnel who previously had made comparisons on the basis of raw totals only. (This is Research Need G.)

Standards and statistics are at the very heart of the measurement and evaluation procedure. Only those who have been involved in the procedure are aware of the great difficulty with which standards are set and promulgated. The profession owes a great debt to those librarians who have spearheaded the work of the U.S.A. Standards Institute Committee Z-39 on Library Work and Documentation; the current Chairman is Jerrold Orne and the Vice-Chairman is Anne Richter.

One of the main lessons of the ALA Pre-Conference Institute on Library Mechanization in June 1967 was that the librarians present were beginning to realize that they could no longer afford to have varying procedures out of sheer obstinacy. They saw that the exchange of serials records, for example, would be impracticable without increased efforts to agree on entries. They saw the need for the Library of Congress to facilitate its dissemination of machineable cataloging information. The serious study that the Library of Congress has undertaken, to result in the announcement of MARC II data elements, will be a major step forward. This emphasis on the desirability of following standards is not for the purpose of achieving peas in pods, but for the maximum utilization of information in the records of special libraries so that we all might expeditiously accomplish our objectives of providing exceptional active services. (Research Need H.)

One evidence of the American Library Association's concern with statistics is the Statistics Coordinating Committee that meets at the annual convention to exchange news on progress in statistics, expecially their collection and evaluation in the various library specialities. Not all news is good at these meetings; for example, at San Francisco, those responsible for reference statistics announced abandonment of efforts to define classes of reference questions for statistics purposes. Unfortunately, special librarians will not be able to accept this finding because the management of commercial organizations demands to know the results of the expenditure of money for library support; so reference questions *have* to be counted. There are those who decry their being counted because of the time needed to do so, but reference questions worth answering are worth recording, as a means of following workload trends in this "queen of library functions." Compilation of good statistics, furthermore, is in the selfish interest of the library profession as well. For example, libraries are the principal customers for the sale of technical books. Virtually any book on a "hot topic" such as lasers, semiconductors, or traffic safety is assured of a commercial success by library purchases alone. The American Library Association has agreed on a standardized library keyboard which makes commercially feasible the manufacture of these typewriters for libraries. Whether it is textbooks, book trucks, telefacsimile machines, record players, or universal book testers, the market studies required are becoming more and more sophisticated, and the library community must have better statistics so that it may receive the attention it deserves and may benefit from the new technology. Their importance to the special libraries scene is shown by their use in answering inquiries received at SLA headquarters from all quarters, including overseas. (Research Need I.)

On September 25, 1964, the Special Libraries Association's Executive Board adopted the objectives and standards for special libraries as prepared by the SLA Professional Standards Committee and Professor Leonard. (The latter subsequently was awarded the SLA Professional Award, the Association's highest honor, for her contribution.) These objectives and standards were published in *Special Libraries*.[40] Some criticisms of these standards have appeared in the literature, but one of the more careful evaluations was done by Randall[41] who considered the standards in the light of lessons learned at the Thomas J. Watson Research Center Library, Yorktown Heights, New York, which serves the most sophisticated audience in the company and is in the upper 5 percent of special libraries in Kruzas' statistical tabulations. His article was prepared as an American Management Association talk. He had available for cross-checking the work that had been under way for a couple of years within IBM by a group called the "IBM Librarian Standardization Committee." As of 1964, the latter were considering such tasks as functional evaluation, standard recording format, microform standards, periodicals handling, clerical performance standards, professional job codes and descriptions, service standards, and statistical reporting standards for library operations. Section I of the SLA Objectives and Standards is devoted to objectives, and these have been covered earlier in this paper. As to staff, the committee recommended the ratio of two professionals to three non-professionals, while Randall thought that larger staffs — that is, those having eleven or more persons — should have a larger ratio of clericals. He further suggests, for minimum services, one staff member per hundred potential users or one for seventy-five actual users.

In regard to collections, which the Committee asked to be intensive and extensive enough to meet needs, Randall suggested one journal subscription per user and fifteen books per user. He did not consider the number of internal reports per user or other non-book items. As to the comprehensiveness of the collection, he felt that if a library could supply 95 percent of requests made, its acquisition rate was acceptable, but if it was necessary to borrow 15 percent of the inquiries, it should increase the acquisition rate. Special libraries are not going to be able to continue increasing in size indefinitely, and he suggests that, as the space for the collection tightens, the weeding rate should approach the acquisitions rate, and hazarded the guess that ten years from now the book collection of his library will be the same, whereas the periodicals collection will have doubled.*

---

*The differentiation between interlibrary loan and interloan was not made clear in his figures, and it would seem that a larger proportion of requests from other libraries within the company can be tolerated than requests to libraries outside the host organization.

As to services, circulation came in for prime attention and Randall felt that circulation statistics in themselves are not particularly relevant, but that the ratios related to them could lead to the eventual development of a circulation standard. First, on the ratio of loans to acquisitions, he notes that his library has a ratio of six to one. A second ratio, of loans to total book collection, was nine to ten in his library. On the circulation per user per year, his library showed a range of twenty to thirty items loaned per user per year. He suggests that a definite loan period and recall procedure be included in the standard.*

As to physical facilities, the standards call for convenient location. Randall has suggested that location near the cafeteria might be appropriate, that an area of 25 to 75 square feet per reader be reserved, that small tables or carrels are to be used rather than large tables seating many people, and that the library should be attractive physically.**

The standards say that the budget should be based on the recommendation of the library administrator, that the larger proportion should be devoted to staff salaries (about 60 to 79 percent of the total), and that the administrator should have the authority and the responsibility for expenditure of the funds. Randall's comments were that the first priority should be given to increasing the proportion of the budget for book collection instead of for staff, and that part of this increase should be secured by more effective utilization of personnel, machines, and good management practices.***

On evaluation, Randall points up the advantage of mechanized procedures for obtaining better data for the determination of how well the library is doing. Among other applications, he finds it possible to evaluate vendors on the basis of factual data on performance. He evaluates cataloging procedures and keeps track of processing delays by means of "exception reporting" procedures and for the evaluation of work methods he finds the time-tried method of "doing it yourself and if you find out better ways to do it, pass it on to the staff" as being hard to surpass.

There is perhaps more division of opinion on the actual degree of cooperation existing between libraries than on any other topic. The International Cooperation Year was 1965, and provided the occasion for a number of presentations on library cooperation in the special libraries area, including Gordon Williams' keynote address at the SLA Annual Convention. He pointed out the dilemmas of special libraries, which need to provide all information required by their patrons although it is impossible for any library to be self-sufficient. "To satisfy librarians by trying to make every library big enough to satisfy all of its patrons' needs from its own collection and its own bibliographic descriptions is not practical. Cooperation is indeed the key to greater library resources."[42] (We note here the implied necessity for standardization in bibliographic data elements.)

Charles A. Nelson, whose firm, Nelson Associates, Inc., has prepared an increasing number of surveys that impinge on library cooperation, stated at the same conference that "characteristically cooperation tends to be an ancillary activity engaged in usually with some reluctance by institutions or organizations whose primary interests are directed elsewhere. It tends often to be stimulated by some outside force and thus is likely to persist only if the effort reaches sufficient maturity to culminate in a professionally staffed effort, which then can defend its interests in cooperation in the face of the normally independent and centrifugal tendencies of those institutions whose cooperation is sought. Perhaps it is not too much to say that the natural forces at work in society are essentially *dis*-integrative and that this may serve to explain why cooperation is so often so slow and so painful and tentative in character."[43]

The reaction of Richard Logsdon, of Columbia University was that "real progress in the area of cooperation, or more precisely, progress toward pooling and conserving resources, will require: (1) that we put our own house in order; (2) that we develop appropriate programs, see that we tell state legislature or Congress

---

*The desirability of a definite load period and the necessity for a recall period would seem to vary with the type of clientele, and the physical relationship of the library to the remainder of the host organization, among other factors. In the writer's experience the propensity of research personnel for frequent moves of offices prevents a significant loss of library material. The individual department should always have the option of purchasing materials through the library from its own funds with the understanding that the library will not recall them for circulation to others.

**The advantage of an attractive library from the public relations point of view is recognized by some industrial concerns which have the library on their regular tour route for distinguished visitors — one of the attractions is that it does not reveal proprietary information to the casual observer — and it is increasingly used recruiting aid for interviewees. The typical special library is receiving an increasing proportion of its requests by phone which makes the location somewhat more negotiable than before.

***There is a trade-off that needs exploration between staff and collection. There are circumstances in which an exceptional librarian can effectively be used as catalyst in information situations to support highly sophisticated staff with a modest collection. An essentially "self-service" library needs a collection of more than average exhaustiveness. The tendency in some new laboratories to buy scientific periodicals by the foot is not desirable, particularly as the availability of many such periodicals in microforms is increasing.

about them, and with the help of our parent organizations, see them through to enactment."[44]

Scott Adams' contribution dealt with what he felt to be "the challenge facing American librarianship today. Because the functions of research in special libraries are now understood to have a more direct relationship to the growth of national economy, more public and private funds are available to them. At the sametime, revolutionary new technologies have provided us with the capability of producing new forms of service mechanisms. Together these factors require that we think no longer in terms of *ad hoc* cooperative efforts, but in terms of the design of systems, local, regional and national."[45] Thus at this one general session of the SLA convention were brought up most of the important points that have ever been made on cooperation involving special libraries. (Research Need J.)

Woods's other question on association and government as they affect special libraries is related to the above. The library associations did join in the formulation of CONLIS (Committee on a National Library and Information System) which was in effect an answer to the recommendations of COSATI on national document handling systems and which did not give a very large place to the part which libraries would play in the future provision of technical information in the U.S. There are indications that the gathering of library voices speaking in unison had as much positive effect as the pronouncements themselves, and ALA President Mohrhardt has called for continuing inter-association efforts in all fields.

To go from the national scene to the state of New York with its widely known three-R's program will illustrate one more difficulty in cooperation. There the METRO project in New York City and several other regional library systems in the state are prevented specifically by state law from having librarians of profit-making institutions as officers, though in some cases they may have membership in the organization itself. One of the problems being examined by the A.D. Little study for the New York State Library is the relationship between that Library's services to industry and those to be provided by the State Technical Services program. Twenty educational institutions in New York State supply information on contract to the State Department of Commerce on a combination of geographic, area and subject matter bases. For example, the Syracuse University Research Corporation has the responsibility for aiding classes of industry in a six-county region, whereas Alfred University has a state-wide responsibility for assistance to the ceramic industry. (In passing, it should be noted that these State Technical Service organizations are intended to serve groups of companies rather than individual companies.) It is conceivable that the present study will result in a recommendation for a change in legislation permitting special libraries to enter more fully into the cooperative activities of the state.

One of the basic questions facing the individual special library is how much cooperation it can give without disservice to its own primary patronage and without excessive drain on its host organization's need to be a profit-making concern. Special libraries have for years made their materials available under "exceptional circumstances." It is the rare Ph.D candidate who has been turned down by a special library when its exceptional resources (other than company proprietary information) were critical to his research success. The question before the profession now is, "Should our interpretation of 'exceptional circumstances' be more relaxed than in years past?" A desirable education device by which to heighten acceptance of cooperative efforts is to inform management officers when the information that was provided in answer to their specific inquiry came from a public library, the state university, or a professional association's library. The "cookbook" approach to the evaluation of a company library is provided in Eva Lou Fisher's *Checklist for the Organization, Operation, and Evaluation of a Company Library*. She listed points to be noted, functions to be reviewed, breakdowns within those functions, methods of determining what to measure, preliminary steps necessary in conducting a study, and data which should be gathered for the study. She described the questions to be answered in seeking comparable situations in other libraries.[46] While this checklist has been used successfully with company managements who are about to set up libraries or suspect that libraries may be needed, it is also useful as a reminder list to the practicing librarian and is recommended.

So far, we have defined a special library, learned of its environment, described the profiles of typical special libraries, and discussed the problems they face (which include their role, equipment and facilities, collections, services, standards, statistics, cooperation, contributions of associations, and relations to government). We have also indicated topics on which research needs to be undertaken. How are the projects going to be carried out? It will have to be by a team effort which involves persons with many backgrounds and skills and which receives its inspiration from vital special librarians who participate in the program and give direction and interpretation to the findings.

Cleverdon and Harper asked special librarians to use the operations research approach: to define the problem and the objectives of the study, to find out the facts concerning present procedures, to analyze those facts to determine what is necessary, to find out the best solution in keeping with the objectives, and to put the solution to work.[47] Their concern with systems at work is echoed by Rees who says, "It is most important that means be developed to quantify the performance of libraries. Cooperative efforts involving librarians and system analysts will be most productive in the achievement of performance criteria and measurements taking into account both effectiveness and efficiency. Although the assistance of persons trained to analyze and formalize the relationships involved in complex situations is both desirable and useful, only librarians themselves can satisfactorily define library purpose in precise terms. If this were achieved, criteria for determining performance and the development of quantitative measures would then be made possible."[48]

Stevenson sees the need for the librarian to operate in the framework of a professional manager. In this regard, he will help determine the proportion of the research and development budget that should reasonably be allocated to technical information activities; secondly, he will participate in surveys leading to the determination of the proportion of an over-all plant budget that should be allocated for technical information activities; thirdly, he will need to determine the actual cost of performing necessary jobs; and fourth, and finally, he will ascertain how effective the program is from the point of view of those who use its services.[49]

A second Army Technical Library Information Service report recently became available from the Federal Clearinghouse; it abstracts 472 articles in the areas of library and management science that relate to evaluating the effectiveness of library operations and services, and lists an additional 286 articles. This, the first phase of a contract by John I. Thompson & Company, was an assessment of the present state-of-the-art, and will be followed by a Phase II report validating past data uncovered in the first, and securing certain amounts of new data from selected Army Technical Libraries. The final phase will comprise the origination of new criteria and carrying out of a program of testing and evaluation.[50] The heart of the present report is a matrix with the two axes of Potential Library Applications versus Management Techniques, with data points indicating references at those intersections. A portion of the matrix is in Table 3 below. The complete axes are as follows:

Potential Library Applications

Library Mission & Placement in Organization
    Definition of mission of parent organization
    Definition of mission of library
    Types of clientele served
    Placement of library in parent organization
Budget
    Relationship to budget of parent organization
    Allocations for materials and services
Physical Layout
    Geographic location
    Space size and arrangement
    Equipment
      Type
      Amount
      Cost
Staff
    Qualifications
    Size
    Salary
    Utilization
    Professional activities
    Educational activities
    Training programs
    Administrative aids
    Incentive programs

Contents
    Collection
      Orientation to mission
      Orientation to clientele
      Orientation to services provided
      Composition
      Extent
    Procurement & maintenance methods
Contents Control
    Cataloging, classification & subject headings
    Assignments
    Automation applications to operational procedures
    Special systems applicable to subject matter control
Services
    Circulation
    Bibliographic
    Editorial assistance
    Translations
    Special services
    Preparation and dissemination of listings or articles
Additional Areas of Consideration
    Contract performance
    Research in library operations

Management Techniques

Systems Analysis
Cost Effectiveness
  Cost accounting
  Value analysis
  Break-even analysis
  Utility analysis
  PPBS (Planning-Programming-Budgeting System)
  PACER (Production Allocation and Control of Expecting Resources)
Operations Research
  Probability
  Sampling, statistical
  Game theory
  Linear programming
  Queuing theory
  Regression analysis
  Equipment investment analysis
  Correlation analysis
  Simulation
  Monte Carlo technique
  Modeling, mathematical
Charting Techniques
  Flow diagram
  Organization chart
  Process chart
  Layout chart
  Multiple activity chart
  Right and left hand chart
  Production study chart
  Work distribution chart
  Employee utilization chart
Operations Analysis
  Methods study
  Motion and time study

Operations Analysis (cont'd.)
  Standardization
  Performance evaluation
  Standard data
  Work sampling
  Basic motion time study (BMT)
  Group attainment program (GAP)
  Methods-time measurement (MTM)
  UNOPAR (Universal Operator Performance Analyzer and Recorder)
Procurement Inventory Study
  Economic order quantities
Personnel Administration
  Human relations
  Behaviorial science
  Environment analysis
  Personal appraisal methods
  Job description analysis
Economics
  Econometric models
  Input-output analysis
Planning
  Goal-setting
  Budgeting
  PERT (Program Evaluation Review Techniques)
Information Theory
  Data processing techniques
  Electronic data processing
Control
  Cybernetics
  Quality control
Plant Layout Analysis
Organization Analysis
Management Appraisal

Special librarians live in a real world of information transfer where there are important problems to be met, important goals tc be achieved, and ever-present identification with the successes of their host organization. With so little time and so much to be done, only quality research should be undertaken, only valid results should be received, and aggressive steps should be undertaken to achieve the goal of catalyzing the library profession.

TABLE 3

Potential Library Applications vs. Management Techniques

MANAGEMENT TECHNIQUES	Def. of mission of parent organ.	Def of mission of library	Types of clientele served	Placement of lib. in parent organ.	Relationship to budget of par. organ.	Allocations for materials & services	Geographic location	Space size & arrangement	Type	Amount	Cost	Qualifications	Size	Salary
					Budget		Physical Layout		Equipment			Staff		
Systems Analysis	●	●		●									●	
Cost Effectiveness														
Cost accounting						●				●	●			●
Value analysis						●			●	●	●		●	●
Break-even analysis						●					●	●	●	●
Utility analysis						●			●	●	●	●	●	●
PPBS					●	●			●	●	●	●	●	●
PACER						●					●	●	●	●
Operations Research														
Probability														
Sampling, statistical					●									
Game theory														
Linear programming													●	
Queuing theory													●	
Regression analysis														
Equip. investment analysis									●	●	●			
Correlation analysis				●	●							●	●	
Simulation														
Monte Carlo technique														
Modeling, mathematical														
Charting Techniques														
Flow diagram							●	●						
Organization chart	●	●		●				●						
Process chart														
Layout chart							●	●						
Multiple activity chart														
Right & left hand chart														
Production study chart														
Work distribution chart														
Employee utilization chart													●	

APPENDIX
Problem Areas for Special Libraries[9]

Research Needs

A. Formulation of Definitive Role Statements for Special Libraries
B. Survey of the Manpower Requirements of Special Libraries
C. Systematic Evaluations of and Improvements in Library Equipment
D. Authoritative Inventories of Special Library Facilities
E. Authoritative Inventories of Special Library Resources
F. Development of Means for the Objective Evaluation of Services
G. Exhaustive Identification of User Populations and Optimized Fulfillment of Essential Information Needs
H. Identification of Maximum Practicable Areas for Standardization
I. Development of Valid, Objective Statistical Concepts
J. Development of Optimum Means of Facilitating Cooperation

REFERENCES

1. Jackson, Eugene B. "Special Libraries," *Library Trends*, 10:209, Oct. 1961.
2. Special Libraries Association. *Activities & Organizations Brochure*. New York, (n.d.), p. 1.
3. Havlik, Robert J. "The Role of Special Libraries in the United States," *Special Libraries*, 57:236-237, April 1966.
4. Kruzas, Anthony T., ed. Gale Research Company. *Directory of Special Libraries and Information Centers*. Detroit, Gale Research Company, 1963.
5. Kruzas, Anthony T. *Special Libraries and Information Centers: A Statistical Report on Special Library Resources in the United States*. Detroit, Gale Research Company, 1965.
6. "Profiles of Special Libraries," *Special Libraries*, 57:179-184, March 1966; 227-231, April 1966; 327-331, May-June 1966.
7. Jackson, Eugene B. "The Special Libraries Association — American Library Association/Library Technology Program Survey of Library Automation Activities: A Summary Review." *In* Herbert Goldhor, ed., *Proceedings of the 1967 Clinic on Library Applications of Data Processing*. Urbana, Ill., Graduate School of Library Science, 1968, pp. 131-182; a condensed version can be found in *Special Libraries*, 58:317-327, May-June 1967.
8. Bonn, George S. "Implications for the Special Library," *Journal of Education for Librarianship*, 2:201, Spring 1962.
9. Woods, Bill M. Memorandum, dated July 1967.
10. Wasserman, Paul. "Measuring Performance in a Special Library — Problems and Prospects," *Special Libraries*, 49:377-382, Oct. 1958.
11. Rothstein, Samuel. "The Measurement and Evaluation of Reference Service," *Library Trends*, 12:456, Jan. 1964.
12. Hutchins, Margaret. *Introduction to Reference Work*. Chicago, ALA, 1944, pp. 199-202.
13. Tauber, Maurice F. "Survey Method in Approaching Library Problems," *Library Trends*, 13:15-30, July 1964.
14. "A Study of 1967 Annual Salaries of Members of the Special Libraries Association," *Special Libraries*, 58:217-254, April 1967.
15. Fishenden, R.M. "Information Use Studies. Part I — Past Results and Future Needs," *Journal of Documentation*, 21:163-168, Sept. 1965.
16. Barnes, R.C.M. "Information Use Studies. Part II — Comparison of Some Recent Surveys," *Journal of Documentation*, 21:169-176, Sept. 1965.

17. System Development Corporation Appendices to: U.S. Federal Council for Science and Technical Information. Committee on Scientific and Technical Information (COSATI). *Recommendations for National Document Handling Systems in Science and Technology.* Washington, D.C., U.S. Dept. of Commerce, National Bureau of Standards, Institute for Applied Technology, 1965; Auerbach Corporation. *DOD User-Needs Study, Phase I,* Final Technical Report 1151-TR-3. Philadelphia, Pa., 1965, 2 vols; North American Aviation, Inc. *DOD User-Needs Study, Phase II.* Final Report, C6-2442/030. Anaheim, California, 1966, 2 vols.

18. Rosenbloom, Richard S., and Wolek, Francis W. *Technology, Information & Organization; Information Transfer in Industrial R&D.* Boston, Mass., Graduate School of Business Administration, Harvard University, 1967.

19. Jackson, Eugene B. "The General Motors Research Laboratories Library: A Case Study," *Library Trends,* 14:353-362, Jan. 1966.

20. Tauber, *op, cit.*

21. Shank, Russell. Study for METRO (New York Metropolitan Reference and Research Agency, Inc.). This study is still in the editorial stages.

22. Strain, Paula M. "A Study of the Usage and Retention of Technical Periodicals," *Library Resources & Technical Services,* 10:295-304, Summer 1966.

23. Bonn, George S. "Science-Technology Periodicals: A Preliminary Report on a One-Year Use-Study at NYPL," *Library Journal,* 88:954-958, March 1, 1963.

24. Keenan, Stella, and Atherton, Pauline. *The Journal Literature of Physics: A Comprehensive Study Based on Physics Abstracts (Science Abstracts, Section A) 1961 Issue.* New York, American Institute of Physics, 1964.

25. Kilgour, Frederick G. "Use of Medical and Biological Journals in the Yale Medical Library. Part I. Frequently Used Journals. Part II. Moderately Used Journals," *Medical Library Association Bulletin,* 50:429-449, July 1962.

26. Fleming, Thomas P., and Kilgour, Frederick G. "Moderately and Heavily Used Biomedical Journals," *Medical Library Association Bulletin,* 52:234-251, Jan. 1964.

27. Hogg, I.H., and Smith, J. Roland. "Information and Literature Use in a Research and Development Organization." *Proceedings of the International Conference on Scientific Information, Washington, ... 1958.* 1:131-163, Washington, D.C., National Academy of Science, National Research Council, 1959.

28. Hanson, C.W. "Survey of Information/Library Units in Industrial and Commercial Organization," *Aslib Proceedings,* 12:391-396, Nov. 1960.

29. Aitchison, T.M. "Survey of Library Provision in the Aircraft and Guided Weapon Industry," *Aslib Proceedings,* 12:397-406, Nov. 1960.

30. Herner, Saul, and Herner, Mary. "Determining Requirements for Atomic Energy Information from Reference Questions," *Proceedings of the International Conference on Scientific Information, Washington, ... 1958, op. cit.,* 1:181-187.

31. International Business Machines Corp. Advanced Systems Development Division. *Mechanized Library Procedures for the IBM Advanced Systems Development Division Library, Los Gatos, California.* White Plains, New York, 1967. (IBM Data Processing Application No. E20-0285-0.)

32. U.S. Army Engineer Research and Development Laboratories. *An Approach to Cost Effectiveness of a Selective Mechanized Document Processing System,* by Carlos O. Segarra. Fort Belvoir, Virginia, 1967. (Army Technical Library Improvement Studies Report No. 12) (AD 651486.)

33. Special Libraries Association. Government Information Services Committee. "Users Look at Information Centers," *Special Libraries,* 57:45-50, Jan. 1966.

34. Bernal, J.D. "Scientific Information and Its Users," *Aslib Proceedings,* 12:438, Dec. 1960.

35. Fishenden, *op. cit.,* p. 164.

36. Rees, Alan M. "Medical Libraries and the Assessment of User Needs," *Medical Library Association Bulletin,* 54:99-103, April 1966.

37. Rosenbloom and Wolek, *op. cit.,* pp. 38-40.

38. Bare, Carole E. "Conducting User Requirement Studies in Special Libraries, *Special Libraries,* 57:103-106, Feb. 1966.

39. Resnick, A., and Hensley, C.B. "The Use of Diary and Interview Techniques in Evaluating a System for Disseminating Technical Information," *American Documentation,* 14:109-116, April 1963.

40. "Objectives and Standards for Special Libraries," *Special Libraries*, 55:672-680, Dec. 1964.

41. Randall, G.E. "Special Library Standards, Statistics and Performance Evaluation," *Special Libraries*, 56:379-386, July-Aug. 1965.

42. Williams, Gordon R. "Library Cooperation – Key to Greater Resources," *Special Libraries*, 56:570, Oct. 1965.

43. Nelson, Charles A., *et al.* "Library Cooperation: Panacea or Pitfall?" *Special Libraries*, 56:574, Oct. 1965.

44. *Ibid*, p. 575.

45. *Ibid*, p. 578.

46. Fisher, Eva Lou. *A Checklist for the Organization, Operation, and Evaluation of a Company Library.* 2d rev. ed. New York, Special Libraries Association, 1966.

47. Cleverdon, C.W., and Harper, L.J. "Information Services: Assessing Their Value," *Aslib Proceedings*, 8:239-251, Nov. 1956.

48. Rees, Alan M. "Criteria for the Operation of Libraries and Information Retrieval Systems," *Special Libraries*, 57:642, Nov. 1966.

49. Stevenson, C. G. "Work Measurement in Technical Information Activities," *Special Libraries*, 47:409-411, Nov. 1956.

50. John I. Thompson & Company. Wessel, C. J., and Cohrssen, B. A. *Criteria for Evaluating the Effectiveness of Library Operations and Services. Phase I: Literature Search and State-of-the-Art.* (Army Technical Library Improvement Studies Report No. 10). Washington, D.C., 1967.

51. *Ibid*, p. 50a.

General Reference

Rees, Alan M. "Evaluation of Information Systems and Services." *In* Carlos A. Cuadra, ed. American Documentation Institute. *Annual Review of Information Science and Technology.* New York, Interscience Publishers, 1967, Vol. 2, pp. 63-86.

CHAPTER VIII: MEASUREMENT AND EVALUATION IN ADULT EDUCATION

WILSON B. THIEDE
Professor of Adult Education
University of Wisconsin, Madison

We all make value judgments about things going on around us. Evaluation in education means making judgments about the extent to which objectives are being achieved. Before evaluation of education can proceed, objectives and a standard with which to compare progress are needed. If we left Chicago on an automobile trip and we are now at Cleveland, we must know where we were going, what reasonable progress is for automobile transportation, and how much time has elapsed on the way to our goal before we can evaluate our progress. This suggests another element necessary in evaluation. We must be able to measure our progress in some way. Measurement is the process that provides the data used in evaluation. There are two other words in use which generally have the same meaning as evaluation. These are assessment and appraisal. To a large extent in the past, educators of adults (including librarians) have relied on the existence and use of their programs as, *ipso facto*, their own defense.

It is necessary to arrive at one other definition before we proceed. I would define education as the process of changing behavior in desired directions. Some are concerned about "behavior" as the end of education, feeling that there are some things that happen in learning which do not reflect themselves in behavior. I prefer not to deal with this question but rather to say that, as an educator, I am only concerned with those aspects of the individual that reflect themselves in thinking, feeling and acting, all of which I can observe. In this context, the program of the library is educational, with the objective of helping people change their ways of thinking, feeling, and acting in desirable ways. The distribution of books and other materials is not the end of the library but the means to the end of producing desired change in people.

Evaluation serves many purposes and the manner in which we evaluate is determined to some extent by the purposes to be served: "Most, if not all, are included under the following four major purposes: (1) guiding individual growth and development; (2) improving programs; (3) defending programs; (4) facilitating and encouraging staff growth and psychological security."[1] If we evaluate in order to help guide the individual, then we need diagnostic measures which tell us what the individual has learned or not learned and what kinds of problems he is having. If we are trying to improve educational programs and need data, we can obtain it from a small sample of the learners rather than all of them. If we are trying to teach three things, we can ask each of three persons about one of the things rather than the whole group about all three things. To defend programs it may be necessary only to ask specific questions about items of most concern to that defense. In general, evaluation used for program improvement is most useful for facilitating staff growth and psychological security.

There are presently three broad types of evaluation procedures used in adult education: assessment by participants, leaders, and administrators; measures of knowledge, attitudes and skills acquired; and adoption of practices.[2] In the first type, participants may be asked to respond to queries aimed at obtaining their judgments as to whether they think the program accomplished objectives of the leaders and the participants, and as to whether they liked the program. Many studies of this type have been conducted with precision and most evaluative studies reported fall in this category.[3] An example of a carefully designed study of this type is one by Kaplan of 150 participants and leaders in liberal arts discussion programs in the Los Angeles area.[4] He was trying to obtain the participants' judgment of whether they had developed in intellectual growth, in civic participation, or in desire for continued study. Kaplan used direct self-report type questions asking, for example, whether they gained "a great deal" or "some" knowledge and whether they read "more than previously" or "read more serious works." Whether these self-report items have validity and reliability depends on how carefully they are designed and whether the conditions under which they are answered can be assumed to be relatively free of threat or reward so as to permit honest answers. There are many arguments for self-evaluation in adult education. In adult education we are particularly concerned with planning educational programs to suit the purposes of the learner, and the learner ought to be the best judge of whether his purposes have been served.

In the same category of evaluation by participants are assessments of program effectiveness by leaders and administrators. Verner describes four principal ways in which this is accomplished.[5] The first of these is by measuring the program against a standard. For much adult education there are no standards for programs comparable to those established for other levels of education by accrediting associations. There are, of course, the standards of the American Library Association which can be used in the library field. Second is "measuring the program against a hypothetical conception of what a 'good' program should be." But there is no general agreement in this area and judgments depend too heavily on the educator and the community. Third is comparing the programs of one or more communities; this may produce new program ideas but is not of great use in evaluation. Fourth is measuring the amount of participation, which is based on the assumption that if people participate the program must be good.

However, all of these assessments by participants and leaders produce, at best, descriptions of what is happening and thus are not likely to be valid evaluations of program effectiveness. The defense of this last statement lies in the forty years of research in evaluation of teacher effectiveness. "It is widely agreed," say Medley and Mitzel, "that the ultimate criterion of teacher effectiveness must be based on changes in (learners)."[6] An extensive series of University of Wisconsin studies demonstrates that such things as teacher rating scales and supervisors' ratings are uncorrelated with effectiveness as measured by learner change.[7]

While it might be hoped that the effectiveness of educational programs could be judged by asking participants and leaders to rate the characteristics of the learning experiences, there is no reason to assume that the results will be different from those obtained in the research on teacher effectiveness. Paraphrasing Medley and Mitzel,[8] we might ask whether it would seem reasonable to expect even the most experienced researcher to visit a program, watch it in operation, and then judge the effect it would have on even a single learner — that is, to predict the score the learner would attain at the termination of the program, making proper allowances for the score he got at the beginning. The use of such judgmental criteria asks the judge to do this for all participants in the program.

Bernard Berelson in his study of graduate education suggests that there are two subjects to investigate in seeking the answer to the question of how good graduate programs are: content of the programs, and the quality of the product. He does neither and proceeds to deal with what he calls "the next best question, how good people *think* it is."[9] The excellent library studies by Helen Lyman Smith,[10] Margaret Monroe,[11] and Philip Ennis[12] are essentially descriptive or historical, and are evaluative only in the sense discussed above.

The second major type of evaluation procedure depends on measures of knowledge, attitude, or skill. This type is widely used in elementary, secondary, and higher education to evaluate both individual progress and the program. Its major problem relates to the specification of what is to be learned, upon which the construction of the data-gathering instrument depends.

This is an appropriate point at which to discuss the process of evaluation itself, which consists of five steps: (1) determining the objectives, (2) defining the behavior desired, (3) determining acceptable evidence of the behavior, (4) collecting evidence, and (5) summarizing and evaluating the evidence. As I have said elsewhere, "The most common difficulty in evaluation as well as in curriculum (i.e., program) building in adult education is failure to arrive at objectives agreed upon, understood, and accepted by leader and learner .... While it is possible (although not desirable) to build programs on the basis of content, methods, and resources available, it is not possible to evaluate such a program on any other basis than a client 'happiness index'."[13] We frequently build programs based on intriguing methods we have seen or used or on persons known to be available and "dynamic speakers." In these cases objectives must then be inferred and are not available for use in evaluation. An evaluator develops statements of objectives only with patient, painstaking work with the instructor(s) of the program. These objectives are derived by instructors from societal need, learner need, organizational goals, subject matter and learning theory. Excellent expositions on determining objectives are available.[14]

One of the most difficult problems in developing objectives has been the absence of a common language of evaluation so that reference to certain objectives universally raises the expectation of certain behaviors. This deficiency has made it difficult for researchers to add knowledge about the effectiveness of educational programs and for those who use the research in evaluation to understand what has been discovered. A useful beginning in this area which has delineated, defined and classified educational objectives in the cognitive and affective areas has been made by Bloom[15] and Krathwohl.[16] These are particularly useful in indicating the range and sequence of possible objectives. In the cognitive area, for example, objectives are categorized as knowledge, comprehension, application, analysis, synthesis and evaluation.[17] Each of these has a number of sub-categories. In general, they are arranged from simple to complex and each category tends to make use of and be built on the behaviors of the previous category.

After objectives have been stated, it is necessary to define them in terms of the learner behavior desired. These behaviors are used in evaluation to arrive at descriptions of acceptable evidence of the attainment of the behavior. As an example of how one can develop objectives and specify the behavior desired, Miller and McGuire use several areas of liberal adult education. In the political and social area, they state an objective relating to interests: "The individual develops new, broader and more intense interests in this area."[18] They then describe the behaviors which will demonstrate his achievement of this objective:

1. a) continuing to read widely in the field or beginning to read in new fields;
   b) increasing the level and scope of his reading in this field;

2. participating in activities to which he was previously indifferent or hostile;

3. seeking new learning experiences in this area;

4. initiating discussion and attempting to persuade others to share his interests in this field;

5. giving more time to thought about problems or issues in this area;

6. changing his perspective on familiar concepts, activities, etc., and developing new modes of thinking about familiar problems;

7. participating at a different level in activities in this area; and

8. attempting to make independent judgments in these areas.[17]

Following this specification of behaviors desired, one decides what will be acceptable evidence of the behavior and proceeds to construct data-gathering instruments which may be simple statements of activities, mental and physical, presumed to be engaged in by persons who have developed an interest in this area. Such instruments or observations should be administered both before and after the learning experience to be able to judge change in the desired direction. Because adults have had a great range of experience in almost any of the areas in which we program, it is unacceptable to use only "after" measures to judge the amount of learning. Only where we have reason to believe adults have had no prior experience in an area would this be at all acceptable.

In the fourth step of evaluation evidence may be collected by an independent observer, by tape recorders, by films and other recording devices, by tests, by self-reports, and by other evidence from the learner. Observations or records may be obtained in real situations or in simulated situations such as could be provided by written cases, film and video tape, audio tape, and role playing. Further, it may be helpful to gather data several times throughout the learning experience and after a considerable lapse of time at the end since different kinds of learning are acquired at different rates and have different retention characteristics.

The final step in evaluation is summarizing and evaluating the evidence. Data can be summarized by counting, describing and analyzing. Descriptions can indicate that the person or group can do certain things and cannot do others. They abstract out of the record significant things to be taken into account. Data can be presented in tabular form or graphic form. After this the meaning of data must be made clear. Individuals may have learned half of what was expected. They may have been unable to perform some operations at all. They may have learned some things not anticipated. Judgments must then be made as to the progress of the individual, the extent to which the objectives were attained, the extent to which they ought to have been attained, the appropriateness of the objectives themselves, and other aspects of the educational program. As a result of these judgments the educational program may be modified at that point to increase learning, the objectives may be changed, the process of evaluation changed, or the program discontinued.

This digression on the general process of evaluation followed discussion of two out of the three types of evaluation used in adult education, viz., (1) assessment by participants, leaders and administrators, and (2) measures of knowledge, attitudes, and skills acquired.

The third type, adoption of practices, is almost exclusively related to adult education. It was introduced by the Cooperative Extension Service and grew out of the concern of this agency from the first with improving farm production practices. By "adoption" is meant the acceptance of a practice (such as contour plowing) and the introduction of it into one's behavior. That is, it is not enough to know why under certain conditions it is a desirable practice, but the learner must adopt the practice as the end objective. The adoption of a practice as an objective requires special provisions in the education program and is a different kind of educational objective from knowledge itself; for example, stopping smoking is not equivalent to understanding its health hazards, and obtaining regular exercise is not equivalent to understanding its benefits.

In recent years a number of studies of the adoption of ideas and practices have been extremely illuminating and helpful to the educator who is trying to reduce the gap between knowledge and its use.[19] As a result of research in this area we are fairly confident of two conclusions. First, overt behavior is not changed as effectively by the acquisition of knowledge, whether it be by lecture, film, or print, as it is when knowledge is accompanied by discussion of the situation. Second, there is a sequence among people in the adoption of a new practice whether it be an aspect of farm production or the use of a new pharmaceutical by doctors. The first adopters of a new practice are not the group leaders, as one might expect, but are individuals who can be identified as innovators. If these adoptions are successful, then the leaders will try it, followed by early adopters and then by others.

A summary of what may be concluded from the three types of evaluation would be something like this: (1) While what participants, administrators and others think of programs may well affect the life and character of those programs, we have no evidence to indicate that these assessments are in fact related to what or how much is learned by the participant. As long as this is kept in mind and false claims are not made, it is appropriate to continue to investigate these judgments with precision. (2) With regard to measuring knowledge, attitudes and skills, we know how to construct these measures but we have great difficulties in specifying the objectives and in keeping the adult in the learning situation long enough to make a difference. Elementary and secondary education and, to some extent, vocational and higher education have extensive lists of objectives with sequential achievement goals and many kinds of tests for measuring progress. The adult in many instances is in the learning situation for a few days or a few weeks at most, often for only a few hours. The amount of behavior change which should be anticipated is likely to be very small. In much of adult education we do not do any evaluating of this short-term learning. (3) With respect to adoption of practices, the rural sociologists and extension staff members have begun to add substantially to our knowledge of how to bring about adoption of new practices and of how well we are doing in those adult education areas where adoption is an objective.

What is necessary at this point is a look at the characteristics of adult education which have special relevance for evaluation. When the adult comes to the library, to the discussion group, or to the class, he has immediate needs he wishes to satisfy. He wants information on how to be a better parent, how to judge the current international conflict, how to make better barbecue meals, or how to speak German. He only occasionally is seeking to satisfy a remote or deferred goal and almost never learning because society insists on it (e.g., remedial driving schools). The immediacy of adult objectives requires that the educator involve the adult learner and share with him the responsibility for determining the objectives of the learning experience. Learning is more efficient if the learner understands and accepts the objectives. So that the learner and teacher can strive for the same end, joint planning must occur so that the ends of the adult learner will not be put aside. Otherwise if he rejects the purposes evident in the situation he becomes a drop-out. Establishing objectives must be included by the educator as a part of the learning experience. The fact that the adult is task-oriented also provides an opportunity for evaluation. Since the adult will almost immediately practice what he has learned, observation in the life-situation is possible. This makes evaluation considerably more valid than with the use of secondary evidence necessary in high school social studies classes or even of behavior in contrived situations such as case studies or role playing. On the other hand, evaluation in the life situation requires more effort and greater resources since it necessitates going out of the educational setting to collect data.

The aim of the adult educator is always to help the adult become an independent, self-directed learner.

Each learning experience needs to be constructed so that the learner will have less need for the educator next time. This demands that as a part of each learning experience, the adult be helped to diagnose his educational need, plan the learning experience, and evaluate his progress. Anything less than this makes the learner more dependent, not more independent. A special committee of the Adult Education Association reported: "In adult education, methods of evaluation must exemplify that sense of freedom which characterizes the learning process itself.... Methods of evaluation should be internal, not imposed from without. Adult learners, in short, must also learn how to evaluate their own success or failure."[20]

The evaluative process is affected by three variables associated with adult education programs: the primary source of the objectives, the degree of formality of the program, and the length of the program.[21] When objectives are primarily societal in origin, as in a refresher course required for the continued certification of a teacher, self-evaluation by the learner is more difficult and external evaluation more acceptable although not necessarily more desirable. The learner may not have objectives related to learning but only to certification, and thus this situation requires special procedures and efforts to develop objectives in the learner which will be harmonious with the leader's objectives and will in reality be learning objectives. The formality of classes and conferences lends itself to evaluation procedures to a greater extent than does the informality of the activities of libraries or the Cooperative Extension Service. While we would all agree that library contacts with readers are effective in helping them, they are certainly brief, occasional, seemingly unsystematic and difficult to describe in precise detail let alone evaluate. When programs are of long duration such as a class which meets for several months or a residential program of several weeks' duration, the greater amount of learning taking place facilitates measurement. In a short term program of two or three days where objectives may not be sharply specified, evaluation is difficult for both the learner and leader. As programs become more informal, of shorter duration, and deal to a greater extent with goals of the learners, they require greater ingenuity and skill to provide for evaluation.

It will be useful to focus on the questions of what needs to be evaluated and how to go about it. At this time, except for assessment by participants, leaders and administrators, little evaluation of adult education has been carried on. As stated earlier, the continued existence of the program has been its principal defense. Kreitlow summarized needed research in the field and indicated that there exists "a lack of structure and theory which could have been used to launch new research and to integrate that which had been completed."[22] It may be helpful to paraphrase some of his suggestions, giving them particular relevance for the library:

(1) What kinds of materials are of greatest use to new literates?

(2) What methods of materials' dissemination are most effective with the inhabitants of the central city? With youth? With older adults?

(3) What are the most effective ways for the library to relate to adults in other learning situations in order to increase the effectiveness of the use of library materials?

(4) How much do library patrons now learn from their present use of the library?

(5) What innovations in library staff service would increase the effectiveness of the library and to which categories of clientele?

(6) What kinds of contributions can the adult student make to the book selection policies of the library? The reference services? The acquisition and cataloging practices?

(7) What factors prompt adult use of the library? For what specific present purposes do adults use the library?

(8) What are effective ways in which the library can "market" its materials and services to better serve educational needs of adults?

(9) How can the library staff assess the progress of the library user so as effectively to guide his next uses? Would tests be useful? Questionnaires? Interviews?

A few additional ideas may be suggested in thinking about evaluation of adult programs. First is the concept of sampling. In evaluating the learning of an individual it is not necessary to measure everything he intended to learn but only a sample of it. As we know from probability theory, a sample carefully chosen to represent the total population will with much less effort and with predictable precision tell us as much as using the whole population.

If we are evaluating the effectiveness of an educational program it is not necessary to test all individuals nor to test for all learning. It is sufficient for a carefully chosen set of essential questions to be put to a carefully chosen sample of individuals. It is not necessary or even desirable for any individual to respond to all questions. This concept of evaluation underlies the new approach to the national assessment of education for which Ralph Tyler is providing leadership.[23]

Second, one of the current methods in use for evaluating teaching is a detailed analysis of behavior occurring in the learning experience. This method operates first to describe the behavior of teacher and learner and second to test hypotheses about learning under certain variables of teacher behavior and learning situation interaction. The attempt here is to try to accumulate sufficient data to build models of interaction which can be tested for their effect on learning.[24] Can we adapt this to the behavior of the library staff and the adult reader? Suppose we begin by observing and describing in detail the behavior of staff member and reader when the reader is being served. We will need to develop careful descriptions of behavior categories and then checklists or other devices for recording the behavior accurately. These descriptions will need to be related to reader behavior in the library (which must be considered as a part of the learning situation) and then to learning. Can we describe in detail what the reader does while in the library? These observations systematized and organized in detail might help begin a science of library service at present untouched.

Third, could we begin to analyze our library users by sets of categories which demonstrate more precision than those now in use? The categories need to be organized around behavior systems in use by library patrons, perhaps categorization by clientele purposes on some needs rationale such as the developmental tasks of Havighurst.[25] Could we draw samples of the new categories from our files and study in detail our relationships with them, including studies of their purposes, what they learn, and the relative effectiveness of various methods of serving them?

Fourth, the library is almost exclusively oriented to subject matter (in this case, books and materials) and to society in arriving at what materials and services it will render. Earlier it was stated that the sources of educational objectives are the subject matter, the individual, the society, the institution, and learning theory. Could we experiment with the effectiveness of various ways of involving the adult user in determining what purposes we will serve, our book selection policies, our reference and readers' advisory services? The library is confronted with the same problems as the school: limited resources of time, staff, money and facilities in relation to curricular objectives. Now that we are about to accept the idea of the only complete library being the national library system, perhaps we need to reexamine our ways of determining the purposes to be served by local libraries and branches.

Libraries and library schools have been as dilatory as most of the rest of adult education in committing resources of money, staff, and mind to the problems of evaluation. We have all been service-oriented and pressed to greater service demands than the resources provided would support. However, if we wish to have evidence and not just faith that we are a vital force in the education of the people, then we must evaluate. The development of research staff and of library schools is a necessary first step and has been taking place in the last several years stimulated in good measure by the Federal funds specifically and generally available for library programs in the United States. As a sympathetic colleague from a related field, let me assure those in library science that there is not a great deal of help to be had elsewhere in terms of specific methods; you must set yourself down in the middle of the problem and start chipping away.

REFERENCES

1. Thiede, Wilson. "Evaluation and Adult Education." *In* Gale Jensen et al., *Adult Education: Outlines of an Emerging Field of University Study*. Washington, D.C., Adult Education Association, 1964, pp. 291-305.
2. Thiede, Wilson, and Meggers, John. "Evaluation of Outcomes," *Review of Educational Research*, 35:185-190, June 1965.
3. For many examples of this and other types of evaluation studies, see the "Adult Education" issues of the *Review of Educational Research* for June 1959 and June 1965. See also the summer issues of *Adult Education*, "Research and Investigations in Adult Education" for the last several years.
4. Kaplan, Abraham A. *Study-Discussion in the Liberal Arts*. White Plains, New York, Fund for Adult Education, 1960.
5. Verner, Coolie, and Booth, Alan. *Adult Education*. Washington, D.C., Center for Applied Research in Education, 1964, pp. 92-94.
6. Medley, Donald M., and Mitzel, Harold E. "The Scientific Study of Teacher Behavior." *In* Arno A. Bellack, ed., *Theory and Research in Teaching*. New York, Columbia University, Bureau of Publications, Teachers College, 1963, p. 83.
7. Barr, Arvils, et al. *Wisconsin Studies of the Measurement and Prediction of Teacher Effectiveness*. Madison, Dembar Publications, 1961.
8. Medley and Mitzel, *op. cit.*, p. 85.
9. Berelson, Bernard. *Graduate Education in the United States*. New York, McGraw-Hill, 1960, p. 202.
10. Smith, Helen L. *Adult Education Activities in Public Libraries: A Report of the ALA Survey of Adult Education Activities in Public Libraries and State Libraries and State Library Extension Agencies of the United States*. Chicago, ALA, 1954.
11. Monroe, Margaret. *Library Adult Education: The Biography of an Idea*. New York, Scarecrow Press, 1963.
12. Ennis, Philip. *Adult Book Reading in the United States* (National Opinion Research Center, Report No. 105). Chicago, University of Chicago, National Opinion Research Center, 1965.
13. Thiede, Wilson, "Evaluation and Adult Education," *op. cit.*, p. 294.
14. Furst, Edward J. *Constructing Evaluation Instruments*. New York, Longmans, Green, 1958, pp. 19-79; and Tyler, Ralph W. *Basic Principles of Curriculum and Instruction*. Chicago, University of Chicago Press, 1950, pp. 2-40.
15. Bloom, Benjamin, ed. *Taxonomy of Educational Objectives, Handbook I: (Cognitive Domain)*. New York, Longmans, Green, 1956.
16. Krathwohl, David. R., et al. *Taxonomy of Educational Objectives, Handbook II: (Affective Domain)*. New York, David McKay Co., 1964.
17. Bloom, *op. cit.*, pp. 201-207.
18. Miller, Harry L., and McGuire, Christine H. *Evaluating Liberal Adult Education*. Chicago, Center for the Study of Liberal Education for Adults, 1961, p. 49.
19. Lionberger, Herbert F. *Adoption of New Ideas and Practices*. Ames, Iowa State University Press, 1960; and Rogers, Everett M. *Diffusion of Innovations*. New York, Free Press of Glencoe, 1962.
20. Issue Committee and Lindeman, Eduard C. "Evaluating Your Program," *Adult Leadership*, 1:18-19, April 1953.
21. Thiede, Wilson, "Evaluation and Adult Education," *op. cit.*, pp. 303-304.
22. Kreitlow, Burton W. "Needed Research," *Review of Educational Research*, 35:240, June 1965.
23. Tyler, Ralph W. "Changing Concepts of Educational Evaluation." *In* Ralph W. Tyler et al., eds., *Perspectives of Curriculum Evaluation* (American Educational Research Association, Monograph Series No. 1). Chicago, Rand McNally, 1967.
24. Medley and Mitzel, *op. cit.*
25. Havighurst, Robert J., and Orr, Betty. *Adult Education and Adult Needs*. Chicago, Center for the Study of Liberal Education for Adults, 1956.

CHAPTER IX: STATISTICAL INFERENCE

ROBERT E. PINGRY
Professor of Secondary and Continuing Education and of Mathematics
University of Illinois, Urbana

Without question one of the greatest aids to research developed in the last century has been that body of knowledge and methods we call statistics or statistical inference. The social scientist as well as the physical scientist leans heavily on statistical methods in making research decisions. Economists, psychologists, sociologists, and educators are now using rather sophisticated statistical methods and designs such as have been used for many years in fields such as agriculture and engineering.

As the research worker collects data he organizes them and tries to draw conclusions. At times the data are so definitive that a sharp conclusion is possible with very little room for doubt. A scientist who does an experiment to compare the densities of iron and aluminum does not need to resort to statistical inference to draw a conclusion. The variation in the measures he takes is so small compared to the differences in the measures for iron and aluminum that there is little doubt concerning the results.

However, when an agronomist wants to check the yields of two varieties of hybrid corn, the variation in yields due to weather, soil, and cultivation is so great that the scientist needs to investigate how probable it is, under given estimates of variation, that such a yield difference as he has obtained would occur by chance. If the difference could easily occur by chance, then it is possible that there may be no real difference in the yields of the two different hybrids. From the theory of probability, if it is determined that such a yield difference was very unlikely by chance, then one may doubt that a chance difference occurred. The difference may be the result of a true variety difference.

Herein lies one of the chief values of statistical inference, the value of checking the results of an experiment against chance. A medical researcher found that, as a result of a new pill, seven out of ten patients got relief from a common cold. Is the pill a cold cure or is it possible that seven out of ten patients could get relief after taking a sugar pill just by chance? The researcher has through statistical inference a machinery for bringing to bear the theory of probability upon the results of his experiment. It is possible that what may at first appear a difference between two methods may be nothing more than a chance difference.

As will be discussed in this paper, statistical inference also results in a machinery that enables the research worker to control or have knowledge of the probability of errors of decision. Errors may be made, but over the long run the researcher can have some confidence that he has been right a lot of the time.

It has been common in textbooks on statistics to use the expression "statistical inference" to mean an inference about a population by observations on a random sample from that population. For example, one may wish some knowledge concerning the weight of eighth grade students in Illinois. One way to get this information is to weigh every eighth grade student in the state and report the results. No inference would be made in this situation. The results of the measurements would be described. This use of numbers to describe certain characteristics of a population of measures is referred to as descriptive statistics.

However, a research worker would probably not expend the great effort and expense needed to weigh every eighth grader in Illinois to make a decision about the weights. He would probably weigh a random sample of eighth grade students drawn from the population of all eighth grade students and then infer what the average weight in the population would be. Statistical inference then refers to an inference about a measure in a population from knowledge gained from observations on a random sample from that population. There is an arithmetic mean, call it mu (μ), of all weights of eighth grade students in Illinois. Inferences can be made concerning this mean by computing the arithmetic mean $\bar{x}$ on a random sample drawn from this population. The inference is from $\bar{x}$ to μ.

Statisticians have commonly classified the types of inferences which are made into three: (1) point estimation, (2) interval estimation, and (3) hypothesis testing.

The preceding example concerning eighth grade students will be used to discuss the concepts of these three types of inference. Although each of the three will be discussed, the chief emphasis will be placed on hypothesis testing.

POINT ESTIMATION

Suppose that a research worker computed the arithmetic average ($\bar{x}$) of a random sample of eighth grade students to be 100 pounds. This weight (point), 100 pounds, then is inferred to be the average weight (μ) of the entire population of eighth graders. Thus, $\bar{x}$ is considered to be a point estimate of μ. Of course this estimate, $\bar{x}$, might be greatly in error if a random sample had a predominance of cases at one extreme or the other, but much of the time we would expect it to be fairly close to μ.

It could be possible to estimate the average weight of the population of eighth graders (μ) in other ways. For example, one could use the median weight of the weights in the random sample to estimate the arithmetic mean, μ, of the population of weights. One could also at random order the weights from the first weight to the n'th weight in the sample and then choose the tenth measure as the estimate of μ. These three numbers, $\bar{x}$, median, and tenth weight, among others, could each be used as a point estimate of μ.

Intuitively it seems that $\bar{x}$ would be a better point estimate of μ than would the others. But before one can classify one estimate as better than another one must have some criterion for deciding why one is better than another.

Within the limits of this paper, I cannot discuss the common properties desired of an estimator, but for a point estimate they include: (1) lack of bias, (2) consistency, and (3) relative efficiency.

INTERVAL ESTIMATION

In interval estimation of a population parameter, a researcher reports an interval in which he believes the population value lies. Not only does he report the interval, but by use of probability theory, he is able to tell how confident he is that the population value lies in the interval.

Using the example of the average weight of eighth graders in Illinois, the research worker would report some such statement as the following: "I am 95 percent confident that the population average weight is between 97 and 103." Of course, this interval estimate from 97 to 103 was computed on the basis of the point estimate, $\bar{x} = 100$. If the 100 is greatly in error, then the 97 to 103 interval might not include μ. However, all that the experimenter states is that he is 95 percent confident that the mean is between the two limits. He allows some room for error. For this same example the researcher might wish to be more confident than 95 percent, say 99 percent. This desire for greater confidence would lead to an interval which might be from 96 to 104 rather than 97 to 103.

Although the example for confidence interval discussed here has been limited to the population mean, μ, confidence intervals can be given for many population parameters. A researcher might be interested in a confidence interval for a variance, a difference of means, a proportion, a correlation, a linear regression coefficient, or many other parameters.

HYPOTHESIS TESTING

A third type of inference used in statistics is that of testing hypotheses about population parameters. A researcher may believe that the average weight of eighth graders in Illinois is increasing and wish to test his belief. A first step in testing this belief is to state an appropriate hypothesis about the parameters in the populations in such a way that inferences made concerning the parameters can be translated into inferences concerning weights of eighth grade students.

In this example it is possible the researcher would test the hypothesis that

$$H_o: \mu_1 - \mu_2 \geq 0 \text{ or } \mu_2 \leq \mu_1$$

against the alternative hypothesis that

$$H_1: \mu_1 - \mu_2 < 0 \text{ or } \mu_2 > \mu_1$$

where μ_1 is the mean weight of all eighth graders in Illinois today and μ_2 is the mean weight some years later, say ten. In 1977 the researcher would get his random sample and test the hypothesis, H_o.

The example chosen here is admittedly oversimplified for the purpose of discussion. It is likely that a sophisticated researcher would choose some other design and statistical hypotheses to test this belief.

For such a test, if the researcher would reject the hypothesis that $\mu_1 - \mu_2 \geq 0$ he would be stating that he believes that $\mu_1 - \mu_2 < 0$, that is $\mu_2 > \mu_1$. If the researcher does not reject the hypothesis H_o, then he is saying that he has no evidence that eighth grade students are any heavier than they were in 1967.

Suppose ten years from now the average weight of a random sample of eighth graders in Illinois is 102 and today a random sample of 99 is found. Since these are both sample values, each may deviate considerably from the true parameter values μ_1 and μ_2. We know nothing about the population values with surety. It is possible $\mu_1 = \mu_2$, or it might be true that $\mu_1 < \mu_2$ or $\mu_1 > \mu_2$; we cannot tell for sure from the fact that $\bar{x}_1 = 99$ and $\bar{x}_2 = 102$. We can infer a conclusion, but we may be in error. In ten years we might make a common-sense conclusion that, since the average weight is 102 and ten years ago it was 99, there is sufficient evidence that today's eighth grade students are different in weight from those ten years ago, and are heavier. Our conclusion may be a good one or it may be in error.

Errors of Decision

The big advantage of using statistical methods over common-sense methods in making a decision is that we have some knowledge of the probabilities of the possible errors we may make. We can also make our decisions in such a way as to minimize the error of decision. Let us look more closely at these errors:

True Population Values

	H_o is true	H_1 is true
H_o is true	Correct Decision	Type II Error
H_1 is true	Type I Error	Correct Decision

Decision

In the table shown here can be seen four situations that may arise in testing an hypothesis H_o that $\mu_1 \geq \mu_2$ against an alternative hypothesis H_1 that $\mu_1 < \mu_2$. In two of these situations correct decisions are made. If it is true in the population that $\mu_1 \geq \mu_2$ and the research worker decides not to reject the hypothesis H_o then he has made a correct decision. If it is true in the population that $\mu_1 < \mu_2$ and the researcher decides to reject H_o in favor of H_1 then he has made a correct decision.

In the other two cases, however, the decisions would result in an error. When μ_1 is in fact equal to μ_2 in the population and the researcher rejects H_o in favor of stating that $\mu_1 < \mu_2$ he has made an error. This is the error of rejecting the null hypothesis (hypothesis being tested) when it is in fact true. This is called a "Type I error."

Naturally, a research worker would like to avoid each of these errors. By the theory of probability the statistician can establish the procedures for making the decision in such a way as to let the research worker know what the probability is for making an error of decision. Although steps can be taken in the design of the experiment to try to make the probabilities of each of these errors small, it is also the case that some balance must be maintained between these two errors. That is, because the act of rejecting an hypothesis is the opposite of not rejecting the hypothesis, then it must be true that the more rigorously one guards against a Type I error, the more he puts himself in danger of making a Type II error.

Let us return to our example of eighth grade students in Illinois to illustrate these ideas. We wish to test the research hypothesis that eighth grade students will be heavier on the average ten years from now than they are today. Let us decide to use a random sample of 100 students.

Sampling Distribution of Differences

For the simplicity of this discussion the sample will be considered sufficiently large and population variances will be assumed as known so that large sample normal probability methods may be used.

Using independent random samples of 100 from a large population of all eighth graders in Illinois the theory of statistics tells us that sample differences of means will have a nearly normal distribution with variance equal to the sum of the variances of the means as independent variables. Thus

$$\sigma^2_{\bar{x}_1 - \bar{x}_2} = \sigma^2_{\bar{x}_1} + \sigma^2_{\bar{x}_2} \quad \text{or} \quad \sigma_{\bar{x}_1 - \bar{x}_2} = \sqrt{\sigma^2_{\bar{x}_1} + \sigma^2_{\bar{x}_2}}$$

The mean of the sample differences will be the mean difference of the population. Thus, if δ is the true difference between the two population means, that is if $\mu_1 - \mu_2 = \delta$, then the sample difference ($\bar{x}_1 - \bar{x}_2$) will have δ as their mean. Some ($\bar{x}_1 - \bar{x}_2$) drawn at random may be larger than δ, and some sample differences may be smaller. Many differences will be close to δ. Theory tells us then that repeated random sampling would give a distribution of differences that would appear as indicated in the graph.

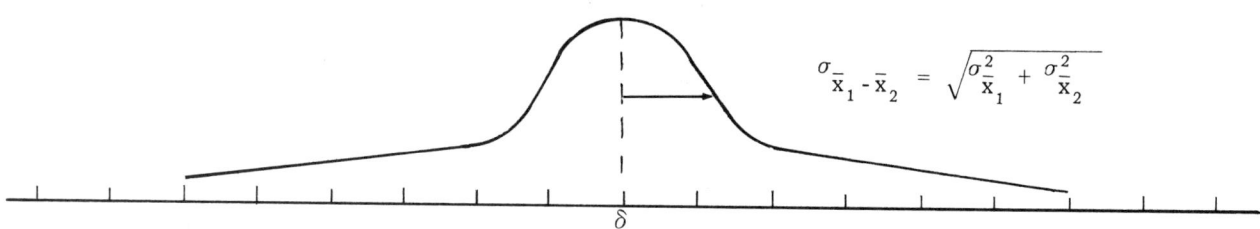

Thus, if the difference in weights between the two populations is $\mu_1 - \mu_2 = 2$

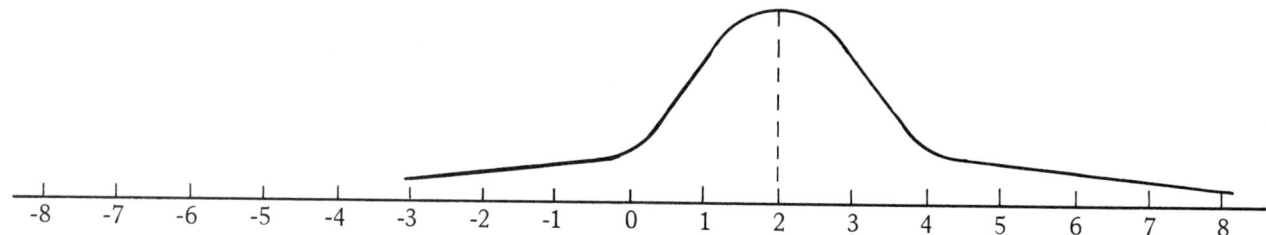

the distribution of sample differences will have 2 as the mean.

If the difference is -3

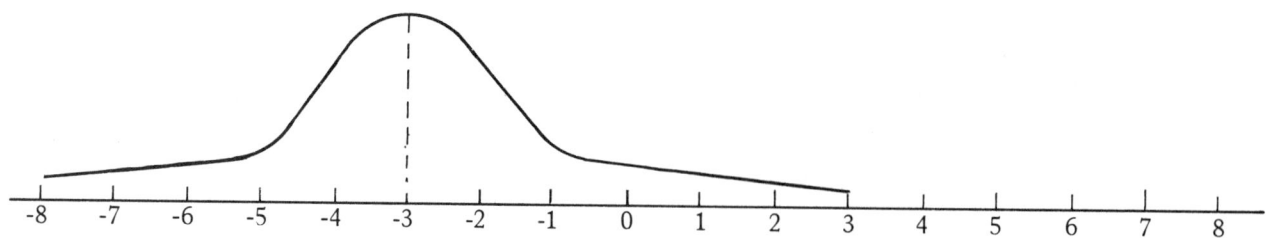

then the distribution of sample differences, ($\bar{x}_1 - \bar{x}_2$), will have -3 as the mean.

If the hypothesis being tested, $\mu_1 - \mu_2 = 0$ is true, then the distribution of sample differences will have 0 as the mean as shown

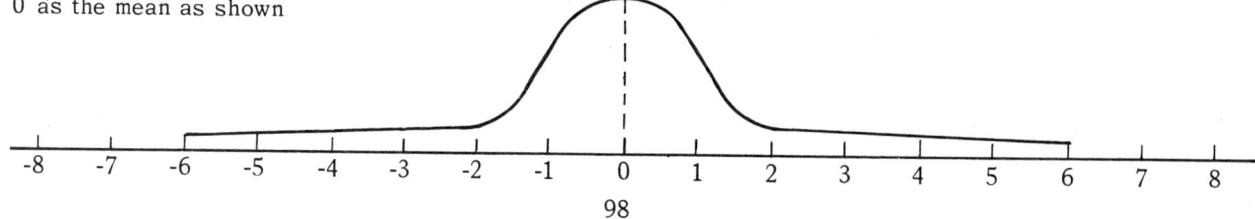

Probability of Type I Error (α)

Using this information we can now establish the boundary for decision in such a way as to limit the probability of making a Type I error. Recall that a Type I error is made by rejecting a true hypothesis. If the hypothesis, H_o, is true, that is, if it is true that $\delta = \mu_1 - \mu_2 = 0$ then the distribution of sample differences of means will be as shown in the graph.

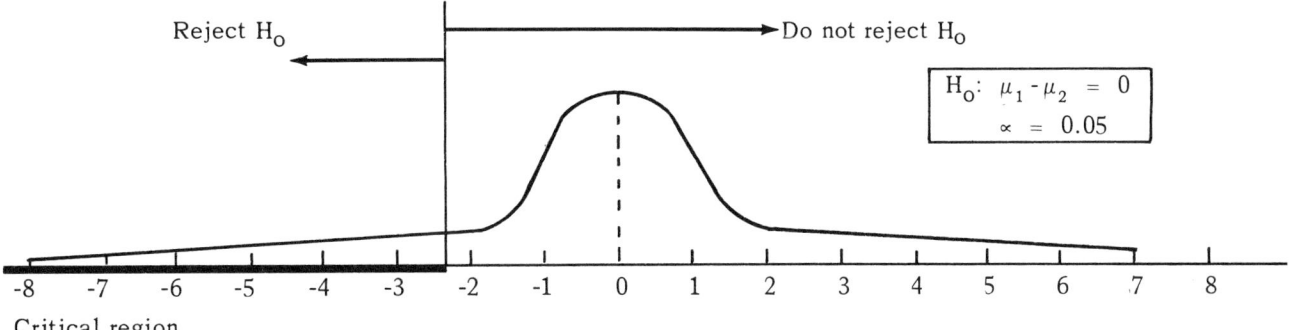

Since this is a nearly normal distribution, then using a table of normal probabilities we can determine that the probability of getting a difference less than -2.3 is 0.05.

Using this information, we can decide that should we get a sample difference of -2.3 or less, then we would reject the hypothesis H_o. Since this is the distribution of differences when the hypothesis is true, and since only .05 of the sample differences are expected to be less than -2.3 then we would expect to reject the hypothesis when true with probability .05. The probability of making a Type I error is thus no greater than .05. Thus, the research worker now has some control on the error of his decision. He may make an error, but he knows what the probability of that error is.

It is common to call the probability of a Type I error, α (alpha). Thus by this decision process, α is limited to be no greater than .05.

If it is desired that α be some smaller number, say 0.001, then the decision process could be described as shown in this graph:

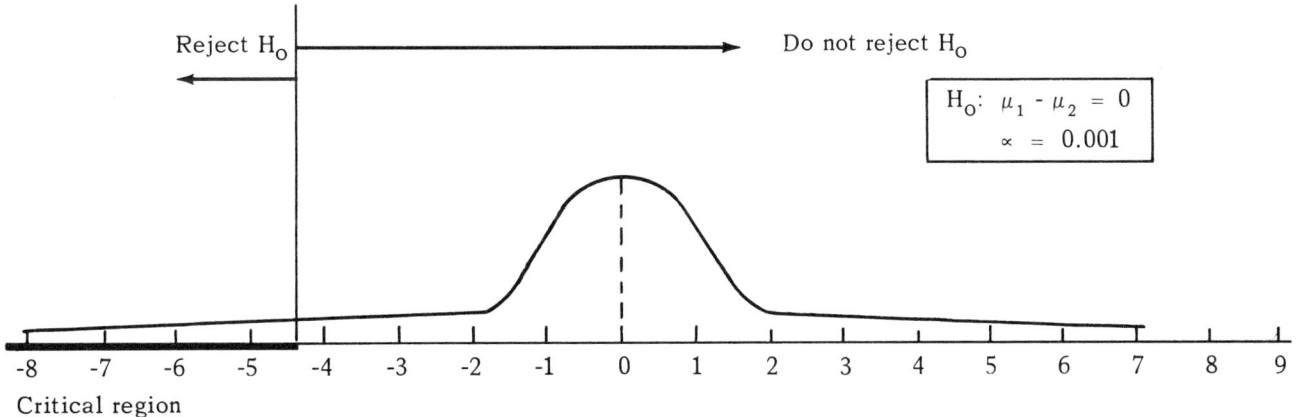

Probability of Type II Error (β)

When H_o is not true and in fact $\mu_1 < \mu_2$ or $\mu_1 - \mu_2 < 0$ then H_o should be rejected. If it is not, then a Type II error has been made.

There was only one value of δ possible for the case where H_o was true namely $\delta = 0$. However, for H_1 being true, i.e., $\mu_1 < \mu_2$, there are many possible values for δ. If $\mu_1 = 102$ and $\mu_2 = 104$, then $\delta = -2$ and H_1 is true. If $\mu_1 = 98$ and $\mu_2 = 99$, then $\delta = -1$ and H_1 is true. Thus H_1 could be true, and H_o false, for innumerable pairs of values of μ_1 and μ_2. Thus, the problem of computing the probability of a Type II error — β (beta) — is not as simple as that of computing a Type I error. As a matter of fact, for one given α for this sample β is a variable dependent upon δ. As you will see, when δ is very small, β will be large and when δ is large in absolute value, β will be small.

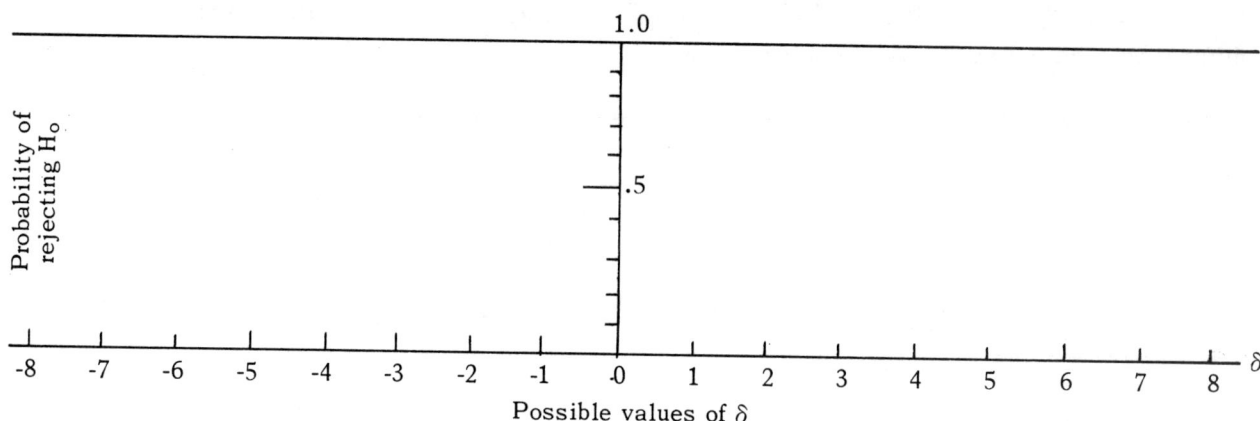

We shall construct a graph of the probability of rejecting H_o for possible values of $\mu_1 - \mu_2 = \delta$ in the population. We shall choose $\alpha = .05$ for this situation. Recalling the decision structure of this example, we decided

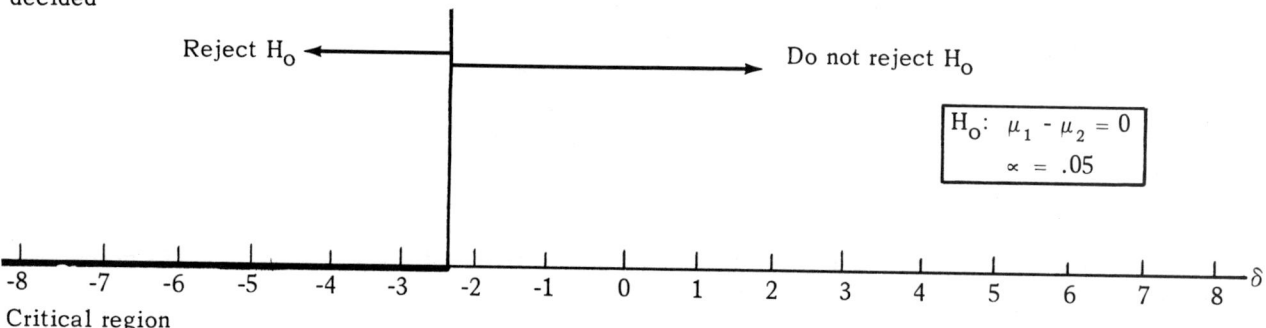

Critical region

that by rejecting H_o for sample values ($\bar{x}_1 - \bar{x}_2$) less than -2.3 and not rejecting H_o for sample values less than -2.3 would lead us to expect a probability of a Type I error (α) no larger than .05. Note that α is not dependent on δ.

Now let us assume that δ has some definite values, and for each value assumed compute the value of β and plot it on the graph.

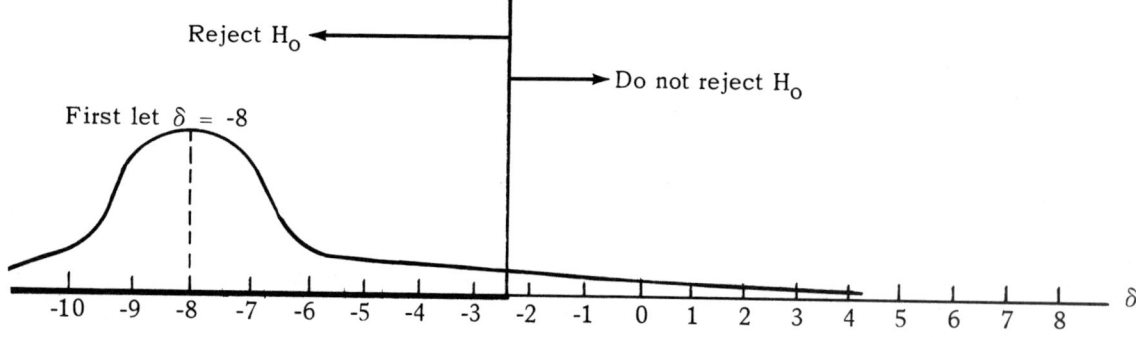

Since the distribution of sample differences ($\bar{x}_1 - \bar{x}_2$) would have -8 as the mean, then almost all of the sample means obtained from such a population would be the rejection region. The probability of rejecting H_o would be approximately .999+. Thus the probability of *not* rejecting H_o and making a Type II error would be nearly zero.

Next consider $\delta = -4$.

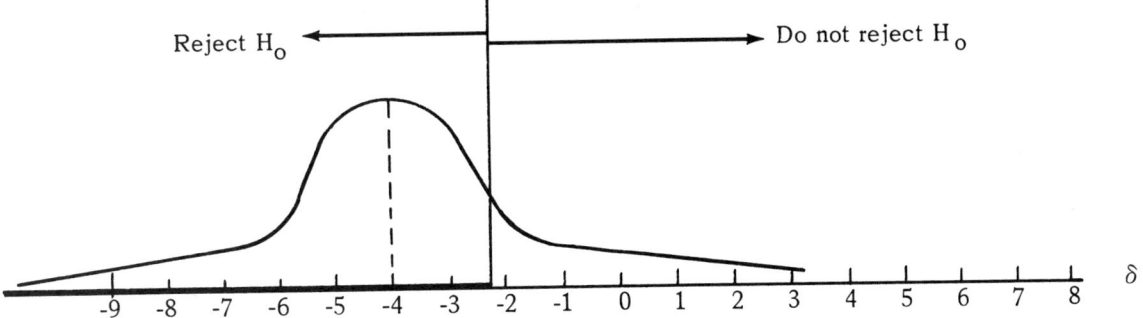

The distribution of sample means would be as shown in the graph above.

The probability of rejecting is still above .5. By using a table of normal probabilities I have computed it to be .88. Thus since the probability of rejecting H_o is .88, then the probability of *not* rejecting H_o is .12 and thus $\beta = .12$.

Next let $\delta = -2.3$.

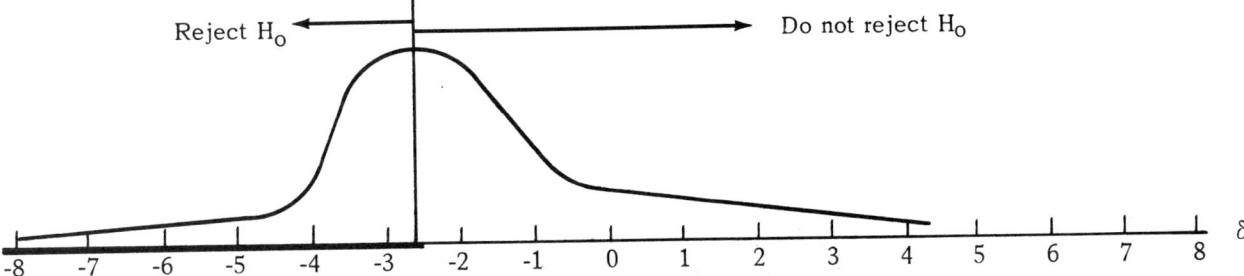

At $\delta = -2.3$ the normal distribution has -2.3 as its mean so the probability of a Type II error is 0.5.

Next let $\delta = +1$.

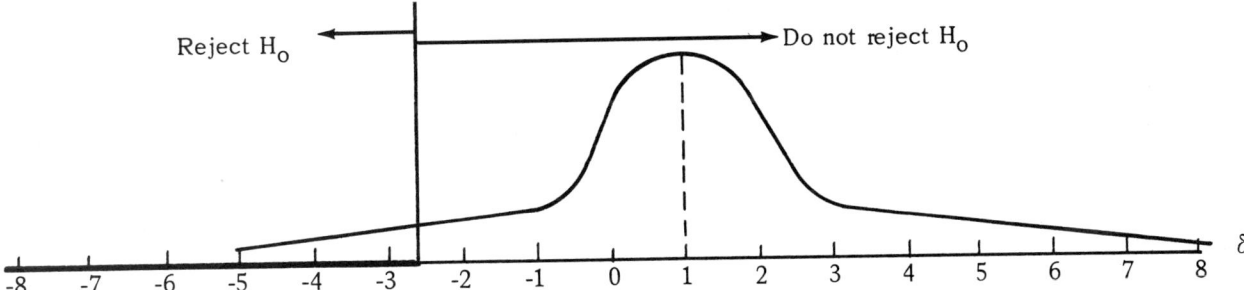

By observing the graph for the case $\delta = +1$ it can be noted that the probability of rejecting H_o is less than 0.05. The probability of not rejecting H_o is thus greater than 0.95. However, since a $\delta = +1$ means $\mu_1 > \mu_2$ then H_o which is $\mu_1 \geq \mu_2$ is in fact true, so no Type II error would be made by not rejecting H_o. Our graph now appears as shown.

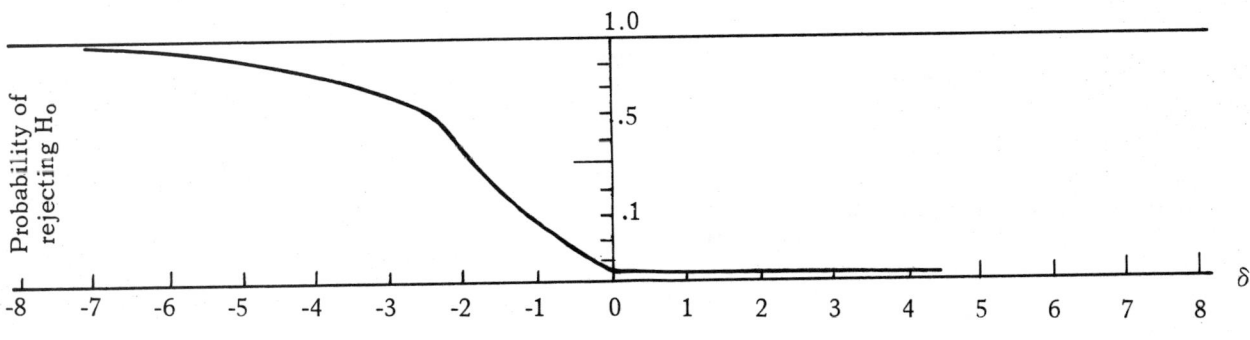

Note the property stated earlier that if δ is near zero, β is large. If δ is far from zero then β is small. From a practical point of view this direction of variation is more desirable than the reverse. That is, if δ is near zero, failure to reject H_o that $\mu_1 - \mu_2 = 0$ is frequently of little practical importance. When δ is far from zero, and the practical importance of the large difference is apparent, then the probability of failure to reject H_o is small.

Relation of α to β

Earlier in the paper, I stated that since the two errors resulted from opposite actions — Type I error is for rejecting and Type II error is for failure to reject — actions taken to avoid one type of error would lead to an increase in the probability of the other type of error. The graph of the power function will help us observe this relation:

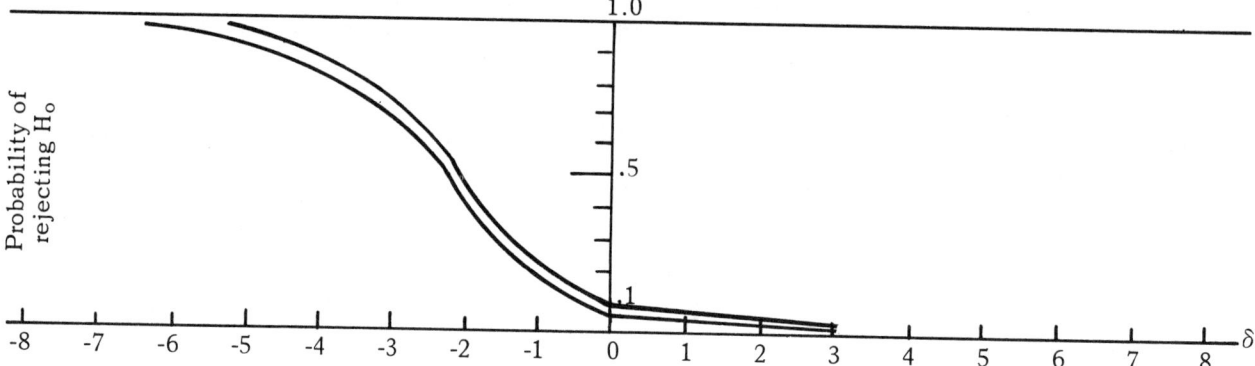

Proceeding in the same manner that we did earlier a power curve is shown graphed here for $\alpha = .10$ on the same coordinates where the graph for $\alpha = .05$ was drawn. As can be seen, the graph for $\alpha = .10$ is above the graph for $\alpha = .05$. This means that everywhere the probability to reject (Power) is greater and that the probability of a Type II error is everywhere smaller. That is an increase in α from 0.05 to 0.10 resulted in a decrease in β for all possible values of the parameter $\mu_1 - \mu_2 = \delta$.

In like manner if α were made smaller than 0.05 then β would increase everywhere. Note that it is always true that $\beta +$ Power $= 1$.

Control of α and β

The research worker then has α under his control. If he chooses to make a decision at the $\alpha = .01$ level he can so choose. For this situation the probability of a Type II error is a variable and may range from a large value to a small value depending on how close the true parameter value is to the hypothesized value.

There is some action that the research worker can take, however, to reduce the size of β while keeping α constant. Previously, in the example concerning eighth graders in Illinois, we were considering a random sample of size 100. If we were to choose a random sample of size 500 the α-level could be maintained as before, but β would be reduced.

Let us choose one example from our previous work, the example with $\delta = -2.3$. When $\delta = -2.3$ in our example with $\alpha = .05$ and $n = 100$ the probability of a Type II error was 0.5 (See graph on page 101).

Since $n = 500$ then $\sigma_{\bar{x}_1 - \bar{x}_2}$ becomes much smaller and the decision point for $\alpha = .05$ is -1.1 rather than -2.3.

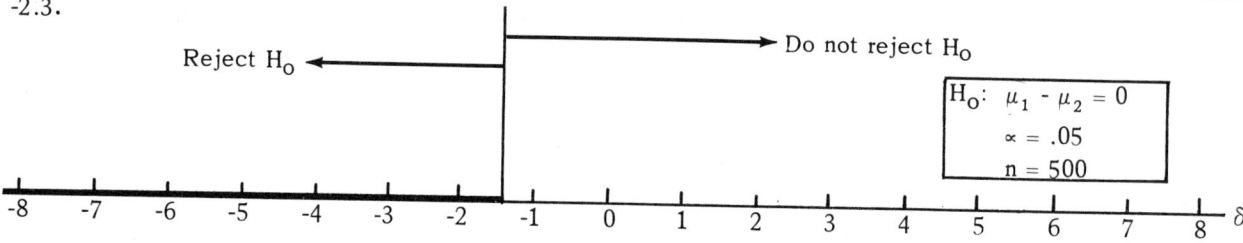

Since the $\bar{x}_1 - \bar{x}_2$ is smaller the distribution of $\bar{x}_1 - \bar{x}_2$ is less dispersed, so that for $\delta = -2.3$ the new graph appears as follows:

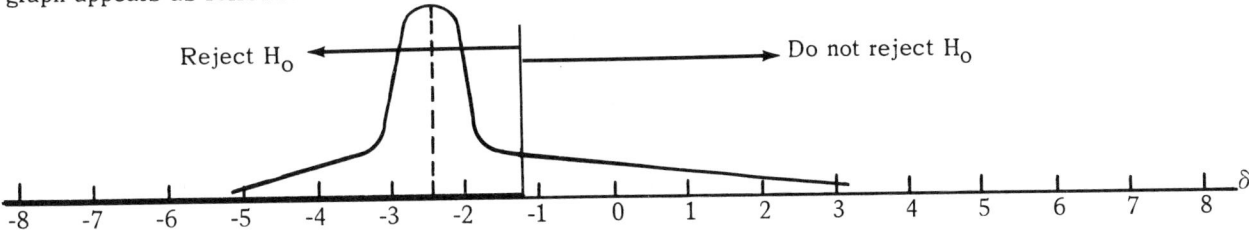

It is apparent from the graph that the β number will be smaller than 0.5.

Thus by increasing the size of the sample and keeping $\alpha = .05$, the size of β was reduced. The power curves appear as follows:

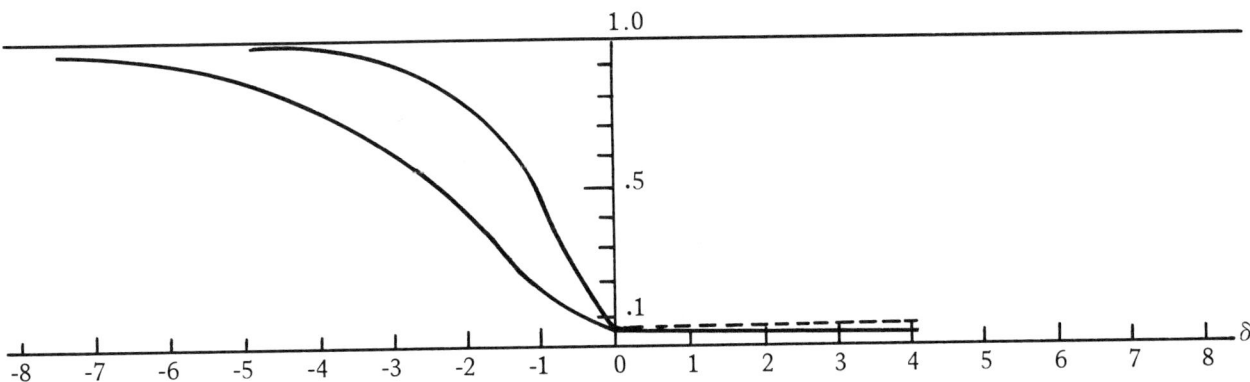

Thus, β is everywhere smaller in the situation where $n = 500$ than it was for $n = 100$, even though α remained the same.

Thus there appear to be two ways in this example to reduce the size of β. One is by increasing α; the other is by increasing the size of the sample.

Choosing a Suitable α and β

In performing a statistical test of an hypothesis, the research worker decides on the size of α and β that he is willing to gamble on for the particular experiment at hand.

In some economic problems it is possible to decide upon the relative size of α and β as related to a loss function that may determine loss in dollars; but for much research in education, psychology, and related fields such sharp loss functions are not possible, so that the decision on an α and β level becomes a judgmental decision by the experimenter. The judgment depends on the dangers involved in making the two kinds of errors.

In some cases it is very undesirable to make a Type I error. In such cases the research worker may wish to choose $\alpha = .001$. In other situations a Type I error, although undesirable, will not mean catastrophe and in the interest of not making a Type II error the research worker may wish to work at $\alpha = .05$ or even $\alpha = .10$. There is nothing sacred about any level of α. The decision to use α at any level is a judgment of the researcher.

If the research is such that no decision is required, then the research worker might better use the methods of interval estimation or simply report the probability level of the statistic found, rather than rejecting or failing to reject an hypothesis.

HYPOTHESIS TESTING OR CONFIDENCE INTERVAL?

Now that I have emphasized the concepts related to hypothesis testing and earlier treated rather lightly the concept of interval estimation, it may appear that I am advocating hypothesis-testing procedures over interval estimation. Such is not the case.

Hypothesis-testing procedures are indeed very useful in situations where decisions must be made. If one conducts an experiment concerning the efficiency and desirability of two different methods of cataloging books in a library and must decide on one or the other of these two methods, then hypothesis-decision-testing procedures would be helpful. However, one could accomplish the same thing with interval estimation because a confidence interval may be thought of as the interval of acceptable hypotheses. The interval of estimation is the interval of all hypotheses that, if tested by the sample statistic on hand, would not have been rejected.

It is not uncommon to see a statement in research literature that a correlation of .58 was computed and found to be significant. What the researcher has said in this statement is that he tested the hypothesis that the population correlation coefficient, ρ, is zero and rejected it. Thus, all that he has said is that he does not believe the population correlation is zero. How much better it would be in many situations if he were to state: "I am 95 percent confident that the true population correlation is between .42 and .65." This statement would be more helpful to many readers than would the statement, "I do not think the correlation is zero."

This has been a rather loose presentation of some ideas of statistical inference, especially of hypothesis testing. The emphasis has been placed on the informal intuitive development of the concepts rather than on a rigorous development of the ideas. The intention was to help the reader gain some general insight into the logic of statistical inference. A more careful development would require considerably more time and space and a more careful buildup of prerequisite knowledge.

CHAPTER X: MEASUREMENT AND EVALUATION OF RESEARCH IN LIBRARY TECHNICAL SERVICES*

MAURICE F. TAUBER
Professor, School of Library Service
Columbia University, New York

This discussion will not try to cover research in all areas of the activities that may be defined as technical services. However, reference will be made to the fields of acquisitions, cataloging and classification and other means of organizing collections, binding and preservation, and photographic reproduction, which cuts across several areas. Circulation systems are mentioned, but there is no effort to cover the full field of circulation service.

The sources of information and suggestion for this presentation cover a wide range: (1) such standards as are applicable to any of the areas of the technical services, (2) dissertations and theses which appear to add quantitative or qualitative measurements to library processes, (3) reports in the journal literature on detailed studies, usually in libraries, which provide data of varying degrees of possible application in other libraries, and (4) surveys of libraries (systems or individual institutions) which seek to apply research methodology or even innovative approaches.

The usefulness of research methodology applied in other fields, such as public administration, management, systems analysis, time and motion studies, cost studies, equipment analysis, and examination of personnel requirements, has been commented upon in the literature, and such applications as appear to be fruitful are noted in this presentation. Because it provides a simple framework on which to base my remarks, I shall discuss the various technical services areas first, and then seek to summarize instruments of measurement that lend themselves to generalization or general applicability, and to indicate areas which appear to warrant study, or in some cases, further study.

Areas included are the following: selection and acquisitions, cataloging, subject headings, filing, classification, binding and preservation, photographic reproduction, automation, circulation systems, scientific operations, library technology reports, matrix of library surveys, summary of methodology, and areas of study.

The literature is full of "this-is-the-way-we-do-it" contributions. Not all of these reports or articles are useless, but a good many are, and unfortunately, some of them are incomplete or misleading. The word "research" is seldom used in terms of controlled studies, and even some of these purported "research" investigations have flaws in sampling, data gathering, or interpretation, usually as the result of bias or limited experience on the part of the writer.

In *Technical Services in Libraries*,[1] issued in 1954 (now in process of revision), one of the primary efforts was to isolate, in the findings of studies which had been carried on either in library schools or in the field, such guidance as would lead to improvement of technical services for any library. In April 1963, Number 58 in the University of Illinois Graduate School of Library Science's Occasional Papers (a revision of an earlier 1960 paper) provided an approach to *The Literature of Library Technical Services*.[2] The important characteristic of the sections of this publication — general technical services, acquisitions, cataloging and classification, serials, document reproduction, interlibrary cooperation, and library resources — is the apparent search for fundamental studies that go beyond what Ralph Esterquest describes as "pious generalizations, detailed reports on specific projects, and ambitious plans or proposals."[3] The late Mortimer Taube referred to them as "glowing promises."

Although it is not my purpose to review the literature of technical services since 1963, it will be necessary, in the development of a pattern of potential research in the field, to refer to some studies, usually as examples, in order to indicate areas on which to build.

Some years ago as chairman of the Committee on Research of the Association of American Library Schools, I encouraged an effort made in an issue of *Library Trends*[4] to single out areas for research. Verner W. Clapp,[5]

---

*The author is grateful to Mrs. Nathalie C. Batts and Mrs. Margaret P. Klein for assistance in preparing this paper.

in a review of this issue, indicated that his reaction to the contents of the papers was that they were traditional and did not lead to a program for the future. He deplored the type of research in some library schools which added few cumulative objective findings which would lead to solution of pressing problems in American librarianship.

The issue cuts across all areas of library service, including various aspects of the technical services. No unifying thread or pattern of integrated research was contained in the set of papers, according to Clapp. Despite an effort by Robert D. Leigh,[6] to refute Clapp on the grounds that the issue was intended to describe the situation so that the pattern envisioned by Clapp might be developed, it appears that Clapp evaluated the situation properly. As late as May, 1967, in a set of papers entitled "A Kaleidoscopic View of Library Research," the *Wilson Library Bulletin*[7] sought to estimate the current level of research. Philip Ennis, of the University of Chicago, characterized it as "non-cumulative, fragmentary, generally weak, and relentlessly oriented to immediate practice."[8]

Measurement and evaluation of technical services, important in themselves under ordinary circumstances, have become more important than ever in terms of financial support now available through Federal and state funds. The funds for research from many governmental and non-governmental sources are greater than ever before, and while they may seem small when compared with those in other fields, they represent an opportunity librarians have never had before. Projects of concern to both the United States Office of Education, and the Council on Library Resources, Inc., relate to indexing, classification or abstracting, cataloging, library technology (which includes physical access), photographic reproduction (now called reprography), and automation. Funds are obviously important because one of the pressures upon library administrators, as well as on budget officers generally, is to keep expenditures for operations in line and still meet growing demands. It would be hard to estimate the amount of money that has been spent annually, and sometimes wastefully, on library operations. Economic efficiency is a major goal, but so are fulfillment of function, accuracy, and promptness in meeting the needs of users.

AREAS OF TECHNICAL SERVICES FOR LIBRARIES

Before discussing the various areas of the technical services, it may be well to refer briefly to the significant developments in the merging of library interests, geographically and without relation to type of library, referred to in Beasley's and Armstrong's papers. There are international, national, regional, state, county and metropolitan movements toward cooperative activities. On the international level, there are the various cooperative acquisitions programs, which affect activities in individual libraries directly, and also the efforts towards the establishment of international cataloging rules to speed up cataloging through the shared cataloging program (which involves international cooperation), besides other activities of the International Federation of Library Associations (IFLA) and other international organizations to improve technical developments in libraries. On a national level we see the work of the Library of Congress in various acquisitions programs, the introduction of the MARC (Machine Readable Cataloging Copy project), the work of the National Library of Medicine and the National Library of Agriculture in developing bibliographical and other services for libraries within the framework of their interests, and the services of the major research libraries in participating actively in national operations.

On the regional, state, and county levels, the introduction of centralized processing centers has had a profound effect upon the operations of individual libraries, not only in what they acquire, but also in what they catalog, classify and retain. We shall come back to this later. The literature reports these activities, and there is the beginning of efforts to evaluate some of them, such as the Farmington Plan, the PL480 Project, the Latin American Cooperative Acquisitions Project (described in a volume by M.J. Savary to be issued by Stechert-Hafner in 1968), and other cooperative acquisitions programs. The establishment of the new Anglo-American cataloging rules, the new edition of the Dewey Decimal Classification, the emergence of the new list of LC subject headings, the return of book catalogs, the invention of new equipment (with the possibility of a full-fledged cataloger's camera), computer applications, and other devices should also help to reduce the time needed at present for repetitive operations. Two current studies at the University of Chicago deal with the nature of the catalog (Don Swanson) and the full-scale effort to automate operations (Herman H. Fussler).

Selection and Acquisitions

Even though selection of materials may be regarded as somewhat outside the orbit of the more technical aspects of technical services, it has a currently significant place in the work of library systems, particularly those related to school and public libraries. In various studies made of book selection in relation to regional processing, it has been shown that unimaginative independence in selection may be a critical barrier to obtaining full cooperation.

At the present time, a full-scale study of acquisitions operations in libraries is under way, under the supervision of the American Library Association, Library Research and Development Office. Results are not yet available, but it appears that its techniques of evaluation are less innovative than might have been expected.

Acquisitional studies, like those which study resources of a library or a library system, are normally combinations of several approaches — questionnaires, examinations of holdings in relation to various checklists (and this has been criticized as a method of evaluating resources), examination of collections by individuals or teams of specialists, review of acquisitional policies and procedures, including personnel, routines, vendors used, equipment, forms, and records. Physical space, type of staffing, transportation and communication conditions, and other aspects of acquisitions are examined by actual observation and study of data, either assembled by the investigator or made available by him.

Beasley, in his paper on "A Theoretical Framework for Public Library Measurement" in this volume, refers to the problem of adequacy of the collections for academic libraries, and mentions the Clapp-Jordan formulae.[9] These indeed did return to the quantitative criteria for measuring collections. The significant part of the article comes at the end where the authors set out questions requiring research; the topics are worth summarizing here:

(1) the need for positive tests of adequacy of collections;
(2) the minimal contents of an undergraduate collection;
(3) the effect on contents of geography, curriculum, methods, teaching methods, intellectual climate, etc.;
(4) the adequacy of collections for particular kinds of materials at various levels — e.g., periodicals, government documents;
(5) the adequacy for needs of faculty, honors students, etc.;
(6) the correlation, if any, between student body and size of collection;
(7) the existence and characteristics of a replacement cycle and its effect on acquisition, weeding, cost of collection-building;
(8) adequate resources for graduate work and research in various subjects and at various levels.

Similar questions might be asked for other types of libraries. This article raises the whole question of the place of formulae in the technical services. Hardly a week goes by when I am not asked for a certain formula in acquisitions, or cataloging and classification. In binding and photographic reproduction there may be a more definite note of progress in development of standards.

In the examination of acquisitional activity in libraries, the equation of staffing must be related to the increase in budgets for books, periodicals, and other materials, the engagement in acquisition cooperative programs, the introduction of blanket or standing orders, and similar steps. The introduction of educational accounting or computer equipment also would involve a relationship to staff composition.

Cataloging

We may now turn to a discussion of cataloging. One of the major reasons for the development of centralized processing is to eliminate or minimize the amount of cataloging prepared in the participating libraries. Acquisitions may or may not be a part of this operation, and the evaluation of studies that have been made on this problem suggests that unless both are included the results are likely to be less beneficial than one expects. The method of examining this situation is to review the literature on projects that have attempted both. Here one may point out some of the results of processing centers, which are summarized in the July, 1967, issue of *Library Trends*, "Cooperative and Centralized Cataloging."[10] Studies indicate that costs are sometimes not reduced, but justification of the centralized services is based on such arguments as the following: (1) elimination of unnecessary duplicated work, (2) release of staff from processing in order to do other things, (3) uniformity in cataloging and processing, (4) availability of consultative services in cataloging and classification, (5) maintenance of the card catalog, (6) improvement of the catalog, and (7) improvement of library services generally in terms of greater utilization of limited staff and of prompter service.

The recent study of the *Emerging Library Systems: The 1963-1966 Evaluation of the New York, New York State Public Library Systems*[11] and the earlier Nelson Associates, Inc. study, *Centralized Processing for the Public Libraries of New York State*[12] represent an effort on the part of one state to take into account the problems of small units in continuing to give proper service by taking care of their individual processing needs. The methodology of the first of these studies is indicated to some extent in Armstrong's papers on "Measurement and Evaluation of the Public Library." In the second, analytical estimates and mathematical projections were made which led to the recommendation of the establishment of a limited number (actually four) of processing units, with special attention to processing in the major libraries of New York City. The various units of the City University of New York similarly have been studied for potential merging of certain operations. These studies indicate the nature of the present thinking about processing, or technical services, and show that the potential extension of this centralized activity is more than likely.

In the discussion of cataloging in 1967 one cannot overlook the issuance of the *Anglo-American Cataloging Rules*.[13] These were a long time coming, and the studies concerning cataloging rules and the implications of modifications in rules could fill a volume. Indeed, there were two conferences on these rules, at San Francisco and Montreal, as well as numerous articles. The studies of the rules themselves represent an interesting application of investigative methods, and some of the papers show imaginative analysis of the conditions involved in establishment of name entries, corporate entries, serial entries, and various special forms of entry under these. The measurement and evaluation of studies of rules represent an important part of the literature on the subject, primarily because there are opposing views on basic issues. Calling them "Rules" does not necessarily mean that everyone is going to follow them. The major problem in relation to the *Anglo-American Cataloging Rules* is the extent to which the Library of Congress will accept them. The Library has already issued its rule of superimposition, which means that LC will continue to use established entries for certain names, but will apply new rules if they have not been involved with them in earlier publications. This does not mean that LC will not in the future change its decisions about some of the older materials, but it has decided that these changes will be made, if made at all, after due deliberation. The differences resulting for libraries using the *Anglo-American Cataloging Rules* and also using LC cards might well result in conflicts in some catalogs. That is, there has not been and is not likely to be complete coincidence of collections of an individual library and those of LC. The problem requires constant attention, and one wonders how evaluative techniques can be applied to research in this area.

Another area of concern that has been supported by the Council on Library Resources, Inc., is the establishment of cataloging rules for publications in the more difficult languages. In 1958 Nasser Sharify completed his code for the cataloging of Persian works,[14] and this summer Abdus S. Qasimi, a Pakistani, completed his code for the cataloging of materials in Pushto, Urdu, and Panjabi.[15] These studies at Columbia University are methodologically important in their intensive examination of names so as to develop transliteration schemes, as well as their integration, so far as possible, with *Anglo-American Cataloging Rules*. The usefulness of these codes would be tested by their use at the Library of Congress and other American libraries, as well as by publishers, librarians, and others in countries which publish books in these languages, as well as in their libraries.

Related to this development is the cataloging-in-source experiment, which was reported on by the Library of Congress in 1960.[16] Dawson has discussed this project in his paper in the July, 1967, issue of *Library Trends*.[17] The significance of this study lies in the fact that it seemed to have the "go" sign — based on support in a consumer study by Esther J. Piercy — but was rejected by the Library of Congress because of difficulties which arose during its operations, not only for LC but also for publishers. In essence, the idea is theoretically sound — the insertion of cataloging text in the book or other publication for the use of the librarian. The pilot project at the Library of Congress represented an impressive departure from the traditional practice. Dawson has said that,

> The brief duration of the experiment produced only some 1,200 entries and made no impact on cataloging; the brevity of the experiment is questionable. Equally questionable was the consumer reaction method of determining usefulness. No matter...Cataloging-in-Source

died. The nearest thing it has had to a resurrection is the program, initiated in 1961 by the Library of Congress, to induce book jobbers to insert sets of LC cards in books distributed to libraries.[18]

In his volume, *The Future of the Research Libraries*,[19] Verner Clapp indicated that perhaps cataloging-in-source programs might be applied to limited programs in special types of materials, such as government documents. Indeed, the possibilities for such applications over and above American trade book titles have not been examined with any seriousness.

Related to the general trend toward making information about holdings of libraries easily available to members of a particular system or area, there has been a resurgence of the book catalog. The examination of the various studies on book catalogs would take an unconscionable time, but it is worth commenting on several developments in regard to them. In the first place, they are growing rapidly, as David Weber shows in his paper on "Book Catalog Trends in 1966."[20] This paper, together with a recent survey conducted at Columbia University, indicates that book catalogs are here again in public, school, college and university, and special libraries. They are likely to grow, and the evaluation presents a formidable problem. Cost can be a considerable factor, even though the merits of using book catalogs can be established, and it may be decisive. There is a need for very careful studies, building on those included in the volume on *Book Catalogs*,[21] which Robert E. Kingery and I edited in 1963. These new studies should have pertinent data to assist librarians in the selection of producers of book catalogs, and should be so worked out that we have clear ideas of format, arrangement, ease of use, and nature of cumulations, and of all of these in relation to cost. In one library with which I am working at the present time, a matrix of the various factors was developed which showed pretty clearly that one could get almost anything one wanted in the way of book catalogs if one wanted to pay the cost. The important decision that has to be made is in relation to what is needed from the catalog, and how to get it most conveniently and inexpensively. Among the criticisms that have been made of book catalogs are slowness in production, inaccuracies, and cost. Weber has detailed statements on costs of producing a book catalog at Stanford University's J. Henry Meyer Memorial Library,[22] as well as statements of librarians who have had difficulties in this approach. It should be remembered in discussing the records of library collections that the important motive has not been economy, but rather better service through improved catalogs and easier and more extensive access. Their appearance marks the turn of the circle, with the book catalog returning because of the development of the sequential camera and chain printer.

One of the on-going projects sponsored by the Council on Library Resources, Inc., is the study of problems of research library catalog renovation, presentation, and maintenance being carried on at the New York Public Library. In 1965, Seoud M. Matta, a doctoral student at Columbia, completed his study of *The Card Catalog in a Large Research Library: Present Conditions and Future Possibilities in the New York Public Library*.[23] Matta's concern was to measure the relationship of the card catalog facilities of the New York Public Library in regard to what had to be done to them if they were to be maintained at a level of usefulness to clientele and staff of the library. He developed detailed statistical analyses through sampling techniques which permitted him to project rate of deterioration and likely costs of rehabilitation, and compared these with costs for providing multiple copies of book catalogs. The Council grant provided for an investigation of the card catalog of the Dance Collection in terms of book catalog conversion. The report on this project has not yet been completed, but it represents again a pilot study for action in relation to the future of the massive card catalog of the New York Public Library. In January, 1967, the New York Public Library started using Library of Congress cards and subject headings for processing its materials. Since it does not use a systematic classification for its closed stacks, it has not applied the Library of Congress Classification.

Another major project of importance in respect to implications for cataloging not only for American libraries but for libraries in other countries as well is the decision in January, 1967, to publish in book form the pre-1956 entries in the National Union Catalog, now on cards, by Mansell Information Publishing Ltd. of London and Chicago. Maintained since 1901 by the Library of Congress, the card catalog is the central location device for research titles in more than seven hundred libraries in the United States and Canada. It contains more than ten million titles that were cataloged before the Library of Congress began in 1956 to issue cataloging entries in book form. In March, 1967, the first 27,000 edited cards were sent to the printer for the first of 610 projected volumes of 704 pages each. It is expected that it will take ten years to complete. Obviously, it will be a tremendous cataloging asset to all libraries as a cooperative library tool.

We could of course spend more time on developments that will enable libraries to take advantage of work at the Library of Congress, and indeed this work should be used to the utmost by all libraries which can do so. The library profession should exert its fullest strength in giving support to LC in its various activities and responsibilities.

Subject Headings

Research in subject headings has made little headway for general library usage. In special libraries, however, and in information centers, there have been a number of studies, mostly appearing in journal articles, of subject analysis, and especially there has been the compilation of so-called thesauri. In engineering, in education, and in other fields the development of thesauri, a type of subject analysis which involves the use of headings in classified array and relationships, has been regarded as a development which goes beyond traditional subject headings. There have been reports on efforts to study the effectiveness of these listings, but they have been of special rather than general application.

The issuance of the Library of Congress' new edition of subject headings raises the issue again of the need of a comprehensive study of subject headings for general libraries. In many libraries which use LC subject headings, there has nevertheless been a need to add headings. Here again, coordinated rather than sporadic studies of subject headings would be worthwhile. Mention may be made of two basic studies at Columbia, which might lead to further progress in respect to the development of additional information, in a cumulative sense, regarding subject headings and their characteristics. Jay E. Daily, in his *The Grammar of Subject Headings*,[24] analyzed completely the structure of subject headings as included in the LC list. Oliver L. Lilley[25] examined the subject headings in the field of English literature. Daily's method was to place each subject heading on a card, and then analyze it by categorization and coding. Unfortunately his work was done before the advance of computer potential; today he would undoubtedly use a computer. At the moment, Jessica Harris, at Columbia, is making a study of the relationship of subject headings to administrative controls, and has found Daily's work most helpful; she will code her material for computer analysis. Lilley's study set a pattern that others working in separate fields could follow. He analyzed all headings in the field of English literature and, as Daily did with the total list, categorized and examined their character and coverage. Carlyle J. Frarey, who has been working on a history of subject heading theory and practice in the United States, should provide a systematic categorization of guidelines, if not principles, of subject heading development.

Filing

The problem of filing into catalogs probably should be isolated at this point. The filing into card catalogs on a manual basis for large records has been a serious problem for librarians over the years. Concentrations of cards at different places in the catalog have made it difficult for users to locate easily items they want, and for library personnel to put new cards and entries into the catalog has become a complicated task.

Now that there are book catalogs, computer-produced, new questions of filing have appeared. Theodore C. Hines and Jessica Harris, at Columbia, have been experimenting with filing arrangements, and last year issued their filing code for the arrangement of entries in files, indexes, catalogs, and other records.[26] In addition, Hines also has been chairman of Subcommittee 13, Z39 Committee, Library Work and Documentation, of the United States of America Standards Institute (formerly American Standards Association), assigned to prepare a draft USA Standard, "Basic Criteria for Filing (Alphabetical Arrangement)." This was issued some months ago, and is now being criticized by a large group of individuals in this country and abroad. This is designed for either manual or computer filing. This is such an important matter, in terms of simpler programming for setting up book catalogs, that Hines and Harris decided to make certain changes in the usual library (ALA) rules for filing, and incorporate them into their code. These are reflected in the proposed standard. A review of the Hines-Harris book by F.C. Kilgour[27] recently indicated that he thought it was not necessary to alter any established filing code to absorb the questions of computer filing. It could be said that there should be re-examinations as to what is established, and that suggestions for change are not necessarily wrong. The Hines-Harris code has been tested in several book catalogs and holds up satisfactorily.

This matter is sufficiently important to observe that the new unit set up in October, 1966, in the Library of Congress Processing Department Office, called Processing Department — Technical Processes Research Office, under the supervision of Richard S. Angell, has the mission of evaluating existing patterns of descriptive cataloging, classification, subject analysis and indexing, investigating alternatives to these techniques, and considering how they will be affected by automation and how the new technology can be be put to most effective use for information storage and retrieval. The first project of the Office, carried on jointly with the Library's Information Systems Office, is to prepare a means of filing catalog entries by computer. This will be done through an analysis of LC filing rules, analysis of the filing of a sample of catalog records, preparation and testing of filing programs, and compilation of a set of computer filing rules. The two units of LC have also begun a descriptive study of LC's author and subject authority records to determine their characteristics in order to prepare a standard computer format and perhaps anticipate problems in converting the 1.4 million records now in existence. Thus, we are on the verge of a series of studies which may have significant repercussions on the total record activity of major forces in bibliographical development, and these will affect all libraries connected with national services.

Classification

With classification, we come to an area with a literature that is both exhaustive and exhausting — exhausting because it represents an area in which great personal and subjective considerations enter, rather than one in which there has been concentrated research leading to positive statements on a wide spectrum of topics, ranging from "no classification" as we understand it in library service, to very detailed and constantly revised systems, as in the Dewey, UDC, and the Library of Congress, among the more important.[28] This is no place to discuss the intrinsic merits of classification systems. In my own studies of the subject,[29] it seemed clear quite early that certain types of libraries, academic and those which collected deeply in particular fields, would probably find the LC more adaptable to their needs than other general, hierarchical systems. With the appearance of the 17th edition of the Dewey Decimal Classification, this became somewhat clearer to librarians generally. The various problems presented by the new Dewey, not only in its relocations but also in the modifications in the instructions, general and internal, and in its inadequate index, together with other innovations in notation, resulted in many libraries, both academic and other types, starting to use the LC schedules. Major libraries which had been skeptical about shifting to the LC system have started using it for new acquisitions and for setting up programs of reclassification. The future is longer than the past, it has been said, and it applies apparently in this situation.

The Pre-Conference of the ALA meeting in New York in the summer of 1966, the Institute on the Library of Congress Classification, resulted in a series of papers, many involving the gathering of new data, by either questionnaire or documentary analysis, and should result soon in a volume from the American Library Association which should provide a basis for more detailed or extensive study of the system. There are many assumptions among librarians as to the acceptance of the LC system, including its compatibility with the MARC program, and its likely aid to libraries on an expanded scale through the distribution of greater numbers of printed cards through the Shared Cataloging program. Suffice it to say that libraries have started using LC to get out of a situation of low production in processing and of growing arrears. The evidence is that this is true, despite the fact that LC brings its own problems. A 1967 article by Richard M. Dougherty entitled "The Realities of Reclassification,"[30] points out that there are certain matters which librarians should consider prior to reclassification. These, I believe, represent a shuffling of concerns that have been discussed in the literature, but Dougherty, while emphasizing the importance of considering all the difficulties involved in reclassification, still sees it as necessary. The amount of reclassification that a library has to do should not be a restraint on its need to eliminate the perpetuation of procedures that are a weight on production, and result in a questionable product.

A study of some magnitude is at present being carried on by Malcolm Rigby and Pauline Atherton, and the American Institute of Physics, on the computerization of the Universal Decimal Classification. This is a matter for special collections, primarily report literature, but is noted because computers have undoubtedly a potential for the upkeep of classification schedules, once certain programs have been worked out.

A third comment about research in classification should be related to the British Classification Group, and its two conferences on research at Dorking and Elsinore. The Atherton volume on *Classification*

Research,[31] a weighty tome, presents some useful suggestions for research, particularly of the faceted variety. It seems unlikely, however, that the proposals will make a serious change in the meagreness of classification research in the United States. Classification here apparently is a pragmatic matter, a practical approach to grouping collections on a systematic subject basis with as little difficulty as possible.

One subject that is now being examined at Columbia in Richard J. Hyman's study is the validity of the concept of browsing.[32] This topic, which may be also called concepts of access to materials through shelf arrangement (without getting into the by-product of serendipity), is one that has been mentioned here and there by writers on classification, and it is hoped that Hyman, through observation, interviews with selected groups, and other means will give us more of an idea of what browsing is. In Dougherty's previously mentioned article[30] he singled out browsing as an unknown activity in terms of availability of actual evidence. In my studies at Chicago and Temple in 1939, samplings of faculty members and users of stacks indicated rather clearly that there was some value in classified arrangements, and that browsing was not impeded by the Library of Congress system. A study by Saul Herner in 1960, *A Pilot Study of the Use of the Stacks at the Library of Congress*,[33] prepared for the Council on Library Resources, Inc., was not conclusive in regard to the helpfulness of classification to browsing *per se*.

Binding and Preservation

In the fields of binding and preservation of collections, librarians are faced — and not so suddenly — with the enormous responsibility of saving collections for posterity. The death in August, 1967, of William J. Barrow meant the loss to librarians and scholars of the greatest researcher in the field of paper deterioration.[34] His laboratory at Richmond, Virginia, had already established norms for good paper, and at the time of his death he had completed phase II of a series of studies on the durability of bindings.[35] Aside from Barrow's work, the only other systematic study of bindings has been carried on by the Library Binding Institute.[36] The general effort has been in the direction of developing standards for binding, as a guide to librarians in the making of proper decisions concerning the care of materials as well as in the careful use of limited funds for his purpose.

One could not bring up the question of binding standards without making it clear that there is a difference of opinion — if that is the proper word — between the library group spearheading the examination of the subject, and the administration of the Library Binding Institute. The LBI standard for library binding has been reduced to a single standard, called Class A Binding, and the members of the Institute agree that there are other ways of handling materials than through this procedure. The ALA Committee on Binding, however, has maintained that there are several standards, so to speak, and that what LBI has is only one of them. This difference must be objectively resolved; it is significant how much conflict can be generated just by terminology.

The Less-Used Materials Specifications (known as LUMSPECS) represent an effort at establishing some sort of "standard" or uniform treatment of certain types of materials. Binders do not refer to this as a standard, but as a way of taking care of the materials through something other than binding.

In any review of binding comment should also be made on the developments and expansion of the work by the binding industry. They have introduced new equipment and new plants, have studied carefully their financing and have tried, although it seems as if they do not make as much progress as some would like, to keep prices down. One of the major problems of binding, of course, and this has received considerable documentation and less systematic study than may be desired, is the pricing of pre-bound or library bindings by certain publishers. Since binding is a marketable item, it is to be expected that the economics of the field should be a matter of constant concern.

One needs to refer only to the fire at the Library of the Jewish Theological Seminary of America in New York in April, 1966, and the flood in Florence, Italy, last November, to realize how fragile rare library materials are. The efforts at both of these places to control the ravages after a fire and a flood are most useful to librarians in their care of materials generally. Various American experts in book conservation and paper technology were sent to Florence to assist in restoration. Despite the history of such disasters, there has been limited research on how to grapple with soaked books, and the different approaches at the Seminary were extraordinary — heating by electric ray, freezing so as to extract water, and finally, the handling of each book with paper wrappers to allow drying and rebinding. The effective control of fungus which developed almost overnight, was also limited.

Photographic Reproduction

The activities of libraries in photographic reproduction have been extended to such an extent that librarians are in need of further guidelines on use of the techniques, care of the materials, and the relation of microforms to other types of materials. The introduction of the Xerox, of course, has modified photographic reproduction tremendously over the past half dozen years, and the likelihood of further developments, such as improvement of print-out machines, will make photographic records much more acceptable to users and librarians alike. There have been studies concerned with such areas as the experimental publication of a scientific journal in microform (as against original journal publication); development of various equipment, such as an experimental high-density direct access photostorage-and-retrieval system for library materials; isolation of the technical elements of a mechanized library system; direct photomemory for storage and retrieval; hand reading devices for microforms; the bibliographical control of microforms; testing of effectiveness of protective film coatings; cost of technical reports on microfiche; standardization of microfiche; demonstration of high-density crystalline photo-storage; and construction of various pieces of photographic equipment associated with library use.

Most, if not all of these projects, have been supported by grants from the Council on Library Resources, Inc. In general they are either connected with surveys of situations, such as the bibliographical control of microforms (which led to a *Guide to Microforms*[37]), or tests (such as protective film), or equipment (which leads to a physical product).

Undoubtedly, there is ferment in this field, and there are numerous projects which require the attention of librarians, even though research may be done by commercial companies for the most part. In *The Future of the Research Library*,[19] Clapp has indicated the need for miniaturizing original records, with the expectation that original size copies can be furnished easily. The growth pattern of library collections described by the Purdue researchers[38] is certainly connected with this possibility. Studies of storage by microfilm, and its relation to service, are necessary for making this possibility a reality.

The life of microfilm and other microforms is a pertinent matter for systematic examination by researchers. The development of so-called "measles" on older microfilm has directed attention to the need to make sure that we do not have to replace much copied material in the future.

AUTOMATION

In the July, 1967 issue of *American Documentation*,[39] Burton W. Adkinson and Charles M. Stearns have provided an up-to-date review, "Librarians and Machines — A Review." It may be worth taking a moment to isolate the essential points made by these authors, since they have been close to developments, and have been interested in research projects that will build on what is known. They call attention to the fact that "A library is essentially a set of files." Moreover, "the Library of Congress is a basic set of files that in all contains some 42 million items."[40]

They wrote further,
> The point is that libraries are collections of files, files that have to be updated and manipulated so that you can search them from various angles. No one can challenge the fact that file manipulation is a task of the sort that EAM and EDP devices are good at, providing some one can write instructions for them.

However, libraries are evolving rapidly beyond the status of passive archives that scholars browse in. In science and technology, they are challenged with ever-increasing urgency.[41]

They raise four points in regard to degree and rate of adoption of computers by the library:[42] (1) libraries cannot shut down during a re-tooling for computerization, (2) large economic gains must be evident before old capabilities are eliminated, (3) new capabilities will not be acceptable unless it is clear they meet a real user need, and (4) the largest pay-off will come when computer-readable records are interchangeable between libraries, and this introduces the old barrier of lack of standardization.

On the first of these points, the authors demonstrate that libraries cannot shut down. In connection with point (2), they regard the cost-benefit ratio not only as important in itself, but also as psychologically involved. In respect to point (3), despite the efforts and large sums of money spent on identifying the real needs of users, they point out that we are not able to describe them satisfactorily. In connection with standardization, the authors suggest that librarians will have to engage in cooperative load-sharing arrangements to a greater degree than they have in the past because of the bias towards local self-sufficiency. It may be said in summary that the authors believe that "these obstacles are not insuperable; but they need to be recognized more clearly."[43]

Research in automation is overwhelming in quantity and cannot be evaluated here. The hardware and software papers and even books are numerous, and annual reviews are now appearing (American Documentation Institute)[44] which provide a basis for estimating the value of the studies reported.

CIRCULATION SYSTEMS

In the past few years there have been a number of studies of circulation systems. Undoubtedly the introduction of the transaction card system for circulation, as well as an effort to reduce the excessive time spent on circulation service, will lead to further research in this area. The academic libraries still maintain close control over circulated books, and there appears to be no change in this policy for most institutions. Doubts expressed elsewhere in this volume about circulation statistics have been widely supported, but there does not appear to be any real expectation that they will be given up in the near future, as they provide some indication of use.

SCIENTIFIC OPERATIONS

The volume by Dougherty and Heinritz, *Scientific Management in Library Operations*,[45] makes a first effort to identify those areas of library service that can be subject to improved management, covering the character of scientific management, flow charts, flow diagrams, block diagrams, decision flow charting, operations analysis, forms, time studies, sampling, aids to computation, cost, performance standards and control, study of a circulation system, and present and proposed methods. In their chapter on sampling the authors use the 95 percent confidence level. They may have oversimplified scientific management, but the work represents a real step towards catching up with what Armstrong refers to as "bad management."

Mortimer Taube, in his development of coordinate indexing — which had some value in respect to other controls of materials — sought to examine the criteria for any information system. His criteria are indicated in a paper in his first volume on *Studies in Coordinate Indexing*.[46] In connection with automation or the development of a system, among the points regarded as possible measures of efficiency are rapid searching of indexed data, ability to reproduce the final product economically and quickly, access points involved, ease of use, ease of cumulation, ease of change, and cost. There are other factors, but these appeared to be common to many of the systems indicated. Taube studied these on a comparative basis, but this method may be queried. Jahoda, in his study "Correlative Indexing Systems for Control of Research Records,"[47] which was done by questionnaire and analysis of systems, threw some new light on the coordinate indexing system, and may have had some effect on limiting the extension of coordinate indexing installations.

GENERAL INSTRUMENTS OF MEASUREMENT
Library Technology Reports

In the American Library Association Library Technology Project (now Program), librarians are given an opportunity to have some of their practical problems studied, with the goal of seeking solutions. Thus we find in the annual reports of the project, as well as in the "Library Technology Reports," a looseleaf service of the LTP, a listing of the areas of study, and the results of the findings. In the Report of September 1965, for example, there is a detailed examination of the variables involved in the manufacture of domestic book trucks. For many librarians, and particularly those in charge of technical services operations, this can be an important question. Various other aspects of interior materials of buildings are considered. Similarly, there are studies of steel filing cabinets, contemporary desks, insurance policies, labeling and marking, listening equipment, microforms and equipment, photocopying equipment, shelving, storage and shipping containers, and other supplies. Circulation systems, data processing applications, testing of paper, reader-printers, binding, adhesives, catalog card reproduction, duplicating equipment, and other areas of study have been involved in the project's activity.

Matrix of Library Surveys

In order to determine in what ways libraries were studied in survey situations, fourteen reports were analyzed for devices or measures or conditions used to examine the library problems. Although there is no point in listing here all items in the resulting matrix, there were factors which could be subsumed under the major headings of faculty acquisitions procedures: delay in ordering periodicals, non-placement of standing orders, non-use of jobbers for acquisitions, lack of systematic handling of gifts and exchanges, inadequacy of budget for books and periodicals, inadequate staffing for acquisitions searching and other activities, performance of clerical work by professional staff, lack of acquisitional policy, excessive duplication (unintentional), lack of procedure manual, lack of forms, unsystematic book selection, lack of coordination of technical services units, and unavailability of reference sources.

In cataloging, there were measures such as excessive revision, failure to use printed cards, excessive altering of cards, failure to follow standard rules for descriptive cataloging for certain materials, modification of classification schedules, arrearage in cataloging, lack of distinction between professional and clerical activities, inadequate physical conditions (lighting and ventilation), inadequate layout of work, lack of procedure manual, failure to utilize form slips in cooperation with acquisition unit, and high costs of cataloging (on a comparative basis).

Summary of Methodology

In the examination of the various studies of technical services which have been prepared in recent years, one might expect to find radical changes in these services. There have been changes, but the only general comment that can be made is that there is great concern for improving these services in any way possible. The implications for international and national, as well as other multi-library, activity are clear. But there has been no great impact upon technical services, except in the introduction of computer or educational accounting machinery to assist in various ways. The profession is waiting on major projects in acquisitions, cataloging, and automation of operations.

If one tries to relate these studies to measurement and evaluation, it is obvious that they have been fragmentary, but that occasionally they have had an impact on practice.

It is possible to say that within the framework of the studies that have been made one may find examples of the use of the philosophical, historical, descriptive or narrative, experimental and comparative methods, and of the normative survey. Such approaches as documentary analysis, sampling, and statistical analysis are evident in certain studies. The use of various instruments such as questionnaires, checklists, rating scales, and tests has been introduced. Observation, interviews, time and motion studies, pilot studies, and spot checks have been used. Documents, reports, statistical data, and other records have been reviewed.

Whether or not the results of the various studies have brought about observable changes in the patterns of the technical services is the basic question to be answered. One would be inclined to say that they have not changed much. Automation has altered procedures in acquisitions, accounting, serials records, circulation, and other repetitive operations, and undoubtedly can be applied in more areas. Fussler's Chicago study, mentioned above, should help on this score.

The shift to the Library of Congress classification by a large number of libraries has allowed for an important change in organization of personnel. With a shortage of catalogers, it has been possible to shift intelligent clericals to handling LC cataloged materials in processing units. A large number of libraries have been doing this for years, apparently without any serious difficulties. One may have to change a head cataloger, however, if there is resistance to this type of approach.

FURTHER AREAS OF STUDY

It may be worth listing some of the areas for study, or further study, that appear to be possibly fruitful in improving the technical services of libraries. The list is not intended to be complete, and there may be important items omitted. They can be grouped roughly as follows:

Acquisitions:
1. Development of selection tools on a systematic basis for different types of libraries.
2. Continued evaluation of acquisitional policies and programs, particularly in relation to cooperative enterprises.

3. Detailed studies of staffing, facilities, records, and suitability of computerization. Development of applicable formulae.

4. Research into gift and exchange programs; no studies of merit since Thompson's review in 1961.[48]

5. Study of relationships of acquisitions unit to other library units, particularly in connection with foreign acquisitions.

6. Development of formulae for production.

Cataloging and Classification:

1. Evaluation of new cataloging rules for libraries in relation to LC practice, and of extent of recataloging required. Development of more codes in other countries.

2. Evaluation of subject cataloging at this time.

3. Examination of classification problems (Dewey, LC classes or parts of schedules.)

4. Extension of knowledge of reclassification (studies supported by Council on Library Resources, Inc.)

5. Setting up of principles of indexing.

6. Refinement of filing procedures, particularly for computers; development of a standard.

7. Examination of processing units in libraries working with centralized or cooperative services.

8. Development of guidance for divided catalog.

9. Study of the place of the book catalog.

10. Consideration of physical facilities for catalogers (separate offices for improved production?); formulae for production.

11. Assessment of personnel, operations, equipment.

12. Study of reproduction of cards and preparational activities – cataloger's camera and cataloging-in-source.

13. Evaluation of shared cataloging programs.

14. Constant review of centralized and cooperative cataloging programs.

15. Study of regional processing: how large the region?

16. Status study of union catalog development.

Binding and Preservation:

1. Analysis of ALA and LBI differences on standards.

2. Further experimentation in preservation of materials.

3. Extension of knowledge of restoration.

4. Study of relation of reprinting to deterioration of materials.

5. Evaluation of place of microforms and their care.

Automation: Reprography:

1. Systematic application to processes in all areas of library service lending themselves to automation.

2. Further experimentation in content analysis.

3. Study of further uses of photography in technical services.

4. Estimate of place of Xerox in furtherance of library activities.

Scientific Management:

1. Encouragement in libraries and in library schools; use of results of studies as much as possible for improvement.

Finally and emphatically, there should be a tighter relationship among the various agencies working in the fields of the technical services, in the divisions of the American Library Association, the Special Libraries Association, the American Documentation Institute, COSATI and other governmental bodies, the other library associations, and Committee Z39 of the United States of America Standards Institute. Research funds from various organizations – the U.S. Office of Education, the Air Force Office of Research, the National Science Foundation – are available as never before. The possibility of coordinated research among several library schools has been suggested in the past, but this would require an active group of representatives who would really want to undertake major tasks on a broad scale.

REFERENCES

1. Tauber, Maurice, ed. *Technical Services in Libraries.* New York, Columbia University Press, 1954.
2. Welch, Helen M., et al. *The Literature of Library Technical Services* (University of Illinois Graduate School of Library Science Occasional Papers, No. 58). Rev. ed. Urbana, University of Illinois Graduate School of Library Science, 1963.
3. Quoted by Uridge, Margaret D. "The Literature of Interlibrary Cooperation in Technical Services." In Welch, *op. cit.*, p. 35.
4. "Research in Librarianship," ed. by Committee on Research, Association of American Library Schools, *Library Trends*, 6:101-253, Oct. 1957.
5. Clapp, Verner W. "Is there 'Research' in Librarianship?" *Library Journal*, 83:1868-71, June 15, 1958.
6. Leigh, Robert D. "Comments" (on the Clapp article above), *Library Journal*, 83:1871-72, June 15, 1958.
7. "A Kaleidoscopic View of Library Research," *Wilson Library Bulletin*, 41:896-950, May 1967.
8. Ennis, Philip H. "Commitment to Research," *Wilson Library Bulletin*, 41:899, May 1967.
9. Clapp, Verner W., and Jordan, Robert T. "Quantitative Criteria for Adequacy of Academic Library Collections," *College & Research Libraries*, 26:371-380, Sept. 1965. (Corrigenda, *College & Research Libraries*, 27:72, Jan. 1966.)
10. "Cooperative and Centralized Cataloging," eds. Esther J. Piercy and Robert L. Talmadge, *Library Trends*, 16:1-175, July 1967.
11. *Emerging Library Systems: The 1963-1966 Evaluation of the New York, New York State Public Library Systems.* Albany, The University of the State of New York, State Education Department, Division of Evaluation, 1967.
12. Nelson Associates, Inc. *Centralized Processing for the Public Libraries of New York State.* New York, Nelson Associates, Inc., 1966.
13. *Anglo-American Cataloging Rules.* Chicago, ALA, 1967.
14. Sharify, Nasser. *Cataloging of Persian Works: Including Rules for Transliteration Entry, and Description.* Chicago, ALA, 1959.
15. Qasimi, Abdus Subbuh. *A Code for Cataloging Materials Published in Urdu, Pushto, and Panjabi.* D.L.S. dissertation prepared for Columbia University School of Library Service. Issued for limited circulation by the author from the University of Peshawar, Pakistan.
16. *The Cataloging-in-Source Experiment: A Report to the Librarian of Congress by the Director of the Processing Department.* Washington, D.C., Library of Congress, 1960.
17. Dawson, John M. "The Library of Congress: Its Role in Cooperative and Centralized Cataloging," *Library Trends*, 16:90-91, July 1967.
18. *Ibid.*, p. 91.
19. Clapp, Verner W. *The Future of the Research Library.* Urbana, University of Illinois Press, 1964.
20. Weber, David C. "Book Catalog Trends in 1966." *Library Trends*, 16:149-164, July 1967.
21. Kingery, Robert E., and Tauber, Maurice F. *Book Catalogs.* New York, Scarecrow Press, 1963.
22. Weber, *op. cit.*, p. 158.
23. Matta, Seoud M. *The Card Catalog in a Large Research Library: Present Conditions and Future Possibilities in the New York Public Library.* D.L.S. dissertation prepared for Columbia University School of Library Service, 1965. Issued by the New York Public Library.
24. Daily, Jay E. "Subject Headings and the Theory of Classification," *American Documentation*, 8:269-274, Oct. 1957.
25. Lilley, Oliver L. *Terminology, Form, Specificity and the Syndetic Structure of Subject Headings for English Literature.* Ann Arbor, University of Michigan Press, 1959.
26. Hines, Theodore C., and Harris, Jessica L. *Computer Filing of Index, Bibliographic and Catalog Entries*, Newark, N.J., Bro-Dart Foundation, 1966.
27. Kilgour, Frederick G. Review of *Computer Filing of Index, Bibliographic and Catalog Entries*, by Theodore C. Hines and Jessica L. Harris, *College & Research Libraries*, 28:285-286, July 1967.

28. "Statement on Types of Classification Available to New Academic Libraries," (Report of the Classification Committee, RSTD Cataloging and Classification Section, May 15, 1964), *Library Resources & Technical Services*, 9:104-111, Winter 1965.

29. *See* for example: Tauber, Maurice F. "Reclassification and Recataloging of Materials in College and University Libraries: Reason and Evaluation," *Library Quarterly*, 12:827-845, Oct. 1942; "Reclassification of Special Collections in College and University Libraries Using the Library of Congress Classification," *Special Libraries*, 35:111-115, April 1944; "Partial Reclassification," *Journal of Cataloging & Classification*, 12:221-225, Oct. 1956.

30. Dougherty, Richard M. "The Realities of Reclassification," *College & Research Libraries*, 28:258-262, July 1967.

31. Atherton, Pauline, ed. *Proceedings of the Second International Study Conference.... 1964.* Copenhagen, Munksgaard, 1965.

32. Hyman, Richard J. "The Validity of the Browsing Concept for the Organization of Library Materials." (Study in progress at the School of Library Service, Columbia University.)

33. Herner, Saul. *A Pilot Study of the Use of the Stacks at the Library of Congress.* Washington, D.C., Council on Library Resources, Inc., 1960.

34. Poole, Frazer G. "William J. Barrow," *Library of Congress Information Bulletin*, 26:596-599, Aug. 31, 1967.

35. Barrow Research Laboratory. *Permanency/Durability of the Book.* Richmond, Va., Barrow Research Laboratory, 1963-65.

36. American Library Association. Library Technology Project. *Development of Performance Standards for Library Binding, Phase I: Report of the Survey Team... 1961.* Chicago, ALA 1961;... *Phase II....* Chicago, ALA, (1966).

37. *Guide to Microforms in Print.* (Annual.) Washington, D.C., Microcard Editions, 1961-.

38. Dunn, O.C., et al. *The Past and Likely Future of 58 Research Libraries 1951-1980: A Statistical Study of Growth and Change.* Lafayette, Ind., Purdue University, University Libraries and Audiovisual Center, 1967 (3d printing).

39. Adkinson, Burton W., and Stearns, Charles M. "Libraries and Machines — A Review," *American Documentation*, 18:121-124, July 1967.

40. *Ibid.*, p. 121.

41. *Ibid.*, p. 122.

42. *Ibid.*, p. 123.

43. *Ibid.*, p. 124.

44. American Documentation Institute. *Annual Review of Information Science and Technology.* Ed. by Carlos A. Cuadra. New York, Interscience Publishers, 1966-.

45. Dougherty, Richard M., and Heinritz, Fred J. *Scientific Management in Library Operations.* New York, Scarecrow Press, 1966.

46. Taube, Mortimer. "Evaluation of Information Systems for Report Utilization." *In* Mortimer Taube, et al., *Studies in Coordinate Indexing.* Washington, D.C., Documentation Incorporated, 1953, Vol. 1, pp. 96-110.

47. Jahoda, Gerald. "Correlative Indexing Systems for Control of Research Records." Unpublished D.L.S. dissertation prepared for Columbia University School of Library Service, 1960.

48. Thompson, Donald E. "Gifts" and "Exchanges." *In* Ralph R. Shaw, ed., *The State of the Library Art.* New Brunswick, N.J., Rutgers Graduate School of Library Service, 1961, Vol. 1., Parts 4 and 5, pp. 529-592.

CHAPTER XI: ATTITUDE MEASUREMENT

HARRY C. TRIANDIS
Professor of Psychology
University of Illinois, Urbana

For the purposes of this discussion we will define an attitude as "an idea, charged with emotion, predisposing action." It is possible to give more sophisticated definitions, but the present definition has the advantage of emphasizing that attitudes have a cognitive component (the idea), an affective component (the emotion), and a behavioral component (the predisposition to action).

It should be stated, at the outset, however, that this way of defining attitudes is not universally accepted, though it probably is favored by the majority of psychologists. There is another point of view which focuses on the emotional aspect alone and defines attitudes as the degree of positive or negative affect associated with some psychological object.[1] The difference between these two definitions is one of scope. The first definition includes the second, but considers the amount of affect as only one of three components.

Those psychologists who have been mostly concerned with the operational measurement of attitudes have adopted the second definition. It is probable that its greater simplicity and the desire for a unidimensional measure of attitudes are the reasons for the adoption of the simpler definition by the majority of measurement experts.

This paper will describe in some detail a variety of methods that measure the affective component and will indicate other components which may be measured. A brief description of some of the new developments that permit such measurement will also be given.

Before proceeding with the description of attitude measurement procedures, it is desirable to define some terms to be used in the paper. First, I will clarify what is meant by the *reliability* and *validity* of a measurement. Reliability refers to the extent to which information that is free of measurement error is obtained. If an instrument is reliable, the information obtained from it is stable, so that when the instrument is used more than once, to measure the same thing, very similar results are obtained. It should be clear that all measurement involves some error. When you use your bathroom scale, you are likely to err by as much as one pound. The more refined the measurement, the more likely it is that two repeated measures will not give the same scores. The same is true with attitude measurement. If you want to know if Mr. Smith is in favor of school integration or opposed to it, it is a relatively easy matter to establish this point. However, if you want to know whether Mr. Smith is more strongly in favor of integration than Mr. Brown while both of them are for it, this is a more difficult task which requires a very reliable instrument.

Validity refers to whether the instrument measures what we think it measures. We can have a perfectly reliable instrument which has no relevance to what we think it is measuring, but which does have relevance to some other phenomenon. For example, you may ask a student if he likes Negroes, and you may believe that his responses indicate his prejudice against or acceptance of Negroes. Actually, his responses may be a very reliable indicator of whether he thinks that it is socially desirable for him to give a positive or a negative answer, and they may have nothing to do with his prejudice against or acceptance of Negroes.

Another matter that needs to be clarified, in this introduction, is the kind of scale which one obtains with a particular instrument or measurement procedure. There are basically four types of scales. The crudest scales are *nominal* scales. These involve only a categorization of some object in two or more classes. For example, when we classify men and women in two categories and we examine their answers to a question, for which there is only a *yes* or *no* answer, we relate two nominal scales to each other. Notice that with a nominal scale it makes no difference whether we write Men-Women or Women-Men. The order does not mean anything. The next kind of scale is an *ordinal* scale. Here the order *is* important. If we have answers to our question which we classify as *Yes, No* and *Undecided*, the undecided logically belong between the Yes-people and the No-people. If we lay out a table, it would be easier to read it if we placed the undecided between the *Yes* and the *No*, though we could also place them between the *No-* and the *Yes*-people.

Now notice that an ordinal scale says something about the order of the objects, but it does not say anything about the distance between the objects. For example, suppose you ask people to respond with the categories (a) strongly agree, (b) agree, (c) undecided, (d) disagree, and (e) strongly disagree, to a particular question. The distances between these five response categories may be quite unequal. For example, the distance between "strongly agree" and "agree" might be much larger than the distance between "agree" and "undecided." A stronger scale is an *interval* scale. Here we *do* know the distances. An I.Q. scale is an interval scale. Thus, it is meaningful to say that a person with an I.Q. of 120 is as different from a person with an I.Q. of 100, as the latter is from a person with an I.Q. of 80. However, the interval scale does *not* allow us to say whether somebody is twice as intelligent as somebody else. For that kind of statement we need a scale that has a true zero. Such a scale would be not only an interval scale, but also one for which we can define a true zero. This type of scale is called a *ratio* scale. When you measure the height of people you have a true zero, so you can say that Mr. Smith is twice as tall as his son.

Now, in attitude measurement we will find that some scales are more reliable than others; some are more valid for certain purposes; some are crude, with the characteristics of nominal scales; some are a little better, with the characteristics of ordinal scales; some are still better, with the characteristics of interval scales; and there is a way to construct attitude scales with a true zero, thus obtaining ratio scales.

KINDS OF ATTITUDE MEASUREMENT

There are many distinctions that can be made among attitude measurement procedures. For example, there are attitude measurement methods that utilize physiological or verbal responses; standardized or non-standardized procedures; direct or indirect measures; unidimensional or multidimensional analyses of the data; and specific scales, good for only one kind of attitude object, or general scales, good for a class of attitude objects (e.g., people).

Since many of these attitude measurement methods are rather specialized, I will describe them only briefly in the present elementary treatment of the subject and then turn to a more detailed discussion of the more common procedures.

Selected Specialized Methods

Physiological Measures. Westie and DeFleur[2] showed that prejudiced persons respond differently from unprejudiced persons when they are shown pictures of whites and Negroes in a variety of social situations. They studied the galvanic skin resistance (a physiological measure of arousal), finger pulse, and the duration and amplitude of the heart beat. Cooper[3] obtained ratings of twenty ethnic groups on six graded preference categories, such as "like intensely," "dislike intensely." He then presented derogatory statements in association with the best liked ethnic groups and complimentary statements in association with the least liked. He showed that there was a significantly larger Galvanic Skin Response to the "loaded statements" as compared to the neutral statements. In another study Cooper[4] obtained the Galvanic Skin Response first and predicted the preference ranking of nine national groups. A high positive rank-order correlation of .82 was obtained between the rankings of the ethnic groups according to the skin response and the preference response.

Porier and Lott[5] found that the differences between Galvanic Skin Responses obtained in the presence of Negro and white assistants of the experimenter correlated with the E-Scale score of the respondents. The E-Scale is a verbal measure of generalized prejudice. In other words, highly prejudiced individuals showed a greater difference in their GSR responses to Negro than to white experimental assistants, than did non-prejudiced respondents.

Indirect Measures. Campbell[6] has provided an excellent review of such measures. Of particular interest here are disguised measures, such as ambiguous pictures to which individuals respond. Their responses are then subjected to a thematic frequency count. Doll play techniques, in which the respondent is asked to "make a dramatic scene or scenes of the world as you like it to be," have been found to measure intergroup attitudes in meaningful ways. A sentence completion test has been successfully used to measure racial attitudes. In this test critical sentences such as "Skin color...," "Some lynchings...," "Negro body odor...," etc. are interspersed with neutral items, such as "Maybe...," and "I feel...."

Another category of indirect tests appears highly objective to the respondents, and is usually presented as an ability test. Information tests, estimations of group opinion, tests of critical thinking, and perceptual or memory tests which are susceptible to distortion due to respondent attitudes may be included in this category of attitude measures. Here systematic errors or the persistent selectivity of performance are made the bases for the attitude measurement. For example, in order to measure religious attitudes, respondents may be asked to react to an item such as: "During the 1941-1945 period, church attendance increased greatly. During the 1945-65 period it has: (declined slightly; tended to increase still more; stayed at its high peak; returned to its pre-war level; fallen to its lowest point since 1920)."

Very little research on indirect measures has followed Campbell's review, so that it is still too early to tell whether these procedures have higher validity than the direct measures, as claimed by their proponents. On the other hand, it is clear that these procedures have lower reliabilities than some direct measures. A major program of research is now underway,[7] which considers and evaluates a number of these measures.

Some indirect procedures appear extremely promising. For example, DeFleur and Westie[8] had white subjects view a number of colored photographic slides showing a young Negro man and young white woman, or a young white man and a young Negro woman, in a social setting. The subjects described the pictures and answered specific questions about them. Following this phase, the subjects were told that another set of such slides was needed for further research and they were asked if they were willing to be photographed with a Negro of the opposite sex. Finally, the subjects were given "a standard photograph release agreement." They were asked to sign giving permission for the use of the slides for different purposes — ranging all the way from "laboratory experiments where it would be seen only by qualified social scientists" to "a nationwide publicity campaign advocating racial integration." This approach provides a highly realistic, behavioral measure of the subject's attitude towards interracial contacts.

Another promising method is that developed in Canada by Lambert and others.[9] They used tape recordings of a speech recorded by the same bilinguals (in French and English) as stimuli. Their Canadian subjects were asked to evaluate the personality characteristics of the speakers. The comparative favorableness of the evaluations of the French and English guises appears to be a measure of the favorableness of the subjects towards French and English Canadians. Webb and others[10] have reviewed a large number of unobtrusive measures which are quite promising as disguised procedures for the measurement of attitudes.

Multidimensional Scaling. When sets of attitude items are utilized, it is often assumed that the items may be arrayed along a single dimension — from very pro to very con the attitude object. However, in real life it is quite likely that the relationships among the various items are more complex, so that they may have to be ordered in two or more continua. The attitude toward an issue may be the resultant of two or more attitudes towards unrelated issues. For example, a person's attitude toward "Federal aid to education" may be the result of his attitude toward "education" and his attitude toward "Federal aid." It is theoretically possible to be for or against each of these two attitude objects. The person who is for both would naturally be in favor of "Federal aid to education"; the person who is against both would naturally be against it; but the person who is for "education" and against "Federal aid," or the person who is against "education" and for "Federal aid" would produce more complex responses.

Consider an item that is relevant to the attitude towards Federal aid to education. It may reflect the two components of this attitude in different degrees. For example, the item "Federal aid to education should be rejected because it allows the Federal government to dictate educational policy" is likely to be strongly agreed to by those opposed to Federal aid, but those who are for or against education, as such, may not feel very strongly about it. On the other hand, the item "Federal aid to education improves the quality of education and must therefore be supported" may produce more of a response among those who are in favor of education and may not produce a strong response among those for or against Federal aid. As a result, the two statements may not lie on a straight line extending from an extremely positive to an extremely negative point toward Federal aid to education. Instead, the statements may lie on a plane defined by the dimensions (1) for and against "education," and (2) for and against "Federal aid."

Multidimensional scaling techniques allow one to begin with a set of twenty or so statements, and to discover the number and meaning of the dimensions that are required to describe the relationships among the statements. In the previous example, two dimensions would be discovered. In multidimensional scaling the statements are presented in such a way as to require different kinds of judgments. For example, the subject may be asked: "Here are three countries: America, Brazil and Britain. Which one is most different from the other two?" One subject might pick America because it is "stronger" than the other two; another might pick Brazil because it is "less developed," or because it "speaks Portuguese"; and another Britain because it is "smaller" than the other two, or an island. By presenting several such triads it is possible to obtain the important dimensions used by subjects when thinking about the attitude objects. For an introduction to these techniques the papers by Messick,[11] Abelson[12] and Tucker[13] are highly recommended.

Standardized Verbal Specific Methods

This is by far the most popular method of attitude measurement. Edwards[14] has summarized the classic approaches to this type of measurement. They were developed by Thurstone,[1] Likert,[15] Guttman,[16] and Edwards and Kilpatrick.[17]

All of these procedures utilize attitude statements. An attitude statement is anything that can be said about an attitude object. Such statements may be obtained from newspaper editorials, magazines, books, and other materials dealing with the attitude object; or a group of friends may be asked to do some "brain storming" and think of as many statements as possible which refer to the attitude object. Once a pool of these statements has been collected, they should be subjected to some screening. Factual, ambiguous, confusing and excessively long statements should be eliminated. Edwards has provided the following informal criteria for attitude statements:

1. Avoid statements that refer to the past rather than to the present.
2. Avoid statements that are factual or capable of being interpreted as factual.
3. Avoid statements that may be interpreted in more than one way.
4. Avoid statements that are irrelevant to the psychological object under consideration.
5. Avoid statements that are likely to be endorsed by almost everyone or no one.
6. Select statements that are believed to cover the entire range of the affective scale of interest.
7. Keep the language of the statements simple, clear, and direct.
8. Statements should be short, rarely exceeding 20 words.
9. Each statement should contain only one complete thought.
10. Avoid universals such as *all, always, none, never*.
11. Words such as *only, just, merely*... should be used with care and moderation in writing statements.
12. Whenever possible, statements should be in the form of simple sentences, rather than compound or complex sentences.
13. Avoid the use of words that may not be understood ....
14. Avoid the use of double negatives.[18]

Thurstone has provided at least three methods of attitude scaling: paired comparisons, equal-appearing intervals and successive intervals. The first and last of these methods results in an interval scale, while the method of equal-appearing intervals results in only an ordinal scale. Likert's[15] and Guttman's[16] procedures result in ordinal scales that are close approximations of interval scales. The Edwards and Kilpatrick procedure results in interval scales.[17] Thurstone and Jones[19] developed a procedure that results in ratio scales. A technical discussion of these procedures is provided by Edwards.[14] In the present introductory presentation we will only describe them in non-technical and non-rigorous ways.

The basic principles behind Thurstonian attitude measurement are found in Thurstone's "law of comparative judgment."[20][21] This law provides a rationale for psychological measurement. For a technical exposition of this law, the reader is referred to Edwards.[22] The three Thurstone methods, mentioned above, utilize subjects acting as judges of the relative favorableness of attitude statements. The judgments made by these subjects are treated statistically to obtain "scale values" for the attitude statements. Then the already scaled statements are presented to the subjects whose attitude is to be assessed.

The Method of Paired Comparisons. Given n attitude statements, there are n (n-1)/2 possible pairs of statements. If these pairs of statements are given to one hundred individuals, all of whom judge which member of each pair is the more favorable to an attitude object, we obtain a set of frequencies corresponding to the number of times each statement is judged as more favorable than the others. Now consider two statements A and B. If A and B are equally favorable towards the attitude object, then the frequencies when A is compared with B and B is compared with A will be approximately equal. The greater the distance between A and B on the favorableness continuum, the more the frequencies of judgments of A as more favorable than B and

B as more favorable than A will be different. For example, to take the extreme case when A and B are positive and negative toward the attitude object, A will be seen as more favorable 100 percent of the time and B more favorable zero percent of the time. Thus, the frequencies of the favorableness judgments can be used as indices of the distance between two statements on the psychological continuum.

We can obtain a set of numbers that represent the position of the n statements on the psychological continuum by the following simple arithmetic. The frequencies are first converted into probabilities, by dividing the frequencies by the number of judges, and then the probabilities are converted to a statistic called z, by looking up a table that relates probabilities to z values. The method results in n estimates of the position of each of the statements. We can then average these estimates and obtain the mean "value" of the statement on the particular attitude continuum. We can arbitrarily give to the most negative statement the value .000; the remaining attitude statements will then have positive values. The values are on an interval scale. We can now take ten to fifteen statements that have values at approximately equal intervals and present them in a random order to the people we wish to study. We might ask these people to read all the statements and to check the three which best express how they feel about the particular issue. Finally, we can compute the average of the scale values of these three statements. This number represents the attitude of the particular individual, expressed in psychological units identical to those used by the judges.

The Method of Equal-Appearing Intervals. In this method judges are asked to place the n attitude statements in eleven piles, ordered according to their degree of favorableness to the attitude object. The judges are asked to consider the piles as being equally distant from each other, so that intervals between the piles are equal-*appearing* intervals. For each of the n statements we obtain a distribution of judgments from the judges. If the distribution shows too much dispersion, or is bi-modal, this indicates that the statement is ambiguous and it is eliminated from further consideration. For the remaining statements, the median of the distribution of the judgments can be used as the estimate of their scale value. The equal-appearing interval procedure gives only ordinal measurement of the scale values of the attitude statements. The method of successive intervals gives interval measurement.

The Method of Successive Intervals. This method first requires the steps used by the judges in the method of equal-appearing intervals. It employs the frequencies of assignment of the n statements to the eleven categories as the basis for estimating the distance between the eleven piles. The obtained scale values are on an interval scale, and the statements may then be given to individuals whose attitudes we wish to study. They are then asked to check the three statements which most represent their attitudinal positions. The average value of the three checked statements is the individual's attitude.

Thus, in the three methods that have just been discussed (paired comparison, equal-appearing intervals, and successive intervals), judges are employed to obtain the scale values of a set of ten to fifteen attitude statements. The ten to fifteen statements, with values that span the entire attitude continuum, are then given to a sample of individuals whose attitudes we wish to study. Each individual chooses three statements which reflect his attitude. The average value of these statements is used as a measure of the individual's attitude.

Assumptions of the Thurstone Methods. The basic assumption of Thurstone and his collaborators is that the values obtained from one sample of judges will be the same as the values obtained from another sample of judges. It has been shown that as long as the judges are not extremists, on the particular attitude continuum, this assumption is generally safe. On the other hand, with judges who are very ego-involved, this assumption is incorrect. Hovland and Sherif[23] showed that judges who are deeply involved show displacements in the values of the attitude statements. Specifically, highly favorable judges place only a few highly favorable statements in the favorable piles; they displace the remaining statements towards the unfavorable side of the continuum.

Sherif and Sherif[24] and Sherif, et al.[25] used this phenomenon to measure involvement with the attitude object. Their procedure asked their respondents to sort attitude statements in as many piles as they desired. It is therefore called the "own categories procedure." Persons who are extremely ego-involved with the particular attitude issue place statements in fewer categories. The Sherifs have also asked individuals to sort statements in "accept," "indifferent" and "reject" categories. Involved people generally place only a few statements in the "accept" category, and most of the statements in the "reject" category. The Sherifs related this work to standard Thurstone scaling of the statements and found that the "latitude of acceptance" of the involved individuals was relatively small, the "latitude of non-committment" relatively small, but the "latitude of rejection" very large. Thus the ratio of the latitude of rejection to the latitude of acceptance can be used as a measure of involvement. The "own categories" method has the advantage that it measures the individual's attitude without his awareness. His task is simply to sort the statements in as many categories as he desires. The way he sorts them is used to learn his position on the issue.

The Method of Summated Ratings. This method was developed by Likert[15] and has the advantage that it does not require the use of judges. Thus, attitude statements are given a value by a statistical procedure which employs the data from the sample of persons whose attitudes are being studied. The Likert method begins with $\underline{n}$ statements which are given to the sample of individuals who are to be studied. Five response alternatives are allowed: (a) strongly agree, (b) agree, (c) uncertain, (d) disagree, and (e) strongly disagree. The responses of the individuals are first scored "*a priori*" using the investigator's best judgment of whether the statement is positive or negative toward the attitude object. On the basis of this preliminary scoring, the individuals are ordered from most favorable to least favorable towards the attitude object. Following this step, the most favorable 27 percent and the least favorable 27 percent of the individuals are separated so that they constitute a "favorable" and an "unfavorable" group. The responses of the favorable to each attitude statement are compared to the responses of those who are unfavorable. If the attitude statement is "good" it will discriminate between the two groups of persons. A statistical test is used to determine whether the responses of the favorable are significantly different from the responses of the unfavorable. Those statements which do discriminate are then used to measure the attitudes of the entire group of individuals.

Scalogram Analysis. This is a procedure developed by Guttman[16] to check on the unidimensionality of a set of attitude statements. Assume that you have five attitude statements that span the full attitude continuum and five individuals who also span the full attitude continuum. If you rank-order the statements and the individuals so that they are ordered from the most positive to the most negative, you will obtain a pattern of responses (assuming that the individuals are perfectly consistent) such as the one shown in Table 1. A parallelogram of "Yes" responses can be seen.

TABLE 1

Theoretical Perfect Response Pattern of Five Individuals

to Five Attitude Statements

The Individuals	Attitude Statements				
	Very Favorable	Favorable	Indifferent	Unfavorable	Very Unfavorable
Very pro	Yes	Yes	No	No	No
Just pro	No	Yes	Yes	No	No
Indifferent	No	Yes	Yes	Yes	No
Somewhat anti	No	No	Yes	Yes	No
Very anti	No	No	No	Yes	Yes

The Guttman technique involves the analysis of the responses of approximately one hundred individuals to a set of attitude statements. It involves the trial-and-error change of the orders of both the persons and the attitude statements, until the minimum number of inconsistent judgments is obtained. An inconsistent judgment occurs when a favorable person, who has accepted several highly favorable statements, also accepts a statement which is assumed to be unfavorable. Statements that produce too many inconsistent judgments are assumed to belong to a different continuum from that of the majority of the statements, and are therefore eliminated from further consideration.

Scale Discrimination Technique. The equal-appearing interval, summated ratings, and scalogram analysis techniques may be considered as three procedures which accomplish a similar task. The similar task is the elimination of attitude statements that are inappropriate or ineffective. The three procedures use three different criteria for the elimination of statements. The equal intervals procedure eliminates those statements which are not judged consistently and are, in other words, ambiguous. The summated ratings procedure eliminates those statements which do not discriminate between favorable and unfavorable individuals. The scalogram analysis eliminates those statements which do not fall on a unidimensional continuum. The scale discrimination technique of Edwards and Kilpatrick[17] utilizes all three of the previously mentioned techniques, thus eliminating statements according to three criteria. The resulting statements should be neither ambiguous nor poor in discrimination, and should fall on a unidimensional continuum.

Discussion of Above Methods. A sophisticated comparison of the various methods mentioned may be found in Green[26] and Scott.[27] Edwards[14] discusses the advantages and disadvantages of the methods in some detail. In the present section we will only point out that the Thurstone technique makes assumptions that differ from the assumptions of the Likert and Guttman techniques in at least two important respects.

(1) The response characteristics of the items are assumed to be different. Technically speaking, Thurstone items are assumed to be non-cumulative (or non-monotonic); Likert and Guttman items are assumed to be cumulative (or monotonic). Suppose that a subject accepts a favorable item on a Thurstone scale; he is not assumed to be acting inconsistently if he rejects a *less* favorable item. On the other hand, the Likert and Guttman procedures assume that the acceptance of a favorable item implies acceptance of the less favorable items. The work of Sherif and Sherif,[24] on the latitudes of acceptance and rejection of items, suggests that the Thurstone assumption is more realistic than the other assumption. In fact, the Sherifs have shown that highly involved (e.g., militantly pro-civil rights) subjects reject mildly favorable items (e.g., "There should be more discussions between white and Negro leaders") and accept only extremely favorable statements.

(2) The Thurstone procedure requires the use of judges, while the other procedures do not. There are disadvantages in the use of judges: (a) we know that unless the judges are moderate in their degree of involvement, their judgments lead to distorted scale values; (b) it is unclear how much consensus there should be among the judges to establish a satisfactory location for a test item; and (c) the subjects and the judges have different tasks. The subjects indicate agreement with the item; the judges locate the item on a judgmental dimension. That sort of shift in the nature of the task may well introduce measurement errors.

It is clear, from the above, that the arguments under (1) favor the Thurstone procedure and the arguments under (2) favor the Likert or Guttman procedures.

Final Comment on Specific Methods. All of the above-mentioned standardized verbal specific methods are designed for the measurement of the person's attitudes towards a particular (attitude) issue or (attitude) object. Shaw and Wright[28] have reviewed the published scales towards a large variety of attitude objects, e.g., opinions regarding the bringing up of children, disciplining children, freedom of children, children's activities, educational practices, religious practices, heterosexual practices, health practices, etc. Other chapters review scales towards social issues, international issues, political and religious issues, ethnic and national groups, and social institutions. The reader is referred to this handbook for a description of existing attitude scales towards a large variety of issues and attitude objects.

General Methods

The methods reviewed in the previous section are designed to measure the subject's affect towards a specific attitude object, or controversial issue. This means that one must employ a different scale, consisting of different items, for each attitude object. Since the development of such scales is time-consuming and precise measurement of every attitude object is not always required, there have been attempts to develop general scales which are appropriate for a class of attitude objects or for *any* attitude object.

Scales Appropriate for a Class of Objects. Among the scales that are suitable for classes of attitude object we shall list the following: (1) Bues[29] has published scale values of items that may be used to respond to any practice. They range from the item "It is better than anything else" (11.0), through "My likes and dislikes for this practice are balanced" (6.0), to "Is the worst thing I know" (1.0). Two forms of this scale, each containing thirty-seven items are readily available[30], (2) Remmers[31] has published a seventeen-item scale which measures attitudes towards any proposed social action. It ranges from the item "Will bring lasting satisfaction" (10.3) to the item "It is perfectly absurd" (1.0). Two forms are available.[32] (3) Bogardus[33] developed an ordinal scale which is suitable for use with any group. A list of nationalities, races or religions is presented and the subjects are asked to indicate whether they would:

    marry into this group,
    have members of this group as close friends,
    have as next door neighbors,
    work in the same office,
    have as speaking acquaintances,
    have as visitors only in my nation, or
    debar from my nation.

An interval scale of social distance was developed by Triandis and Triandis.[34] It was later employed in Greece,[35] Germany and Japan,[36] as well as America. The cross-cultural work employing this scale has required separate standardizations of the scale in each culture. The results suggested that persons from different cultures react to different characteristics of "stimulus persons" when they make social distance judgments. For example, Greeks show social distance mostly towards people who differ from them in religion; Americans show social distance towards persons who differ from them in race; the Germans and the Japanese show social distance mostly towards persons who are lower class. A review of these studies can be found in Triandis and Triandis.[37]

An extension of this work led to the development of the Behavioral Differential[38] which is a general instrument for measuring the behavioral intentions of subjects towards any person or category of persons. A description of the person to be judged is placed on the top of the sheet. A series of scales permit the subjects to indicate their behavioral intentions towards this person. For example:

A Portuguese 35-year old coalminer

would ___'___'___'___'___'___'___'___'___ would not
obey this person

would not ___'___'___'___'___'___'___'___'___ would
ask this person for advice

would ___'___'___'___'___'___'___'___'___ would not
invite this person to dinner

A typical study is likely to employ about fifty person stimuli and about twenty scales, thus requiring the subject to make one thousand judgments. The stimuli are generated according to factorial designs, i.e., all possible combinations of the characteristics under study and different levels of each characteristic are employed. For example, in studying the attitudes of subjects towards several kinds of European nationalities, Triandis and Triandis[35] employed a preferred nationality (Swede) as well as a non-preferred (Portuguese); in studying the responses of Greeks towards religion, they employed a preferred (Greek Orthodox) and a non-preferred (Jewish) religion; in studying responses towards stimuli of different social class, they presented stimuli that were described as physicians or coal miners. A statistical procedure called analysis of variance allows the estimation of the relative importance of these characteristics in the determination of the judgments made by the subjects.

The sampling of social behaviors requires extensive work. Lists of ten thousand social behaviors were developed by Triandis, and others[39] in each culture. They were subjected to a variety of statistical treatments, including the use of factor analysis, in order to obtain a short list of twenty scales that may be used as the standard set of social behaviors in a given culture. Five major dimensions of social behavior were obtained from this work: (1) *respect:* admire the ideas of, admire the character of, ask for opinions of, learn with help of; (2) *marital acceptance:* marry, fall in love with, go on a date with, make love to; (3) *friendship acceptance:* be partners in athletic game, eat with, gossip with, accept as intimate friend; (4) *social distance:* exclude from my neighborhood, prohibit from voting, not accept as a close kin by marriage, not invite to my club; or (5) *superordination:* treat as a subordinate, command, not obey, criticize work of.

The above-mentioned twenty scales may be used to estimate a subject's behavioral intentions towards other people. These intentions are describable in terms of five more or less independent dimensions. However, the dimensions are further reducible to two clearly independent dimensions: intimacy-formality and positive-negative behaviors. Respect is a cluster of formal-positive behaviors; marital acceptance a cluster of intimate-positive; friendship a cluster of positive behaviors intermediate in intimacy; social distance a cluster of negative-intimate; superordination a cluster of negative-formal. Thus, this work reduces interpersonal attitudes to two basic dimensions. Any interpersonal relationship may be described by the degree of positive-negative affect and the degree of intimacy which characterizes it.

A Scale Appropriate for All Objects. The most general method for the measurement of affect is the Semantic Differential.[40] This instrument allows the researcher to present any attitude object, be it person, issue, institution, practice, picture, musical composition, or anything else. A series of scales, bound by polar adjectives, is employed and the subject reacts to the attitude object on this set of standard scales. For example:

Integrated Housing

good ___'___'___'___'___'___'___'___'___ bad

passive ___'___'___'___'___'___ ' ___'___'___ active

strong ___'___'___'___'___'___'___'___'___ weak

etc.

Extensive work done with samples of adjectives by Osgood and his collaborators in more than twenty cultures suggests that three major independent dimensions underlie the judgments made by subjects. These are evaluation: the object is good, clean, fair, honest, beautiful; potency: the object is strong, big, large, powerful, heavy; and activity: the object is active, hot, fast, alive. Thus, with a short set of nine or twelve scales it is possible to measure the connotative meaning, or affect, experienced by the subject towards the attitude object.

Though the semantic differential is a most general instrument, it can also be made to be quite specific. Thus, if one is interested in the attitudes of persons towards jobs, he can employ a specially designed instrument containing adjective scales that describe jobs.[41] If one is interested in studying only social issues, another set of scales might be used.[42] If one is interested in studying only people, still another set may be most appropriate.[43] The more specific the set of scales the more comfortable are the subjects when they make their judgments, and the more relevant is the information for the particular problem in hand. For example, Komorita and Bass[44] used sixteen evaluative scales and two concepts: "American foreign policy in Vietnam" and "Draft deferments for married men." After intercorrelating the scales and submitting them to a factor analysis they found three factors: functional evaluation (approved, wise, valuable, beneficial, satisfactory), pure affect (pleasant, attractive), and moral evaluation (clean, honest, trustworthy, sincere). This means that many subjects who thought the Vietnam policy wise, valuable, beneficial, etc., also thought of it as unpleasant, unattractive or as insincere and dishonest. It is clear that such subtle points cannot be uncovered with the most general forms of the semantic differential, while specific semantic differentials may probe into quite subtle and intricate aspects of attitudes. On the other hand, there is a great advantage in having a most general instrument applicable to any kind of concept. The fact that the instrument does not have to be standardized every time one is interested in studying a different attitude is a major advantage.

Measuring the Components of Attitude

In the beginning of this paper attitudes were defined as ideas charged with emotion, predisposing action. The methods which were described above are heavily focused on the measurement of the degree of affect associated with an attitude object. However, at this point it is desirable to consider the distinction between the cognitive, affective and behavioral component of attitudes. The cognitive component includes the associations of the attitude object with other concepts. For example, the attitude object CIVIL RIGHTS LAWS may be characterized by its connections to other laws, to various political points of view, and also to a set of characteristics. For example, one possible characteristic of such laws is that they are controversial. Different people may see different strengths in the bond between the concepts CIVIL RIGHTS LAWS and CONTROVERSIAL. Those who see a close connection would have a cognitive component for CIVIL RIGHTS LAWS that implies the concept CONTROVERSIAL. It is clear that different people may have different concepts associated with a particular attitude object.

In addition, each of these characteristics of the attitude object implies a certain amount of affect. Some people "like" controversial laws and others do not. Fishbein[45] has shown that the total affect towards an attitude object is proportional to the sum of the affects experienced towards all objects associated with it, weighted by the strength of the belief that such associations do in fact exist. For example, there may be many characteristics of CIVIL RIGHTS LAWS. The characteristic CONTROVERSIAL is certainly related to them. On the other hand the characteristic FAIR may be strongly related for some people and very weakly related for others. The affect associated with CONTROVERSIAL may be small, while the affect associated with FAIR may be large. In the case of persons seeing a strong connection between such laws and FAIR there will be much affect, while in the case of those seeing a weak connection there will be little affect. Thus, one way to measure the attitude towards an object is to obtain the associations (beliefs about the object) evoked by the object and the evaluations of these beliefs. The attitude towards the object is the weighted sum of these evaluations:

$$A = \sum_{i=1}^{n} B_i a_i$$

where A is the attitude towards an object,
B_i is the belief strength that the object has a characteristic i,
a_i is the affect toward the characteristic i,
and n is the number of characteristics (or beliefs) associated with the attitude object.

According to our analysis the B_i's constitute the cognitive component of the attitude towards the attitude object. The A constitutes the affective component. The behavioral intentions towards the attitude object (see discussion on the Behavioral Differential above) constitute the behavioral component. Thus, three kinds of scales may be used to measure the three components. Davis and Triandis employed a method which they called the "implicative meaning method" for the measurement of the cognitive component. It presents attitude objects (e.g., integrated housing) and the implications of such objects. For example,

If you have INTEGRATED HOUSING then you have:

Justice

improbable ___'___'___'___'___'___'___ probable

Slums

improbable ___'___'___'___'___'___'___ probable

More crime

improbable ___'___'___'___'___'___'___ probable

Better relations between the races

improbable ___'___'___'___'___'___'___ probable

etc.

The responses of subjects to such scales measure aspects of their cognitive component towards INTEGRATED HOUSING. In addition, the affective component was measured by regular semantic differentials. Finally, the behavioral component was measured by asking the subjects to respond on behavioral differentials to stimulus persons supporting or opposing INTEGRATED HOUSING. The correlations among the three components were positive, but not very high. Thus, though there is consistency in the three components, knowing the degree of affect does not allow one to predict the other two components, with any degree of precision. In order to measure attitudes completely it is necessary to employ separate measurements of each of the components.

SUMMARY

In this paper attitude was defined as "an idea, charged with affect, predisposing action." The reliability and validity of measurement of this construct were discussed. Different kinds of scales of measurement — nominal, ordinal, interval, and ratio — were described.

There are many kinds of measurement procedures — physiological or verbal; standardized or non-standardized; direct or indirect; unidimensional or multidimensional; and specific or general. Each of these kinds of attitude measurement was briefly described and illustrated. Particular attention was given to standardized verbal specific methods, since they are widely used in attitude measurement. In addition, some of the general methods were described in some detail, because they are easily employed by non-specialists.

The final section dealt with the measurement of some of the major components of attitudes. It is shown that separate measurement of each component is at times highly desirable; because although the components are interrelated, each component involves aspects which do not overlap with the other components. The complete and adequate measurement of attitudes is a highly complex matter, involving the measurement of many components, and requiring a variety of measurement strategies. Nevertheless, a first approximation can be obtained with some of the general methods of measurement described in this paper.

REFERENCES

1. Thurstone, L.L. "The Measurement of Social Attitudes," *Journal of Abnormal and Social Psychology*, 26:249-269, Oct-Dec. 1931.
2. Westie, Frank R., and DeFleur, Melvin L. "Autonomic Responses and Their Relationship to Race Attitudes," *Journal of Abnormal and Social Psychology*, 58:340-347, May 1959.
3. Cooper, Joseph B. "Emotion in Prejudice," *Science*, 130:314-318, Aug. 7, 1959.
4. Cooper, Joseph B., and Pollock, David. "The Identification of Prejudicial Attitudes by the Galvanic Skin Response," *Journal of Social Psychology*, 50:241-245, Nov. 1959.
5. Porier, Gary W., and Lott, Albert J. "Galvanic Skin Responses and Prejudice," *Journal of Personality and Social Psychology*, 5:253-259, March 1967.
6. Campbell, Donald T. "The Indirect Assessment of Social Attitudes," *Psychological Bulletin*, 47:15-38, Jan. 1950.
7. Cook, Stuart W., and Selltiz, Claire. "A Multiple-Indicator Approach to Attitude Measurement," *Psychological Bulletin*, 62:36-55, July 1964.
8. DeFleur, Melvin L., and Westie, Frank R. "Verbal Attitudes and Overt Acts: An Experiment on the Salience of Attitudes," *American Sociological Review*, 23:667-673, Dec. 1958.
9. Lambert, W.E., et al. "Evaluational Reactions to Spoken Languages," *Journal of Abnormal and Social Psychology*, 60:44-51, Jan. 1960.
10. Webb, Eugene J., et al. *Unobtrusive Measures: Nonreactive Research in the Social Sciences.* Chicago, Rand McNally, 1966.
11. Messick, Samuel J. "The Perception of Social Attitudes," *Journal of Abnormal and Social Psychology*, 52:57-66, Jan. 1956.
12. Abelson, Robert P. "A Technique and a Model for Multi-Dimensional Attitude Scaling," *Public Opinion Quarterly*, 18:405-418, Winter 1954-1955.
13. Tucker, Ledyard R. "Systematic Differences Between Individuals in Perceptual Judgments." In Maynard W. Shelly and Glenn L. Bryan, eds., *Human Judgments and Optimality.* New York, Wiley, 1964, pp. 85-99.
14. Edwards, Allen L. *Techniques of Attitude Scale Construction.* New York, Appleton-Century-Crofts, 1957.
15. Likert, Rensis. "A Technique for the Measurement of Attitudes," *Archives of Psychology*, 22:44-53, No. 140, 1932.
16. Guttman, L. "A Basis for Scaling Quantitative Data," *American Sociological Review*, 9:139-150, April 1944.
17. Edwards, Allen L., and Kilpatrick, Franklin P. "A Technique for the Construction of Attitude Scales," *Journal of Applied Psychology*, 32:374-384, Aug. 1948.
18. Edwards, op. cit., pp. 13-14.
19. Thurstone, L.L., and Jones, Lyle V. "The Rational Origin for Measuring Subjective Values," *Journal of the American Statistical Association.* 52:458-471, Dec. 1957.
20. Thurstone, L.L. "A Law of Comparative Judgment," *Psychological Review*, 34:273-286, July 1927.
21. Thurstone, L.L., "Psychophysical Analysis," *American Journal of Psychology*, 38:368-369, July 1927.
22. Edwards, op. cit., pp. 20-28.
23. Hovland, Carl I., and Sherif, Muzafer. "Judgmental Phenomena and Scales of Attitude Measurement: Item Displacement in Thurstone Scales," *Journal of Abnormal and Social Psychology*, 47:822-832, Oct. 1952.
24. Sherif, Muzafer, and Sherif, Carolyn W. "The Own Category Procedure in Attitude Research." In Martin Fishbein, ed., *Readings in Attitude Theory and Measurement.* New York, Wiley, 1967, pp. 190-198.
25. Sherif, Carolyn W., et al. *Attitude and Attitude Change.* Philadelphia, Saunders, 1965.
26. Green, Bert F. "Attitude Measurement." In Gardner Lindzey, ed., *Handbook of Social Psychology.* Vol. 1, Cambridge, Mass., Addison-Wesley, 1954, pp. 335-369.

27. Scott, W.A. "Attitude Measurement." *In* Gardner Lindzey and E. Aronson, eds. *Handbook of Social Psychology*. Rev. ed. 1967 (in press.)

28. Shaw, Marvin E., and Wright, Jack M. *Scales for the Measurement of Attitudes*. New York, McGraw-Hill, 1967.

29. Bues, Harry W. "The Construction and Validation of a Scale to Measure Attitude Toward Any Practice," Purdue University. *Studies in Higher Education*, 26:64-67, Dec. 1934.

30. Shaw and Wright, *op. cit.*, pp. 124-126.

31. Remmers, J.J. *A Scale for Measuring Attitudes Towards Any Proposed Social Action*. Lafayette, Ind., Purdue Research Foundation, 1960.

32. Shaw and Wright, *op. cit.*, pp. 190-191.

33. Bogardus, Emory S. "A Social Distance Scale," *Sociology and Social Research*, 17:265-271, 1933.

34. Triandis, Harry C., and Triandis, Leigh M. "Race, Social Class, Religion and Nationality as Determinants of Social Distance," *Journal of Abnormal and Social Psychology*, 61:110-118, July 1960.

35. Triandis, Harry C., and Triandis, Leigh M. "A Cross-Cultural Study of Social Distance," *Psychological Monographs*, 76:Whole No. 540, 1962.

36. Triandis, Harry C., et al. "Some Determinants of Social Distance Among American, German and Japanese Students," *Journal of Personality and Social Psychology*, 2:540-551, Oct. 1965.

37. Triandis, Harry C., and Triandis, Leigh M. "Some Studies of Social Distance." *In* I.D. Steiner and M. Fishbein, eds., *Current Studies in Social Psychology*. New York, Holt, Rinehart and Winston, 1965, pp. 207-217.

38. Triandis, Harry C. "Exploratory Factor Analyses of the Behavioral Component of Social Attitudes," *Journal of Abnormal and Social Psychology*, 68:420-430, April 1964.

39. Triandis, Harry C., et al. *Some Cross-Culture Studies of Subjective Culture*. (University of Illinois, Dept. of Psychology, Group Effectiveness Research Laboratory Technical Report No. 45). Urbana, Ill., 1967.

40. Osgood, Charles E., et al. *The Measurement of Meaning*. Urbana, Ill., University of Illinois Press, 1957.

41. Triandis, Harry C. "A Comparative Factorial Analysis of Job Semantic Structures of Managers and Workers," *Journal of Applied Psychology*, 44:297-302. Oct. 1960.

42. Davis, Earl E., and Triandis, Harry C. *An Exploratory Study of Intercultural Negotiations*. (University of Illinois, Dept. of Psychology, Group Effectiveness Research Laboratory Technical Report No. 26). Urbana, Ill., 1965.

43. Davis, Earl E. *A Methodological Study of Behavioral and Semantic Differential Scales Relevant to Intercultural Negotiations*. (University of Illinois, Dept. of Psychology, Group Effectiveness Research Laboratory Technical Report No. 32). Urbana, Ill., 1966.

44. Komorita, S.S., and Bass, A.R. "Attitude Differentiation and Evaluative Scales of the Semantic Differential," *Journal of Personality and Social Psychology*, 6:241-244, 1967.

45. Fishbein, Martin. "A Consideration of Beliefs, Attitudes and their Relationships." *In* Ivan D. Steiner and Martin Fishbein, eds., *Current Studies in Social Psychology*. New York, Holt, Rinehart and Winston, 1965, pp. 107-120.